J Rogoff

JOHN S. GOFF

ARIZONA CIVILIZATION

BLACK MOUNTAIN PRESS
CAVE CREEK, ARIZONA

AUTHOR'S FOREWORD

Second Printing of the
Third Edition
August 1976

THERE ONCE WAS A TIME when a book on the subject of Arizona history and government could be published and remain current for many years. The reason was that almost nothing ever seemed to change. This is no longer true. In 1968 the first edition of this little volume appeared and by 1970 a second edition was necessary due to events. Now with the passage of more time a third edition is offered. Then as now this work is intended to function as "an introduction to Arizona."

A debt of gratitude is acknowledged here to those who have aided in the preparation of these three editions. L. Max Connolly has ably handled technical production matters. Several colleagues in the junior colleges and high schools have made useful suggestions. However, I must take personal responsibility for the statements made herein. In the textbook field there is an almost universal rule that a work must be written in such a bland way as to offend no one and to create no controversy. Some opinions are here expressed with which some will disagree. Disagreement leads to thought and perhaps new ideas. One of the main goals of this small volume is to stimulate an examination of the Arizona past, present and possible future.

JOHN S. GOFF, Ph.D.
DEPARTMENT OF SOCIAL SCIENCE
PHOENIX COLLEGE

JANUARY 1, 1974

ARIZONA CIVILIZATION

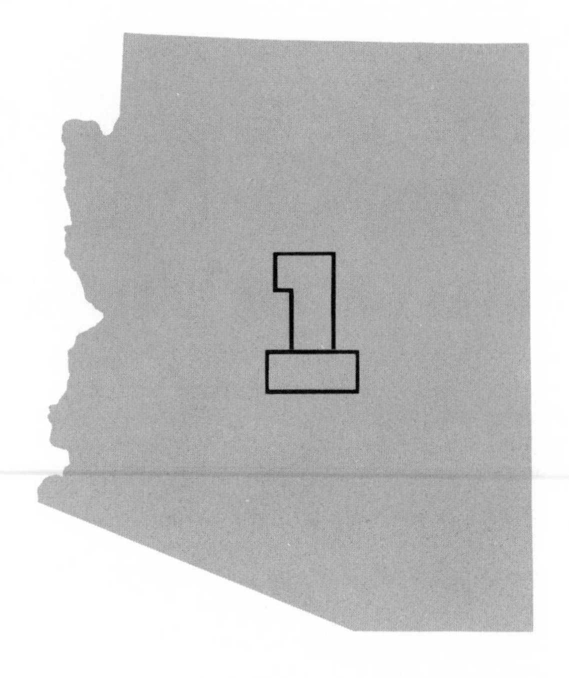

Creating the Territory!

PRESIDENT ABRAHAM LINCOLN posed for this photograph by Mathew B. Brady, sometime in 1863, not long after he approved the Arizona Territorial Act on February 24, 1863.

LIBRARY OF CONGRESS PHOTO

"THE ORGANIZATION of the Territory of Arizona has been a matter of constant importunity upon the Government for more than seven years," declared the powerful Chairman of the Senate Committee on Territories, Ben F. Wade of Ohio, early in the debate on the Arizona bill.

It was now February 20, 1863. Nine months before the House of Representatives had passed a bill to separate Arizona from New Mexico, but its approval had been blocked in the Senate. Opponents repeated familiar objections: Arizona's population was too small, a government already existed, and organization would be costly.

* * *

The Territorial movement in Washington had a strange counterpart in the Southwest where on August 1, 1861, Arizona was proclaimed a Confederate Territory! Tucson itself was occupied in February of 1862 by Confederates but they retreated when the California Column arrived in May.

* * *

February 20, 1863, was a jubilant day for Charles Debrille Poston, called the "Father of Arizona," who in 1864 became the first legally elected Territorial Delegate. He listened to Senator Wade from the gallery and witnessed passage of the Arizona bill, 25 to 12. Four days later President Lincoln placed his signature in approval on the parchment which created Arizona Territory.

Thirty-seventh

At the Third Session

BEGUN AND HELD AT THE CITY OF WASHINGTON

in the District of Columbia

on Monday the First day of December one thousand eight hundred and sixty-two.

AN ACT To provide a temporary government for the Territory of Arizona and for other purposes.

Be It Enacted by the Senate and House of Representatives of the United States of America in Congress assembled

That all that part of the present Territory of New Mexico situate west of a line running due south from the point where the southwest corner of the Territory of Colorado joins the northern boundary of the Territory of New Mexico, to the southern boundary line of said Territory of New Mexico, be, and the same is hereby, erected into a temporary government, by the name of the Territory of Arizona: Provided, That nothing contained in the provisions of this act shall be construed to prohibit the Congress of the United States from dividing said Territory, or changing its boundaries, in such manner and at such time as it may deem proper: Provided, further, That said government shall be maintained and continued until such time as the people residing in said Territory shall, with the consent of Congress, form a State government, republican in form, as prescribed in the Constitution of the United States, and apply for and obtain admission into the Union as a State, on an equal footing with the original States.

Sec. 2. And be it further enacted, That the government hereby authorized shall consist of an executive, legislative, and judicial power. The executive power shall be vested in a Governor. The legislative power shall consist of a council of nine members and a house of representatives of eighteen. The judicial power shall be vested in a supreme court, to consist of three judges, and such inferior courts as the legislative council may by law prescribe; there shall also be a Secretary, a Marshal, a District Attorney, and a Surveyor general for said Territory, who, together with the governor and judges of the Supreme Court, shall be appointed by the President, by and with the advice and consent of the Senate, and the term of office for each, the manner of their appointment, and the powers, duties, and the compensation of the governor, legislative assembly, judges of the supreme court, secretary, marshal, district attorney, and surveyor general aforesaid, with their clerks, draughtsman, deputies, and sergeant-at-arms, shall be such as are conferred upon the same officers by the act organizing the territorial government of New Mexico, which subordinate officers shall be appointed in the same manner, and not exceed in number those created by said act, and acts amendatory thereto, together with all legislative enactments of the Territory of New Mexico not inconsistent with the provisions of this act are hereby extended to and continued in force in the said Territory of Arizona until repealed or amended by future legislation. Provided, That no salary shall be due or paid the officers created by this act until they have entered upon the duties of their respective offices within the said Territory.

Sec. 3. And be it further enacted, That there shall neither be slavery nor involuntary servitude in the said Territory, otherwise than in the punishment of crimes, whereof the parties shall have been duly convicted; and all acts and parts of acts, either of Congress or of the Territory of New Mexico, establishing, regulating, or in any way recognizing the relation of master and slave in said Territory are hereby repealed.

Galusha A. Grow

Speaker of the House of Representatives.

Solomon Foot,

President of the Senate pro tempore.

Approved, February 24. 1863 Abraham Lincoln

Proclaiming the Territory!

PROCLAMATION.

TO THE PEOPLE OF ARIZONA:

I, JOHN N. GOODWIN, having been appointed by the President of the United States, and duly qualified, as Governor of the TERRITORY OF ARIZONA, do hereby announce that by virtue of the powers with which I am invested by an Act of the Congress of the United States, providing a temporary government for the Territory, I shall this day proceed to organize said government. The provisions of the Act, and all laws and enactments established thereby, will be enforced by the proper Territorial officers from and after this date.

A preliminary census will forthwith be taken, and thereafter the Judicial Districts will be formed, and an election of members of the Legislative Assembly, and the other officers, provided by the Act, be ordered.

I invoke the aid and co-operation of all citizens of the Territory in my efforts to establish a government whereby the security of life and property will be maintained throughout its limits, and its varied resources be rapidly and successfully developed.

The seat of government will for the present be at or near Fort Whipple

JOHN N. GOODWIN.

By the Governor:

RICHARD C. M'CORMICK,

Secretary of the Territory.

Navajo Springs

~~FORT WHIPPLE~~, ARIZONA,

December 29, 1863.

Governor Goodwin issues a proclamation to inhabitants of the newly created Territory of Arizona. The document was signed at Navajo Springs where the party of officials stopped on their way to the temporary capital 'at or near' Fort Whipple.

Formation of the State!

President Taft signs the Arizona statehood proclamation February 14, 1912. This particular photograph was presented to the Governor of Arizona by Senator Robert A. Taft of Ohio, the grandson of the President, 1973

□

AN EXACT REPRODUCTION of the statehood proclamation follows on the succeeding three pages. It was made from the original which is in the National Archives, Washington, D.C.

BY THE PRESIDENT OF THE UNITED STATES OF AMERICA,

A PROCLAMATION.

WHEREAS the Congress of the United States did by an Act approved on the twentieth day of June, one thousand nine hundred and ten, authorize the people of the Territory of Arizona to form a constitution and State government, and provide for the admission of such State into the Union on an equal footing with the original States upon certain conditions in said Act specified:

AND WHEREAS said people did adopt a constitution and ask admission into the Union:

AND WHEREAS the Congress of the United States did pass a joint resolution, which was approved on the twenty-first day of August, one thousand nine hundred and eleven, for the admission of the State of Arizona into the Union, which resolution required that, as a condition precedent to the admission of said State, the electors of Arizona should, at the time of the holding of the State election as recited in said resolution, vote upon and ratify and adopt an amendment to Section one of Article eight of their State constitution, which amendment was proposed and set forth at length in said resolution of Congress:

AND WHEREAS it appears from information laid before me that the first general State election was held on the twelfth day of December , one thousand nine hundred and eleven, and that the returns of said election upon said amendment were made and canvassed as in Section seven of said resolution of Congress provided:

AND WHEREAS it further appears from information laid before me that a majority of the legal votes cast at said election upon said amendment were in favor thereof, and that the Governor of said Territory has by proclamation declared the said amendment a part of the constitution of the proposed State of Arizona:

AND WHEREAS the Governor of Arizona has certified to me the result of said election upon said amendment and of the said general election:

AND WHEREAS the conditions imposed by the said Act of Congress approved on the twentieth day of June, one thousand nine hundred and ten, and by the said joint resolution of Congress have been fully complied with:

NOW THEREFORE, I, WILLIAM HOWARD TAFT, President of the United States of America, do, in accordance with the provisions of the Act of Congress and the joint resolution of Congress herein named, declare and proclaim the fact that the fundamental conditions imposed by Congress on the State of Arizona to entitle that State to admission have been ratified and accepted, and that the admission of the State into the

Union on an equal footing with the other States is now complete.

IN TESTIMONY WHEREOF, I have hereunto set my hand and caused the seal of the United States to be affixed.

DONE at the City of Washington this fourteenth day of February, in the year of our Lord one thousand nine hundred and twelve and of the Independence of the United States of America the one hundred and thirty-sixth.

Wm H Taft

By the President:

Huntington Wilson

Acting Secretary of State.

RECLAMATION ARRIVES WITH STATEHOOD

*Still the world's largest masonry dam,
historic Theodore Roosevelt Dam today is more vital
to Arizona's economy than it was
at its dedication on March 18, 1911.
One of the greatest welcomes ever given
a distinguished visitor was accorded Teddy Roosevelt
when he arrived to dedicate the dam
named in his honor. He is pictured below
leading the trek to the dam.
Seated in the rear, between Teddy and driver,
can be seen Arizona's last Territorial Governor,
Richard E. Sloan (in derby hat).*

First Political Salvo!

ANNOUNCEMENT

Globe, Arizona, September, 21, 1911

TO THE PEOPLE OF ARIZONA:

I desire to announce that I am a candidate for the nomination by the Democratic party for the office of Governor of the State of Arizona.

In times past my fellow citizens have repeatedly honored me with positions of trust and responsibility. I shall tire no one with an extended review of my record. It is or easily can be known to the voters of the Territory. To it I feel that I can safely refer, and shall say of it no more than that it has been my constant endeavor, in so far as it lay in my power, to repay the confidence reposed in me with my best and most earnest service.

Neither do I wish to tire anyone with extended promises of what I shall do as governor, if elected, for I believe that the voters of the Territory will realize that the past record of a public servant is a better criterion of fitness to hold public office than future promises, be those promises ever so numerous or alluring.

As to my platform, however, I feel that I should say that I heartily endorse our Constitution. As a Member and President of the Constitutional Convention, I devoted my best energy towards securing the embodiment in our Constitution of those principles of self government by which the control of the government may really abide in and with the people. Our Constitution puts us in the very front of those of our sister states which are now engaged in making our state governments truly representative. I realize, however, that a constitution, however good, is of itself helpless to secure anything and that relief can come only from good principles of government earnestly and uncompromisingly enforced by executive officers. If elected to the office of Governor, I shall devote every talent I possess to carry into effect, for the benefit of the people of our new State, the principles of the Constitution, and to secure and enforce laws which are called for by the Constitution and which shall partake of the same spirit as the Constitution.

I believe that the one way in which the people can secure to themselves the full effect, or any effect whatsoever, of the provisions of the Constitution, is to elect to the various offices of the State, not only honest men, but men in full accord and sympathy with our Constitution. As one of those men who have at all times stood for those principles, I announce my candidacy for the office of Governor.

With a profound sense of gratitude to those who have hitherto honored me with their trust and esteem, and with a deep realization of the high honor and responsibility that will come to the first incumbent of the office of Governor, I solicit the support and aid of all citizens who sincerely believe in the rule of the people by the people themselves.

GEORGE W. P. HUNT

Senator Barry Goldwater

States His Plans For 1964

Ever since the last Republican convention thousands of Americans have asked me to seek the Republican presidential nomination in 1964. I have withheld a decision until now, not because of any attempt to be politically coy, but because I have been giving every aspect of such a decision the most serious consideration.

Today, here at our home, in the State I love, with my family and with the people whose friendship and political interest have placed me where I am, I want to tell you two things.

First — I want to tell you that I will seek the Republican presidential nomination. I have decided to do this because of the principles in which I believe and because I am convinced that millions of Americans share my belief in those principles. I have decided to do this also because I have not heard from any announced Republican candidate a declaration of conscience or of political position that could possibly offer to the American people a clear choice in the next presidential election.

One of the great attributes of our American two party system has always been the reflected differences in principle. As a general rule one party has emphasized individual liberty and the other has favored the extension of government power. I am convinced that today a majority in the Republican Party believes in the essential emphasis on individual liberty.

I have been spelling out my position now for 10 years in the Senate and for years before that here in my own state. I will spell it out even further in the months to come. I was once asked what kind of a Republican I was. I replied that I was not a "me-too" Republican. That still holds. I will not change my beliefs to win votes. I will offer a choice, not an echo. This will not be an engagement of personalities. It will be an engagement of principles.

I have always stood for government that is limited and balanced and against the ever increasing concentrations of authority in Washington. I have always stood for individual responsibility and against regimentation. I believe we must now make a choice in this land and not continue drifting endlessly down and down toward a time when all of us, our lives, our property, our hopes, and even our prayers will become just cogs in a vast government machine.

I believe that we can win victory for freedom both at home and abroad. I believe that we can be strong enough and determined enough to win those victories without war. I believe that appeasement and weakness can only bring war. I have asked and will continue to ask: Why not victory — why not victory for sound, constitutional principles in government — why not victory over the evils of communism?

I am convinced that in this year 1964 we must face up to our conscience and make a definite choice. We must decide what sort of people we are and what sort of a world we want — now and for our children.

My candidacy is pledged to a victory for principle and to presenting an opportunity for the American people to choose. Let there be a choice — right now and in clear, understandable terms. And I ask all those who feel and believe as I do to join with me in assuring both the choice and the victory.

The second thing I want to tell you is that I will continue with all my strength to work for America and for Arizona in my service in the Senate. I have previously announced that I will file for reelection to the Senate. I find no incompatability in these two candidacies.

BARRY GOLDWATER

TABLE of CONTENTS

1

The NATURAL SETTING

THE LAND CALLED ARIZONA derives its name not from a corruption of the words arid and zona or zone, as some people have thought, but from an Indian term meaning land of little springs or land of few springs. A general area in the eighteenth century, it did not exist as a definitely fixed area until 1863, when its boundaries were defined by an act of the Congress of the United States. Arizona's only natural boundary is the Colorado to the west, while the southern boundary with the Republic of Mexico was decided by treaty. The limitation of land area on the east with New Mexico was artificially set as was that of Utah to the north. A Rocky Mountain state, Arizona is today the sixth largest state within the Federal Union. A maximum width of 337 miles and a maximum north and south distance of 391 miles combine to give a total land area of 113,956 square miles.

The state lies entirely west of the Continental Divide and has three distinct geographical zones. The low desert in the southwest, the mountain ranges generally running from the northwest to the southeast, and the high plateau country in the north provide great varieties in landscape and terrain. In the southwest corner of the state the land is at sea level while in the north central mountains, Humphrey's Peak rises 12,670 feet above sea level. Arizona has been called "geology by day and astronomy by night." The high clear atmosphere at Flagstaff early attracted those working in the science of astronomy while more recently Kitt Peak in the south has become another center for that area of human activity. Without doubt Arizona's most spectacular natural wonder is the Grand Canyon although the area also features such lesser rivals as the Painted Desert, the Petrified Forest, and other canyons such as those formed by the Salt River in its winding through the eastern part of the state. When it comes to scenery in general, Arizona presents many wondrous things to behold.

Much of the story of Arizona centers around its rivers and indeed it is generally thought that human civilization itself at the outset took shape from societies living near great sources of water. The river-centered civilization is especially a feature of one located in a land of limited rainfall which Arizona is. While some areas receive as high as an average of thirty inches of rain per year, there are areas with as little as an average of two inches, and one-half of the state's present population lives in the Phoenix metropolitan area where the average is only seven inches a year. The water problem is compounded by temperatures which may range up to 127 degrees F. or as low as 40 degrees F. below zero. The Colorado River is the major stream while the Little Colorado, Gila, and Salt Rivers play important secondary roles. The dependency of the inhabitants of Arizona on water is the fact of life first recognized throughout the entire period of human habitation of the land.

If Arizona was not favored by nature in the matter of water, it was in the area of mineral resources. First gold and silver, then copper and its by-products of lead and zinc, and later asbestos, manganese, tungsten and uranium, have provided great wealth for the state and those who have exploited these gifts of nature. In the late nineteenth century, some coal was found, but like petroleum later, it provided a small quantity of marketable products and was economically disappointing. More unfortunate was the discovery of diamond mines which proved to be a total failure since the whole thing was a man-made fraud anyway.

In the matter of plant life, once again Arizona offers great variety. Some of the land is timbered and suitable for commercial lumbering, although this area is unfortunately limited. More common are the Christmas tree type of forests, and the desert trees such as the palo verde with its lovely yellow blossom. This last mentioned tree is the official state tree, designated by act of the legislature. There are several dozen types of cactus ranging from the giant saguaro, (the blossom of which is the official Arizona flower), to the barrel, organ pipe, prickly pear and the different varieties of the cholla, or jumping cactus. Sagebrush, grasses of many types and sometimes strange and unusual plants complete the picture. Visitors to Arizona will find many attempts directed toward showing and preserving the non-animal life of the state. The national forests occupy sizeable portions of Arizona and the Organ Pipe National Monument, Saguaro National Monument, and such private facilities as the Arizona Sonora Desert Museum, near Tucson, display the natural wonders of the state.

There was once a time when the animal life of Arizona consisted of dinosaurs and giant ground sloths, but in more recent times there have been deer in abundance, elk and antelope, as well as a few bighorn sheep and buffalo. The unfortunate mountain lion has been hunted to such an extent that the balance of nature is threatened. In the Grand Canyon area, for example, the deer which are such cuddly, attractive creatures have caused much destruction of vegetation because they have not been limited in numbers by their natural enemy, who is just not an attractive pet-type animal. The roll call of wild life also includes the javelina, which is a peccary, now and then a bear, some wild-cats, foxes and wolves. Smaller animal life is represented by the beaver, raccoon, muskrat, and the rabbit. Birds also evidence a great variety of types ranging from eagles, hawks, and owls, to doves, sparrows and on to the tiny hummingbirds. Fish seem to be ever present as are reptiles of many types including the notorious rattlesnake and the equally unpopular Gila monster. Insects, too, seem often more than plentiful.

It is difficult to be neutral about the climate and geography of Arizona. Some love it and would live no other place, while others have an equally negative reaction to it. Still no one would deny that in Arizona there is much to see and the eye is rarely bored. Even if it is not a place where one would live, or like to live, it is one to visit and explore. There are various forces at work on the natural features of the state, and the least

The original portion of the Arizona capitol looks today much as it did in 1901.

kind of them all is man. He has polluted the air with the wastes of his industrial society to such a point that this problem is one of the most pressing now being considered by our governmental operations. He has placed ugly billboards about the land and added insult to injury by even lighting them at night. He has built horrible pre-fabricated slum housing for the future and ignoring those styles of architecture which would seem to fit or blend into the natural surroundings, has attempted to wed desert landscapes with New England Cape Cod, Southern pre-Sherman, or even Polynesian styles with almost unbelievable results. Row upon row of shoddy American apple-box residences which start to crumble long before the mortgage is taken care of will present great problems to future generations interested in slum clearance.

The natural features of Arizona have influenced the history of civilizations founded within the land in many ways. Since the coming of the Anglo-Americans, for instance, the climate has tended to make an impermanence of settlement. Due to this and the material resources of Arizona, there has been a tendency of people to come in the hope of making a fortune and then depart for more comfortable surroundings. Actually it was not until the mid-twentieth century that some parts of the state were made livable all the year around. Refrigeration has certainly been one of the great additions to the Arizona scene and one which contributes to a more permanent population group.

After decades of squandering energy resources it became evident during the last third of the twentieth century that shortages in this area exist. As efforts were made to find and conserve energy producing materials it occurred to people that aside from such projects as atomic energy plants, which remain somewhat controversial, it might be possible to harness more natural forms of energy. Two examples were being talked about in Arizona. During the first half of the decade of the 1970's experiments were made in the central part of the state to tap geothermal energy, the heat within the earth, and some test wells were drilled. There were no immediate commercial results and the project soon became dormant. By the mid-1970's there was much discussion of solar energy and on a limited scale houses and other buildings were constructed which would utilize this great resource. There was also much interest in obtaining for Arizona a Federal research installation where important experiments would be conducted. □

2

PRE-COLUMBIAN CIVILIZATIONS

THE HISTORY OF THE NEW WORLD prior to the coming of the first European is the subject of much conjecture and educated guessing. In the absence of written records, it is necessary to speculate, excavate, theorize and debate, before reaching generally held conclusions as to the stories of civilizations which once held sway over this large area. It is, for instance, usually believed that man has lived in the New World for a much shorter period of time than he has lived on other parts of the globe. This leads most to conclude that some ten to fifteen thousand years ago, human beings crossed from what is now Soviet Siberia into Alaska and then being intelligent creatures they headed south toward a warmer climate. In time, they populated North and South America and, misnamed Indians by Columbus, built great societies and civilizations. Some peoples, less fortunate, existed as small pockets of human habitation barely eking out a living in remote and sometimes desolate places.

The problem of reckoning time in ancient days is always present. In recent years the Carbon 14 and Potassium Argon processes have aided archeologists, but for the record of man in the New World, these systems are not as helpful as they might be, for the time-error beyond which they cannot calculate is considerable. When there is a possbility of something being plus or minus ten thousand years, and man has been here little more than that time, the difficulties become very evident. An Arizonan, Dr. Andrew E. Douglass, (1867-1962), originally an astronomer, contributed a new science, dendrochronology, to the archeologist. Douglass concluded that certain trees each year produce a ring within the trunk of the tree which over decades can be pieced together to form a master time chart. As the exhibits in the Arizona Museum on the University of Arizona campus show, these rings form a pattern of different widths. Thus if a log is found in the site of an ancient dwelling, it can be compared to the master time chart and from the pattern of wide and thin rings, its approximate time can be told. While not absolutely accurate, this method has been of great value.

Arizona was never the center of great civilizations as modern-day Mexico, Guatemala and Peru were, but rather was in the back water of these areas of early human life. The other societies were much more complex and sophisticated than the organization of life found here. Still some

Montezuma Castle photographed before ramps were constructed to take visitors into the ruins.

interesting records of past civilizations have been unearthed in Arizona. Some ten thousand years ago, Cochise man lived in the Sulphur Springs Valley of southeastern Arizona. Around 2000 B.C., a primitive type of farming is believed to have been developed and other trappings of civilization, such as governments, religion and a social order, were also gradually taken on. Evidently in the earlier period these Arizonans, scattered around the area which forms today's state, lived in caves as well as pit houses and other crude shelters. Their principal problems in life were obtaining enough water and food and avoiding troubles with their neighbors. The inter-relationships among these groups of early peoples is of great concern to the student of pre-Columbian cvilization, but there will always remain an element of the unknown. About the time of the start of the Christian era there was a three way division among the peoples of Arizona. The Anasazi were the peoples of the high plateau country and later they were often called the Pueblo culture. From them sprang another group the Sinagua, meaning "without water" which inhabited north central Arizona. The Mogollon culture was that of the mountain people while those of the desert were known as the Hohokam. The word Hohokam does not indicate a tribe in the modern sense, but merely identifies those who have disappeared or vanished. These "Indians" inhabited much of what is now Arizona and their civilization has been the subject of many studies. In modern times, for example, Snaketown, a site to the south of Phoenix was excavated with good results and much new knowledge was gained.

For the student of pre-Columbian or pre-Cortezian life which would be a better term, there are several sites of ancient inhabitation which have been preserved and are open to the general public. The city of Phoenix, which is unique in that its municipal government has a department concerned with archeology, operates and maintains the Pueblo Grande site where one can gain an insight into those who long ago lived in the Salt River Valley and who built an amazing canal system in order to bring water to their parched earth. Modern man has built his canal system along the same lines to a surprising degree. One of the most famous archeological sites within the state is Casa Grande, now a national monument not far from Florence. It was first viewed by a European in 1694. This apartment house, as well as shopping center, a self-contained unit for living, is something of a mystery. Built of caliche and some forty feet high it was constructed of blocks piled one on top of another. In places the walls were more than four feet thick which was not only necessary to support the weight of the roof, but also helped to adjust the climate to a more constant temperature.

In the Verde Valley of central Arizona there are other sites of now vanished life. This life, both human and animal, centered around what pioneers of the nineteenth century called Montezuma Well. The legend concocted claimed that the leader Montezuma had escaped from Cortez in Mexico City and with his retinue came north to live in exile. Actually people probably arrived in the area some four thousand years ago. They too built a canal system to water their farm lands and in search of protection built homes under the limestone cliffs not far away. A surviving apartment community is called Montezuma Castle, and is also a national monument. Somewhat to the north and east, near the present-day city of Clarkdale, a site was excavated in 1933 and 1934, and named Tuzigoot, also now a national monument. The Tuzigoot peoples used their hill-top home as a place of refuge when trouble came to their farm land area below.

Other parts of the state of Arizona also have their ancient sites. Not far from Roosevelt Dam is the Tonto National Monument. There cave dwellers arrived around 900 A.D. and like other groups finally vanished from the scene. Northeast of Flagstaff is Wupatki National Monument, an area of nearly 35,000 acres containing many pre-historic Indian ruins. The well-known Canyon de Chelly, "discovered" in 1849, was another early residence, and is also worthy of attention. Located in the northern part of the state, Canyon de Chelly is not only an important site of the past, but also here modern Indian history is blended with the pre-Columbian civilizations. Some areas of Arizona have been continuously inhabited for about as long as man has lived in the New World.

When the first Europeans arrived in this area in the sixteenth century, the ancient order had greatly changed from what it had been earlier. The modern tribal system was reasonably well developed. Some sort of great upheaval must have taken place in Arizona in the twelfth and thirteenth centuries as we reckon time, or perhaps it took place even later. Some think that wars or disease disrupted the flow of civlization, while others emphasize the idea of a major and prolonged drought which in time resulted in a great famine. At any rate peoples abandoned long inhabited areas and moved about the land. Some groups disappeared entirely and those who survived had their way of life greatly changed. Probably the full story of those years prior to the arrival of the European will never be known, but it must be conceded that this is a fascinating area in which to work and to attempt to push back the horizon of the unknown as far as it is humanly possible to do. □

3

The INDIANS

THE TERM INDIAN became applied to peoples of the New World, as is widely known, because Christopher Columbus believed he had reached the coast of India instead of discovering a new continent. By the standards of western European civilizations these were primitive peoples and they remain so to this day to most Americans. But, primitive by whose standards, one must ask. Certainly they did not think of themselves as being such and in many instances they led a life which brought more satisfaction to them than did the life led by those who invaded their lands. It is so very easy to conclude that the most advanced society is the one where automobiles exist to control the increase in population, and psychiatrists thrive in an attempt to make life more tolerable to those who have to endure it. It must be noted that the Indian was here first and the European or American, as citizens of the United States call themselves, arrived later and attempted to super-impose their way of life upon the older established civilizations. Of course the invaders succeeded but it was necessary to spend a great deal of time, energy, and human lives to do so. In the process, Indians generally declined in numbers, partly due to the wars but partly due to disease brought upon the scene by the outsider. For instance, chicken pox was a mild annoyance to the Spaniard but fatal to the Indian for this disease had been unknown in the New World prior to contact with Europe. In the process of dealing with the Indian the new arrival learned some things. A love of the out-of-doors, common in the American civilization, is derived from the Indian who was much more in tune with nature than the European who was often trying to escape from it. Also various foods, herbs and medicines were borrowed from the native cultures.

The Indian civilizations all possessed the essential ingredients of life although there was great variety in cultures and social orders. There was a family structure, a society, a governmental system, and a religion as well as some relationship to the arts and sciences. Any one of these points may be used for comparative purposes and for arranging the tribal relationships into logical order. However, most generally the Indian peoples are arranged according to language factors and thus Arizona tribes represent the Yuman, Athapascan, and Uto-Aztecan peoples. The history of these tribes and groups has been more or less recorded for some four hundred years now but still much is uncertain and disputed. For example, is this a tribe, or a sub-tribe, how large a group was it in say 1600, and where did these peoples then live? Indian history is less an exact science than history can be. Whatever the Indian population of Arizona may have been at a given time, it is now the largest of any state in the Union with several tribes represented.

Perhaps the most famous Indian group to be found in this state is the Apache which is divided into several different sub-tribes. There is some indication that these peoples were relatively late comers to Arizona, probably related to the plains Indians, and driven perhaps by the Comanches to the west and south.

The Apache really never became a united group in the sense of the other tribes but were always composed of several bands which took their name from a Zuni term meaning enemy. These people were fierce and nomadic and led by chiefs who were elective in a sense and to be followed so long as they were victorious. Much effort had to be expended to bring the Apache under control and they were the last of the Arizona Indians to be forced onto reservations. A near relative, it is believed, are the Navajo, who have the distinction of being the only people to grow in numbers after contact with the European. The Navajo have a reputation of being good traders with a well-developed sense of property, and they are famous for their silver-work and weaving. Early in the period of European contact, the Navajo acquired horses, previously not known in the New World. This tribe then proved to be rather difficult to control from the Anglo-American point of view at a later time and it was not until 1868 that this was accomplished.

The only pueblo Indians found in Arizona today are the Hopi, long known as the peaceful ones who live in the high country on land which has always been marginal at best. An interesting fact of family life is that of reckoning descent through the female line, something also found among some other tribes. These farming peoples are considered conservative in the sense that they tend to resist change and to cling to old ways. A prominent feature of life is an elaborate system of rituals and ceremonials, which on occasion feature the use of rattlesnakes.

Though considered one family basically, the Pima and Papago are two separate tribes. Both are a desert people who tilled the soil and were

The north rim of the Grand Canyon,
Arizona's most famous natural wonder.

always non-warlike. The Papago had the first contact with the Europeans and were the most adaptable to the European ways. They were generous to all who entered their territory with the possible exception of the Apache whom they considered a traditional enemy.

The Mohave Indians of the northwestern part of the state were once the largest and most war-like of the Yuman speaking groups, but are now a relative few in number. The Yuma Indians who proved to be a source of trouble to the Spanish were likewise eventually reduced in number until only a few were left. Other Arizona tribes included the Maricopa, relatives of the Yumas whose traditional lands are on the Gila River; the Yavapai, called the people of the sun; the Hualpai, "pine-tree folk" of the Colorado River living north of the Mohave; and the Havasupai. The last mentioned group make their home at the bottom of the Grand Canyon, and probably never numbering more than one hundred, took their name from the blue-green water of the river.

In a sense the Indian civilizations were doomed from the start and one of the principal reasons for this was that although they won battles they lost the eventual war because they could never make common cause against the intruder. It was possible to pick off one tribe at a time as in the instance of using Papago scouts to track down Apaches. As one lists the Arizona Indian tribes, it becomes evident that many names now used were borrowed from these older civilizations and this is especially true in the names we give cities and counties. Recently it has become fashionable to pay attention to the Indian, his life and his ways. Since the coming of the Anglo-American this life has not been easy, for people find themselves caught between an old order which is really disappearing or difficult to keep alive, and a new order which is only partially understood and is often decidedly hostile to the Indian. □

Manuelito, last Navajo war chief, and wife Chiquita

4

The SPANISH PERIOD

IT IS COMMONLY SAID THAT what is now the United States was, at the start, fundamentally the transplanting of western civilization, or more specifically European civilization, into the "New World." Few people stop to ask why it was Europe and not Asia which became interested in new worlds to first "discover," then explore and finally colonize. It seems enough to point out that Europe did create great empires in both North and South America. The threads of the history of western civilization are to be found running through Greece, then Rome and finally expanding into Europe of the Middle Ages. About 1000 there was the beginning of the decline of the feudalistic system and a new spirit came upon the European scene. People became restless, interested in the world about them, and for one reason or another there began a renewal of trade with the Orient.

Trade then became the first link in the chain which would lead into America. Since the Italian city-states developed a monopoly on this eastern trade and since they charged high prices and hurt other national prides, the rulers of the various other European domains became interested in opening up still newer trade routes. One such ruler, or in this case rulers, were Ferdinand and Isabella of Spain. In reality much of the credit goes to Isabella for her husband was often otherwise too occupied to concentrate on this matter. There came along also, Christopher Columbus, who in the popular mind was the first man to conceive of the world as being round. The fact that he was some two thousand years late in bringing that notion into existence does not harm his reputation. In 1492, with the backing of the Spanish empire, Columbus started west and in October of that year, felt that he had found something. His main trouble was that he could never accept just what he had found. While to his dying day, Columbus insisted that he had reached the east, it was plain to many that there was something out in the ocean, some new land. Just what it was, how large it was, and what its value might be would occupy Europe's time and efforts for many years.

Father Kino, 'The First Arizonan'
a statue on Arizona capitol grounds, Phoenix.

If the discovery of America was an accident, and an unwelcome one at that, and if some spent years trying to find a way to get around it so as to reach the true east, there were those who came to appreciate its value. Columbus brought back to Spain, among other things, trinkets of gold which whetted the appetites of the naturally greedy.

European nations of that period operated on the mercantile theory of trade which held that the importance of a nation should be determined not alone by the size of its military forces, but by the gold, silver and precious stones in its treasury. This was an eminently down-to-earth approach to the problem, for, if one had a small army but a large treasury, the former could always be rented in time of trouble. Soon the search for gold, silver and other possible wealth, became the next link in the onward rush toward America. In the race for New World possessions, Spain was to be on hand first and for many decades was the most successful empire builder.

In the year 1519, Cortez began his epic conquest of Mexico. Once established in Mexico City, that capital became the hub of the fan out from which spread conquistidores in all directions. From the area called the "northern mystery" there filtered back stories of great wealth to be found in the Seven Cities of Cibola and elsewhere. In the 1530's the Viceroy of New Spain decided to check on these tales and sent Fray Marcos de Niza, accompanied by a Moorish slave named Esteban, who had earlier been on some exploring junkets, to the area north of settlement in Mexico. Fray Marcos was told to treat the Indians well, to look carefully at the land, to find places for missions, and very importantly to take possession of the land for the King.

The expedition ran into trouble. Esteban, who had gone ahead, sent back to Fray Marcos optimistic reports of the territory ahead, but then managed to get himself killed by the Indians. In due time de Niza returned to Mexico and said he had seen one of the golden cities, at a safe distance of course, but it is now generally believed he saw what he knew his superiors wanted him to see.

Next on the path of exploration came Coronado who started on his junket in the spring of 1540, with the backing of the Viceroy and accompanied by Fray Marcos de Niza. Coronado not only traversed the eastern part of what is now Arizona, but side groups of his party were responsible for the discovery, by Europeans, of the Colorado River and the Grand Canyon. Although the Coronado expedition went as far as the central part of Kansas, in the end the results were disappointing. Viceroy Mendoza was not pleased for the "northern mystery" was not as rich as it was hoped to be. Although Coronado and others helped to keep alive Spanish interest in the north, little was done to make use of the potential of the area until the very end of the sixteenth century. Then Juan de Oñate established a permanent settlement in northern New Mexico and also found time to explore the area to the west. Oñate is credited with being the first European to appreciate the mineral wealth of Arizona, as well as having seen more of Arizona than any other Spaniard before him.

Up to this point, Spanish interest had largely been built upon economic motives, but unlike the colonial programs of the other European nations, Spain took seriously its responsibility to bring Christianity to the peoples of the New World. As a result the Spanish Empire developed a two-armed system of administration and control for New Spain. The military and the Church worked hand in hand, although not always amiably or in harmony. The presidio, mission and pueblo were to be the institutions by which European civilization would be brought to the wilderness. The Church, Roman Catholic, since no other was tolerated, meant to Arizona principally two orders, the Jesuits and later the Franciscans.

Over the decades and centuries hundreds of priests labored in the area, but none has greater nor more deserved fame than Father Eusebio Kino, often called the "first Arizonan." Long years later, in the nineteen-sixties, Arizona would honor this man by having his statue placed in Statuary Hall in the capitol at Washington where states are invited to place likenesses of their two most distinguished deceased citizens. (The other Arizona entry is Colonel John C. Greenway, Rough Rider of the Spanish American War and mining man.) Ironically, it was the desire of Father Kino, Italian born and German educated, to devote his career as a Jesuit priest to the Orient, and yet he came instead to the New World. Born in 1645, he arrived in New Spain in 1681, and in Arizona a decade later. Kino spent the years until his death in 1711 exploring, Christianizing the Indians, increasing their material well-being, and establishing missions. Cattle, sheep and goats, as well as new agricultural products were brought to the peoples of the land now called Arizona.

Within the modern day state today there are only two tangible evidences of the life and labors of Father Kino. One is the lovely San Xavier del Bac, and the other is what survives of Tumacacori, now a national monument. San Xavier, the "white dove of the desert," is near Tucson and was first utilized as a mission in 1700, although the church was not finally consecrated until 1797. Meanwhile, it was once abandoned and at least once sacked by the Indians. During the Mexican period it was secularized and not reoccupied until 1859, while restoration of the misson to its present state was not begun until 1906. Tumacacori, not far away, was a mission site from 1696, and likewise knew Indian attacks, and abandonment. The present building was dedicated in 1822, but a few years later ceased to be used for religious purposes and was never again reoccupied. In 1908 the ruins were created a national monument and now are under the jurisdiction of the National Park Service. Located to the south of San Xavier, it is visited by many.

Following the passing of Father Kino from the scene there elapsed a quarter of a century before there would be appreciable activity in Pimeria Alta, as the area was then known. Although the missionaries remained, it once again took economic developments to interest the Spanish government in this remote region. The discovery of silver deposits in the late 1730's created at least a brief stir. A report describing developments for the first time used the word, "Arissona." Unfortunately throughout this period Spain was beset by troubles. As an empire and first-rate world power, it was now well past its prime. Its government was creaky and archaic, and above all else Spain was underpopulated and having great difficulty in managing to hold on to possessions long ago acquired or claimed. There was also the constant threat of Indian wars in New Spain. The threat erupted into a major revolt in 1751, as well as several other minor ones from time to time. The greatest outburst resulted in the Spanish getting somewhat more interested in holding on to their northern areas and in 1752 a presidio was for the first time placed in Arizona. It was located at Tubac, south of present day Tucson. Never heavily garrisoned it declined in power over the years and there was also an accompanying decline in interest on the part of the Church.

In 1767, the Jesuits were expelled from the Spanish Empire and in Arizona their work was continued by the Franciscans. The new arrivals were soon busy and a plan was fashioned to take more effective control of the upper part of Arizona's western neighbor, California. One involved in the project was Father Francisco Garces, who had taken charge of San Xavier in June of 1768. No less able nor energetic than Kino, Garcés was soon exploring Arizona and in 1774 made the trek to California to help mark a trail into that area.

The next year Father Garcés was also a member of a sizeable party which departed from Tubac to establish a new outpost in what eventually became the city of San Francisco, California. Today Tubac lives on as a small settlement and historical site, while mighty San Francisco thrives! Tubac's fate was sealed in 1776, an important year in many respects, when the garrison stationed there was moved to the pueblo of Tucson which would in time become the center of non-Indian life in Arizona.

Father Garcés became interested in establishing an outpost near the junction of the Gila and the Colorado rivers and while engaged in that task became a martyr in an Indian uprising in July 1781. When this great man died there was seemingly no one on the scene who could effectively succeed him in his important work. Other priests continued to labor but by the latter part of the eighteenth century the sun was setting upon the Spanish New World empire. New eras in the history of Arizona were about to open. □

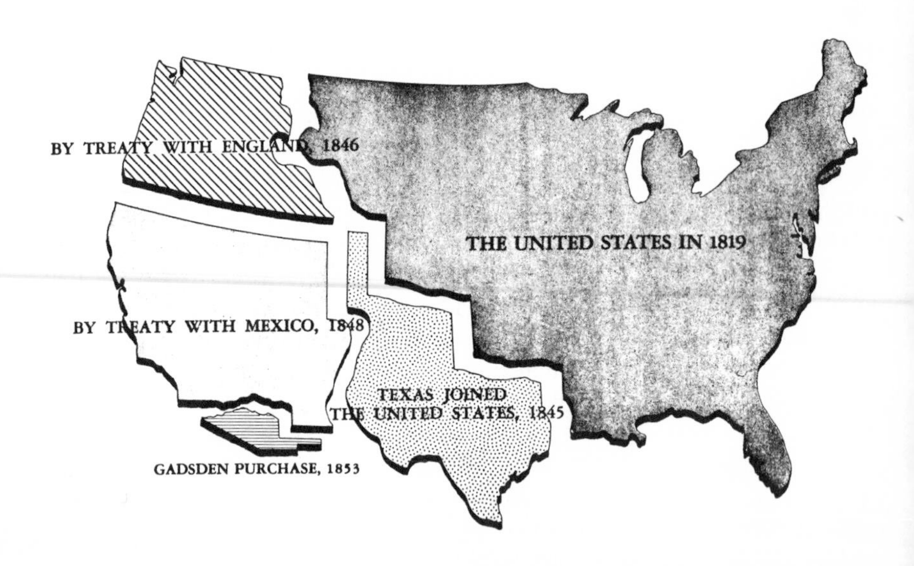

5

MEXICO, MOUNTAIN MEN and MANIFEST DESTINY

IN THE YEAR 1788, His Majesty King Charles III of Spain died, and that year and that event seems to accurately mark the start of the final downfall of the Spanish Empire. The New World peoples, long troubled by oppressive taxes and trade policies, had none the less remained remarkably loyal. Spanish colonists were noted for their docile nature but new outside problems were being felt. To the east of New Spain, there was a new nation, the United States, on the rise; Great Britain was a threat to the north, and there were other troublesome powers such as the Russians. It would be difficult now to even make a pretense at holding on to the Empire. At the end of the eighteenth century, that part of Arizona as we know it which was located to the north of the Gila was virtually unknown. The southern part was lightly held by missions, a small garrison and some settlers and miners. These people faced the constant threat of hostile Indians. Even the parts of Spain's northern empire were for the most part isolated one from the other. There was virtually no east-west contact among California, Arizona, New Mexico and Texas, and little in the way of north-south relations either. Each part was largely now on its own and hopefully could be self-sufficient.

Charles III fortunately did not live to see the events which transpired immediately after his death. 1789 was not a good year for monarchs all over the western world, for the French Revolution erupted. That and its aftermath, Napoleon Bonaparte, would in the next two decades shake the old order to its very foundations. True there had been a revolution in some British colonies earlier, but Spain had managed to cooperate with her ally France against the English, while at the same time avoiding an open siding with a nationalistic revolution. Somehow the French Revolution would have a more profound effect upon the Spanish Empire in the New World.

In 1808, Napoleon on his rampage through Europe, marched into Spain and with the mother country now beset with internal problems, the Latin American colonies became restless. While it is true that the Spanish authorities managed to frustrate the aims and principles of Father Hidalgo in Mexico in 1810, the ideas remained alive and for years Mexico battled to win independence. The old ties with Spain were at last cut in 1820 and 1821, and the new Republic of Mexico was formally launched. Unfortunately whereas the British had trained their colonists in self-government, the Spanish had not and Mexico entered upon a long era of political turmoil and instability. In the spring of 1822, President Augustin de Iturbide decided to make himself emperor, but was overthrown the following year and executed the next. Other governments and other presidents would now follow.

In 1824, the Mexican Congress created the state of Occidente which combined Sinaloa and Sonora and extended perhaps as far north as the Gila River although the boundaries were admittedly a little hazy. This state was to be a member of the new Federal republic but soon internal difficulties appeared and in 1830, Occidente was dissolved. Arizona north to the Gila was now simply a part of Sonora. All of this meant relatively little to Arizona since effective government, or even government of any sort, was virtually non-existent. At this point in its history, once more Arizona would be influenced by events far beyond its control and distant from its boundaries.

Citizens of the United States have always been restless adventurers and the notion that this nation was at one time somehow isolated from the rest of the world is pure nonsense. The United States did not develop in a test tube apart from all outside forces, but rather as an integral part of that which we call western civilization. From the time of its birth as an independent power, the people of the American nation have been going here and there. The China trade and commerce with other parts of Asia dates from the 1780's. In the 1790's American ships were at Monterey and other California ports, and sometime in the first decade of the nineteenth century, traders first put in an appearance in Santa Fe. All such trade with Spanish colonies was of course illegal, but flourishing none the less.

Not only were there adventurers and traders, but there was the mountain man — fur trapper, Indian fighter, explorer and general hell-raiser. If the fur trade was the principal economic pursuit of the mountain man, the raising of a general disturbance in a given area was his chief recreation. Such a gathering of good fellows was regularly held in the 1820's at Taos, north of Santa Fe. Also in the 1820's there was regular trade between the United States and the Mexican province. Goods came in over the fabled Santa Fe trail. In addition to this important stream of commerce, by 1830 the old Spanish trail running through Colorado, Utah,

Nevada and on into California was in operation. Furs and blankets went east while cloth, hardware and various luxury goods went west.

The area which is now Arizona was not especially imposing as a center of commerce and trade, or even a particularly good place for fur trappers; nevertheless the mountain men and others began to wander over the land. The famous Kit Carson traversed Arizona several times; so did Sylvester Pattie and his son, James Ohio Pattie, while William Sherley ("Old Bill") Williams and Pauline Weaver were more or less permanent residents. Sadly, one John James Johnson, whose main claim to fame was to arrange an Indian massacre in 1837, was also a part of the scene. If such could be possible, it seems that in the 1830's relations between Indians and non-Indians became even worse. The Mexican officials even paid bounty hunters to turn in the scalps of murdered Indians. Prices offered were one hundred dollars for a male Apache scalp, fifty dollars for a woman's and twenty-five dollars for that of a child.

The Mexican era did not last long in Arizona although technically it did not come to an end until the spring of 1856, when twenty-six Mexican soldiers walked out of Tucson where they were stationed and headed south. Still the effects of the period on Arizona would be felt for many years to come. Arizona would have a reasonably large Latin American population and the civilization to the south would be felt in the manners and customs of the new "American" civilization.

Throughout the first half of the nineteenth century, expansion was the life blood of the American republic. Starting with the Louisiana purchase in 1803, and ending with the Gadsden Purchase a half-century later, the United States enlarged its original territorial holdings many times over. The notion of expansion, generally always popular, was particularly in vogue in the decade of the eighteen-forties. In the presidential election of 1844, the victorious Democratic party promised to reacquire both Oregon and Texas. The term reacquire was used because there was the political fiction that both areas had once been ours. Manifest Destiny, as such goings on were called, was at its peak and the United States had, so people thought, been ordained to round out its natural boundaries whatever they might be.

The Texas situation was a potentially explosive one from several angles. In 1819, the United States in the Adams-Onis Treaty with Spain, had solemnly renounced all claim to the land called Texas, which was generous of the United States since it had no claim whatsoever to renounce. In the decade which followed several thousand "Americans" were welcomed by Mexico into Texas upon the condition that they renounce their United States citizenship and also agree to become members of the Roman

Catholic faith. By 1835 there were about 30,000 new Mexicans in Texas and trouble developed. Fundamentally there was a clash between an Anglo-American civilization and a Latin-American civilization, but there was also a clash over slavery which Mexico intended to abolish. The Texan Mexicans, desiring the same degree of self-government they had enjoyed as citizens of the United States aided General Santa Anna in winning power in Mexico after he had promised them autonomy in return. Soon, however, they found the new dictator would not keep his promises. The disputes ended in the declaration of Texas independence on March 2, 1836, which then became a reality a few weeks later with the battle of San Jacinto. There was considerable sentiment in the United States for the annexation of Texas but the President merely recognized the new independent republic. To do otherwise would be to enrage Mexico as well as anti-slavery voters in the United States who did not desire more land for cotton farming, which coincidentally was more land for slaves and slavery.

The United States both prior to 1836 and afterward made attempts to purchase Texas but to no avail. For nine years the Republic of Texas was a sovereign nation. In 1844 a treaty of annexation was rejected by the United States Senate but after the election of 1844 had produced a mandate for expansion, Texas was annexed by a joint resolution of both Houses of Congress which required only a majority vote rather than the two-thirds necessary for a treaty. President John Tyler signed the resolution in March 1845, and there now arose the question of the boundary between Mexico and the new part of the Union. Mexico insisted it was the Nueces River which was quite correct, but unimportant since the United States was prepared to defend the Rio Grande as the line separating the two republics. Diplomatic relations had already been broken, due partly to the Texas dispute but also because of Mexican objections to the activities of Amercan agents in California, another Mexican possession about to fall from the grasp of the troubled Latin American nation.

In June 1845, General Zachary Taylor in command of United States troops in the southwest with headquarters in Louisiana, was ordered to occupy a point "on or near the Rio Grande," for the defense of the territory of Texas. Taylor, who had half of the total troops of the entire army then in service with him, at last placed his force of thirty-five hundred men in the desired position in April 1846. Meanwhile President Polk had tried the unsuccessful Slidell Mission which in the summer of 1845 had attempted to again purchase the desired and disputed lands. Now the Mexican general ordered Taylor to withdraw to the Nueces River and when he did not the opening shots of the war were fired. In his message to Congress,

The 'White Dove of the Desert' . . lovely San Xavier Mission.

Polk said, "Mexico has . . . shed American blood upon the American soil," a statement which Representative Abraham Lincoln of Illinois with his "spot resolutions," tried to get the President to prove. The resulting conflict would be unpopular in anti-slavery quarters but it should be noted that the North got what it wanted, namely Oregon, by peaceful means, while the desires of the South resulted in an armed conflict.

President Polk was soon unhappy with "Old Rough and Ready," as General Taylor was nicknamed and so placed "Old Fuss and Feathers," General Winfield Scott, in charge of the planned invasion of Mexico. Ultimately in September 1847, Scott occupied Mexico City. Of more concern to the Arizona story were matters transpiring elsewhere. In many ways the history of California parallels that of Texas. Always lightly held, California was by 1840 obviously about to fall into someone's hands, the only question to be decided was into whose. The Mexican War settled that. As was usually the case, the area now known as Arizona was not to be in the center of events, but was located in the path of these approaching events. When war came Colonel Stephen Watts Kearny began collecting a force known as the "Army of the West." It started from Fort Leavenworth in June 1846 in small detachments going one at a time, and was augmented by eight hundred mounted volunteers from Missouri led by Colonel Alexander W. Doniphan. Altogether Kearny had a force of some twenty-five hundred men who would gather at Bent's Fort, a fur trading post in southeastern Colorado. There the group was also joined by some four hundred wagons loaded with a million dollars in merchandise waiting to be escorted over the trail to Santa Fe.

Kearny displaced Mexican authority in Santa Fe with no difficulty and then with three hundred men pushed down the Rio Grande, his ultimate destination being the southern part of California. In October 1846, he encountered Kit Carson who was heading east but whom he ordered to turn around and accompany the army west. Along the way the party enjoyed friendly relations with the Indians and in late November forded the Colorado River and passed into California. They had deliberately avoided Tucson. The capture of that small but significant settlement would be accomplished later by the Mormon Battalion. This group, numbering some five hundred forty men, recruited with the blessing of President Brigham Young of the Church of Jesus Christ of Latter-Day Saints, had been organized in Iowa but with somewhat reduced numbers set out from Santa Fe in October 1846, under the command of Captain Philip St. George Cooke. The Battalion raised the American flag over Tucson, achieved without bloodshed on December 17, 1846, before it too passed out of what is now Arizona and into California. □

6

PEACE and a DECADE OF PROBLEMS

BY THE END OF 1847 so much Mexican territory was under the control of the United States that the war was virtually over. Nicholas P. Trist, a State Department diplomat sent along with General Scott and later dismissed by President Polk, disobeyed his orders to quit his post and on February 2, 1848, the Treaty of Guadalupe Hidalgo was signed. The document, technically of questionable legality, was approved by the United States and what is now Arizona south to the Gila River became a part of the North American republic.

The next event of consequence to influence Arizona was the discovery of gold in California. Thousands flocked to the new El Dorado and not only was Arizona driven and walked over, but it too received some of the wealth seekers who reasoned that if California were a promised land, perhaps the surrounding areas would also yield riches. The Mexican War, controversial as it had been, now left problems which threatened to disrupt the Union. Henry Clay introduced and Stephen A. Douglas got passed a series of laws in the fall of 1850 which postponed the Civil War for a decade. As a part of this Compromise of 1850, not only was California admitted to the Union but the territory of New Mexico, including Arizona, was created with a capital at Santa Fe. Wisely it was decided to apply the doctrine of "popular sovereignty" to the slavery question in the area. When the territory was ready for statehood the inhabitants would vote on whether they wished to permit slavery, but by the time that day arrived, the question had long been settled.

In the decade of the 1850's the great dream of many in the United States was to build a transcontinental railroad linking the East and the West. As was the case with most of the issues of the time, the railroad question had sectional overtones. The South wanted a line from New Orleans to Los Angeles and obviously such a route would cross Arizona. There was also discussion of the thirty-fifth parallel route across the northern part of Arizona which was traversed by a party led by Francois X. Aubrey in 1853. However, this form of transportation would be in the future and meanwhile wagon roads provided the current method of getting from one place to another. The Mormon Battalion had traced Cooke's Wagon Road, which was the main southern trail into California, but which was unfortunately mostly located in Mexico. During the first half of the 1850's various roads, trails and possible railroad sites were surveyed and marked. The United States Army, largely responsible for this work, delegated it to a group of young officers who would later make names for themselves or leave their names on Arizona's geography or history. Amiel W. Whipple, Joseph C. Ives, John G. Parke, George Stoneman, Lorenzo Sitgreaves, and Edward F. Beale all had a hand in these projects, and Beale, a naval lieutenant during the Mexican War, is perhaps better remembered for his part in the celebrated camel project. In 1855 Congress authorized the purchase of these beasts of burden under the theory that they would be an ideal form of transportation in the far western territories. Beale and his men ultimately brought nearly three dozen of the animals from Texas overland into Arizona. The project was abandoned before long with most people feeling that it had been a failure.

The War Department established its first military outpost on land now included in Arizona in 1851 when Fort Defiance was built in present-day Apache County. In part this action was made necessary by the terms of the Treaty of Guadalupe Hidalgo which held the United States responsible for controlling the Indians in the areas bordering on Mexico. Relations with that Republic also featured squabbles over the exact location of the United States southern border.

In 1853, James Gadsden, a South Carolina politician and promoter of the southern transcontinental railroad idea, was dispatched to Mexico as the American minister. His mission was primarily to acquire new territory, which would be a difficult task. At last on December 30, 1853, the treaty bearing his name was signed. The document was ratified April 25, 1854 after the Senate balked at the promised fifteen million dollars to Mexico and paid instead only ten million. This sum was, however, accepted. Proclaimed in effect June 30, the Treaty also ended United States responsibility for Indian troubles and silenced the question of fifteen to thirty million dollars in damages claimed by Mexico under Guadalupe Hidalgo.

The Gadsden purchase would in time add 29,670 square miles to Arizona. It is often observed that the United States paid Mexico only fifteen million for the entire Mexican Cession while ten million dollars were advanced for a much smaller and less valuable piece of property. There is a strong hint that there was an element of conscience involved in the second transaction. A popular legend in Arizona proclaims that originally the boundary with Mexico was to run straight west from about present-day Nogales, thus giving Arizona an outlet on the gulf. However, it is said that the surveyor in charge reached a point where he either got drunk, or wanted to get drunk, and so headed off in the wrong direction. The story is of course not true, but unfortunately for the future of Arizona, Gadsden tried but was unable to secure a port for the United States on the Gulf of California.

The new area was added by Congress to the territory of New Mexico, whereupon the legislature at Santa Fe extended the western boundaries of its domain into the Gadsden acquired land. There were altogether seven relatively narrow counties which ran east and west through New Mexico. Unfortunately the government at Santa Fe could pay little attention to its western area and before long there was talk of the creation of a new territory. A meeting was held at Tucson to demand the action. In August 1856, two-hundred and sixty citizens framed a petition to Congress on the subject and also elected Nathan P. Cook as its delegate to Washington and Granville H. Oury its representative in Santa Fe. Although Cook in early 1857 presented his petition to Congress, nothing came of it. There was the same result from President James Buchanan's suggestion on the subject of Arizona contained in his annual message to Congress in December 1857. In the next three years various proposals were made on the issue, including that of Senator William M. Gwin of California to create a new political subdivision out of the Gadsden area. One such proposal, introduced into the Senate by Jefferson Davis of Mississippi in December 1859, endeavored to create the territory of "Arizuma."

In 1858 and 1859 there were various mass-meetings held in Arizona to demand action. Then in 1860 a group at Tucson met to draw up a temporary constitution for Arizona, which would be in effect until Congress acted, and to elect a governor of the Arizona fashioned out of the southern part of New Mexico. This movement also failed to win approval but did probably prompt the legislature at Santa Fe to make the western part of one of its larger counties into Arizona county with Tucson as the new county seat. This was done in February 1860, but the act was repealed two years later having never been operational anyway.

Part of Arizona's difficulties in being made a separate territory stemmed from its remote and sparsely settled nature, but there was an even more significant problem. This was the coming disruption of the American Union which became a reality in late 1860. No longer able to achieve a compromise over the many issues prying North and South apart, open war flared in the spring of 1861 and the American people were involved in the most bloody war in their history. Ironically the area eventually formed into Arizona represented one of the unsolved problems which prevented any further compromises. In a last ditch attempt to avert the war, Senator John J. Crittenden of Kentucky and others proposed that the line 36° 30' first drawn in the Louisiana purchase territory, be extended westward and that slavery be allowed south of that line, or at least the issue would be submitted to a vote in the area. President-elect Lincoln, uncertain as to what to do about slavery in the states where it already existed, was absolutely certain that it must not be allowed to spread into any additional territory. Thus because slavery might have gone to New Mexico and Arizona the last hopes of a compromise disappeared. □

Carl Hayden

7

CIVIL WAR and the CREATION OF ARIZONA

THE NEWS OF THE COMMENCEMENT of hostilities in 1861 was slow in reaching Arizona, which only served to point up the remoteness of the area and its great distance from the scenes of the war. The chief import of the war for Arizona, at first, was the ending of the protection afforded the settlers by the troops of the United States. Some officers and men departed to join the Confederacy while others went to New Mexico to serve the one remaining loyal Union commander in that territory. The Indians, seeing a family squabble among the whites, seized upon the opportunity to renew their own wars against the settlers. What of the future of Arizona?

The seceded states, which then formed themselves into the Confederacy, held to the compact theory of the Union which maintained that the Federal association was no more than the sum of the total of its member states. Accordingly each state was entitled to its fair share of the property of the now disbanded Union. The eleven Confederate states saw nothing wrong in laying claim to some western areas and a portion of the people living there were in agreement. There is an assumption that the bulk of the settlers then to be found in Arizona favored the cause of the Southern government. If this be true, it was probably motivated in part by the hope that the Confederacy would establish a more effective government than Washington had. As for the Richmond government, its main interest in Arizona was in securing an outlet to California through the southwestern area, with a secondary desire to enrich its treasury with the products of Arizona gold and silver mines.

Another mass meeting was held at Tucson in August of 1861, and those attending not only asked to become a territory of the Confederacy but Granville Oury was chosen the Arizona delegate to the Congress meeting at Richmond, Virginia. On August 1, 1861, Lieutenant-Colonel John R. Baylor, C.S.A., issued a proclamation announcing the creation of the Territory of Arizona which was to consist of New Mexico south of the thirty-fourth parallel. Later that year, Baylor's senior officer, General Henry H. Sibley affirmed this action. There followed some fighting in the

Rio Grande valley of New Mexico and a rebel force marched west and took control of Tucson.

In April 1862, a Union force heading east collided with a Confederate group in Picacho Pass. The resulting engagement, sometimes called the westernmost battle of the Civil War, was considered a Union victory for the Confederates retreated to the east and the Union forces continued on and assumed control of Tucson. Martial law was declared and taxes were collected for the support of the Federal government. During the remainder of the Civil War, Arizona was quiet as regards the Union-Confederate struggle but not in the matter of the Indian-settler feud. The proclamation by Jefferson Davis, President of the Confederate States of America, creating the Territory of Arizona along the lines of the Baylor proclamation, now had mere historical significance.

If the Confederate territory of Arizona had no lasting importance, the action of the United States Congress at roughly the same time and on the same subject did. Once again in March 1862, a bill was introduced to divide New Mexico at the 109° meridian as once suggested by the New Mexico legislature. There now enters upon the scene a most colorful Arizona character, Charles D. Poston, remembered as the "Father of Arizona Territory." This man, a Kentuckian by birth, was an early arrival in the southwest and in the 1850's became a leading public relations man for Arizona as well as miner, surveyor, irrigation expert, religious philosopher, and politician. Unfortunately in his old age, Poston's stories of his exploits became more involved and elaborate and doubts have been cast upon his account of the creation of Arizona territory. At any rate in December 1862, Poston was in Washington and met with President Lincoln and others in an attempt to get the Arizona bill passed. Since the Civil War was in its darkest days there was not much interest in the project except among certain members of Congress. Poston later told of an oyster supper he gave for various officials including some recently defeated Congressmen. He stressed, in his discussion with these about-to-be-retired men, that Arizona territory would offer new job openings and supposedly the group was interested to the point of apportioning out the offices. Finally Poston said he asked, "Gentlemen what is to become of me?" The answer was, "O, we will make you Indian agent." The bill formally creating Arizona, which was called the Organic Act, passed both Houses of Congress and was signed into law by President Lincoln on February 24, 1863. Early the next month he appointed the first territorial officials and the roster included only two lame ducks, the governor-designate and John N. Goodwin, who was to be chief justice. Poston was indeed made Indian agent. John A. Gurley, slated to be the first governor of the new area, died in

On May 24, 1869, Major Powell, one-armed Civil War veteran, and a handful of men left Green River City, Wyoming, to begin an epic first journey down the Colorado River. They traveled in four small boats one of which was soon wrecked. Three of the men refused to risk the falls and rapids encountered and in attempting to reach civilization on foot perished. Another boat was lost, but after many adventures Powell and the other survivors reached the mouth of the Virgin River at the end of August where they were greeted by Mormon settlers. Powell, who for some years was director of the United States Geological Survey, made other explorations, but the 1869 trip remains his most famous exploration.

JOHN WESLEY POWELL

August 1863, before he set out west and his place was filled by Chief Justice Goodwin. Richard C. McCormick of New York was appointed the first territorial secretary.

As soon as Governor Goodwin received his appointment, he began to organize the party for the westward trek and most officials started over the Santa Fe trail in late September 1863. On November 26, they arrived at the New Mexico capital and later went on to Albuquerque where they were met by a military escort which would take them to their new domain. The eastern boundary of Arizona was not exactly known to the party but they estimated that on December 27, they crossed into the territory and two days later the group halted at a place called Navajo Springs. Here in the midst of a snow-storm, prayer was offered, the flag was raised, oaths of office were taken, and Secretary McCormick made a speech. He also read the Governor's proclamation addressed, "To the people of Arizona." Following the ceremonies hot toddy was brewed for the entire group, the washtub of the expedition being the only vessel large enough to hold sufficient quantity of liquid for all concerned.

The destination of the party was at or near Fort Whipple, a new installation being built in the Chino Valley. On January 22, 1864, they arrived at Del Rio Springs and settled down to work. On March 9, the youthful and energetic Richard McCormick utilized his small hand printing press to issue the first edition of the *Arizona Miner,* the first newspaper published in Arizona north of the Gila. In May it was decided to move the fort and a new site was selected. McCormick named the town Prescott in honor of the American historian and here the territorial government was to be located for the next three years. This was a wild and unsettled area, and although there was the matter of the Indian menace, it was said that the soldiers at Fort Whipple had more to fear from the rambunctious miners than from the natives of the area.

Soon the territorial officials were settled into the routine of establishing a civil government for a large and sparsely-settled area. Governor Goodwin made a tour of Arizona to visit the citizens, a junket considered successful, particularly in light of the fact that at the second election for territorial delegate to Congress, he was selected to that office despite the handicap of being a Maine Yankee in a largely pro-Confederate territory. Six thousand dollars were appropriated to build a log cabin capitol and governor's mansion. Some may joke of Arizona's log cabin but it was still preferable to the present situation where the governor of the state is given no residence.

With a view of establishing permanent government, throughout the territory a census was taken which showed 4,573 non-Indians, and then elections were held. The first territorial legislature convened at Prescott in the fall of 1864 and between September 26 and November 10, accomplished some notable work. The Howell Code, named for its author Justice William T. Howell of the Arizona Supreme Court was enacted into law and based primarily on the laws of New York and California. A new territorial seal was adopted, utilizing the motto, "Ditat Deus." According to law it was to show, "A view of San Francisco mountain in the distance, with a deer, pine trees and columnar cactus in the foreground." Four counties, Mohave, Yavapai, Yuma and Pima, were carved out. A small sum was appropriated to aid the few schools in operation or in contemplated operation. A company of rangers was organized to attempt to cope with the Indian problem.

An almost perpetual issue in this period and for many years ahead was the matter of the permanent location of the capital. Several places were suggested but in 1867, the government offices were moved to Tucson for a decade and then back to Prescott in 1877, and finally in 1889 to Phoenix.

When Governor Goodwin resigned his office to succeed Charles D. Poston as territorial delegate in Washington, Richard C. McCormick was advanced to the top post in Arizona. McCormick would remain an influential figure in Arizona long after he returned to his native New York, but meanwhile he held the governorship until 1869. By that time, Anson P. K. Safford became the third chief executive of Arizona, and the territory was firmly established although there remained many problems to be solved. Governor Goodwin in his 1864 first message to the legislature had predicted:

> The day is not distant when Arizona will occupy a first rank among the wealthy and populous States of the Union. The hostile savage swept away; its mountains and valleys musical with busy implements of mining and agriculture, its unrivalled pastoral regions white with flocks, the wealth of its varied resources made apparent to the world, and its people thrifty and happy, the wonder will be that it was ever neglected by the government, and by capitalists, as an insignificant and unpromising possession.

Unfortunately that optimistic vision would wait years before coming to fruition. Particularly was there a long standing problem with the sweeping away of the "hostile savage." Indian wars would perplex Arizona for two decades. It seems unnecessary to point out that the Indians were here first and had a rather natural and understandable desire to protect what they considered to be rightly theirs. The settlers, on the other hand, generally believed the adage "the only good Indian is a dead Indian." During the brief existence of Confederate Arizona, Colonel John R. Baylor had attempted to solve the Indian issue in his own way. In March 1862 he issued an order to "use all means to persuade the Apaches or any tribe to come in for the purpose of making peace and when you get them together kill all the grown Indians and take the children prisoners and sell them to defray the expense of killing the Indians." Jefferson Davis did repudiate the order later, but unfortunately the Union people were little better in their treatment of the native Arizonans.

While it is true that King Woolsey, who led the massacre of Bloody Tanks near Globe in 1864 where a supposed peace conference was turned into an ambush, was a strongly pro-Confederate man as well as a pioneer rancher and politician, still such activities could not be blamed on the southern government. It is generally said that Bloody Tanks did more than any other single event to arouse the hatred of the Apache for the settlers. In 1867, Governor McCormick in his message to the legislature insisted that the Indian must be taught to accept the white man as his master. The Indian did not take kindly to that notion even if he had never heard that the recent Civil War had been fought in part to do away with such social relationships.

By 1868 when the Navajos were placed on their reservation, only the matter of the Apache remained unsettled. The War Department was hard-pressed to control a vast area with the relatively few troops at its command. Unlike later legends and literature, the cavalry generally did not come racing up at the last minute with bugles blaring. Often it did not get to the scene of trouble at all. The regular army was at times supplemented by volunteers and later a militia which utilized other Indians as guides and spies against the Apache, but General John S. Mason after a fact-finding tour in 1865 concluded that the best to be hoped for was to hold the forts then established and to escort supply trains through the area. In the following several years various army commanders tried to remedy the situation, or to at least maintain the status quo. General George Stoneman, explorer and surveyor of the 1850's, sought to persuade the Indians to settle on reservations, but angered the whites for, among other things, attempting to reduce the number of military forts. The forts, in addition to giving a degree of protection, contributed greatly to the economy of the territory and local merchants and traders had a vested interest in keeping them in operation.

In April of 1871 the terrible Camp Grant massacre occurred when peaceful Apaches were slaughtered near Tucson. This time the outcry raised reached the ears of the normally unconcerned President Ulysses S. Grant and the chief executive dispatched a concilliator, Vincent Colyer, a Quaker who now really incurred the wrath of the Arizona citizenry. Shouted a newspaper, the people "ought, in justice to our murdered dead,

Arizona Territorial Officials, 1863 — Standing, from left: Henry W. Fleury, Milton B. Duffield and Almon Gage; seated are Joseph P. Allyn, John N. Goodwin and Richard C. McCormick.

dump the old devil into the shaft of some mine, and pile rocks upon him until he is dead." The man of peace was further spoken of as a "treacherous, black-hearted dog." Colyer's efforts were followed by those of more military men. General O. O. Howard did make a peace treaty with Cochise which quieted the situation so long as that great figure lived. However, after his death in 1874 there was again scattered fighting until General George Crook arranged another truce.

After the start of the second half of the 1870's warfare seemed a thing of the past. Much credit is due to John P. Clum, a notable Indian agent who did fine work. In time it developed that it was one thing to get the Apache onto the reservation and quite another to keep them there. The last Arizona Indian battles took place in the first half of the 1880's. Geronimo and others fled the reservation but ultimately in 1886, Crook arranged and General Nelson A. Miles got the immediate credit for bringing Arizona's Indian wars to a final close.

Sizeable Indian reservations were created within Arizona. Now a curious quirk in the American character manifested itself. The "noble savage," now vanquished and at the mercy of his conquerors, replaced the "hostile savage," and people began to feel sorry for the lot of the Indians. In the 1880's there was a debate in Congress and elsewhere over the future of the tribes, and the Dawes Act of 1887 marked the apparent triumph of the forces who believed in the assimilation of the Indian into the mainstream of American life. Unfortunately for many years the policy of the Federal government was to ignore the whole issue as much as possible. The long promised Indian citizenship did not materialize until the 1920's and in Arizona it was actually 1950 before reservation Indians could vote. It was 1973 when the state supreme court ruled an Indian living on a reservation could be a member of the county board of supervisors. Caught in the cross-fire between an old and traditional civilization and a new and not always kind and benevolent "survival of the fittest" society, the story of the treatment of the Indian remains a sad chapter in the history of the United States.

At last with the start of the Presidency of Franklin D. Roosevelt in 1933, traditional Federal policy was changed and renewed emphasis was placed on tribal organizations. Slowly attention began to be paid to trying to rehabilitate the Indians, but problems created over the decades and even centuries do not evaporate overnight. Today the Arizona reservations, nominally held in trust by the Federal government, comprise 19,411,691 acres or, over one quarter of all land in the state. Ironically the system of government now applied to the reservations in many ways resembles the original concept of Indian nations within the larger American nation, rather than the 1880's idea of assimilation. There still remains the question of the future of Federal Indian policies. □

8

The TERRITORIAL PERIOD

THE GROWTH OF ARIZONA from the establishment of the territory until the end of the nineteenth century, insofar as population is concerned, was steady if not spectacular. The census of 1870 revealed total inhabitants of only 9,658, but by 1880 the total was 40,440. Then in in the next decade the population more than doubled and in 1890 it was reported at 88,243, while in 1900 the number had climbed to 122,931. During this time Arizona was transformed from a wild, remote, inaccessible area to a settled relatively comfortable place.

In as large a territory as this was, transportation and communication would naturally be a problem. By the early 1870's the telegraph had linked Arizona to the outside world. For many years most goods and products were brought in by way of the steamboats which plied the Colorado River and then commerce was hauled into the interior settlements by freight wagons pulled by bull teams and oxen. This era began to vanish when the first transcontinental railroad to pass through Arizona, the Southern Pacific, was finished in 1881, and was further pushed into history when the Santa Fe completed its line across the northern part of the territory in 1885. Shorter lines were then also built to connect the larger roads to cities and towns. The lonely isolation which had so characterized pioneer life now gave way to a new order and way of life. Not only was it possible to know almost at once what was going on in all parts of the outside world, but it was also now possible to reach that outside world in the matter of a few days instead of the weeks and months formerly required.

Over the years, cities and towns sprang up around Arizona. Some places such as La Paz, Gila City and Ehrenberg had their brief day and then vanished, while others although they would have their ups and downs, would remain as permanent and lasting settlements. Various factors led to the founding of these towns. The activities of the Mormon Church resulted in the starting of Littlefield, Fredonia, Springerville, St. Johns, Show Low, Snowflake, Joseph City, Mesa, Holbrook, Benson, St. David and other communities. Railroading brought forth Flagstaff, Ash Fork and Seligman.

The mining industry gave birth to such famous places as Tombstone, Jerome, Globe and Wickenburg. Some towns came into being because of their strategic location. Nogales is a logical entry point from Mexico as Yuma is from California. Such places as Phoenix, Florence and Tempe (once known as Hayden's Ferry) were agricultural or trade centers. As the years passed, once important cities rested on their laurels and were surpassed by lesser rivals. Maricopa was once a more important place than Phoenix, while Crown King in the Bradshaw Mountains, now a sleepy hamlet, was once one of the largest cities in Arizona and could even boast it had a railroad linking it to other places.

When settlers arrive in a new place they naturally must have some sort of economic activity to pursue. Often they are drawn because the activity is there first. Mining in all forms and aspects has always been important to Arizona. Once it was gold, and in its day the Vulture Mine at Wickenburg is said to have produced ten million dollars worth of ore, while La Paz mines gave up eight million and those around Gila City (located west of Yuma on the Gila River) yielded two million. Then silver had its reign. The famous Mowry mine near Patagonia was well known in the days before the Civil War, while seemingly all the world has heard of Tombstone, another great silver producing area.

By the early 1880's the world of electricity was at hand with its telephones, motors, and lighting, and copper essential to all of these, would prove to be more valuable to the economy of Arizona than gold and silver combined. Famous copper mines included the Copper Queen at Bisbee and the Old Dominion at Globe, while there were several important copper producing areas. These included Jerome (and later Clarkdale), Globe and Miami, Clifton and Morenci, Bisbee and Douglas, as well as the Ray-Superior-Hayden area. Since the machinery needed to work the mines in the most profitable manner was expensive, outside capital was vital and so Easterners, and often Europeans too, invested in the material wealth of Arizona. While this got the job done it also led to one of Arizona's favorite grumbling points of the late nineteenth and early twentieth centuries, the problem of absentee ownership and control of the economy. Some charged the wealth of Arizona was being taken out with little being reinvested in the territory.

While mining was the most spectacular aspect of the Arizona economy, livestock and agriculture were very important too. Father Kino is credited with having brought the first cattle to Arizona and prior to the Civil War herds of animals were driven in from Mexico, California, and Texas. On through the territorial period there were great cattle ranches in operation. However, the industry had its troubles. Indians raided the stock; water was often in short supply; and in the 1880's there was a collapse of the price structure due to the over-production of meat animals. By the end of the century a new cattle industry had taken over with emphasis on improving the breed of livestock, scientific feeding, and taking care of the animals, while the old open range system had simply allowed the herd to look after itself. At roughly the same time the cattlemen appeared, so too did the sheepherder, and according to legend the two were not exactly on the best of terms. The cattleman also failed to subscribe to the notion that the "cow-man and the farmer should be friends."

The farmer was lured out west in part by the Homestead Act of 1862, and other promises of Federal land, but often suffered cruel disappointments. The land was far different from that to be found east of the Mississippi. Everyone it seemed needed more water and the crude earthen dams connected to the canal systems were not always dependable. For instance in the early 1890's there was the terrible Walnut Grove disaster when a dam gave way and swept everything and everyone in the wake of the water. For years Arizonans agitated for the Federal government to do something to provide an adequate and dependable supply of water. More and more irrigation seemed to be necessary to the territory. Still with the water available, Arizona farmers produced wheat and corn as main crops, then alfalfa and eventually cotton. Vegetable farming was also found to be profitable as was citrus raising which was first introduced on a commercial basis in 1891.

The old Governor's Mansion at Prescott is now a museum.

In the history of the frontier and the West of the United States there is always the question, just who went west? Was it the brave, hardy, noble pioneer, or the social misfit who could not make a go of it elsewhere? It is said that some went west because they were not wanted, while others went west because they were. Indeed all types helped to populate Arizona. There was the sturdy God-fearing and strong type (and inter-mixed were a good number of "free thinkers" too), but also the alcoholic, the confidence man, and the drifter. In one respect Arizona was fortunate in the fact that there was a prevailing notion that the place was a good one for health seekers. Several valuable and worthy pioneers came because they were in ill health or had members of their family in poor physical condition.

There is no doubt but that some of the early settlers led colorful lives and often of the type that would tend to embarrass sensitive future generations. There is a natural tendency for succeeding members of a family to forget the pioneering generation's limitations, especially after that generation has disappeared and is no longer around to display its eccentricities. Indeed it seems fashionable to dehumanize all of the past and to place the halo of nonhumaniness around the heads of all who have gone on before us. Regardless of which type of pioneer is under discussion, it must be admitted that they lived pretty much as they pleased, were really rugged individualists and cared little for the stifling trappings of conformity.

In commenting on the Arizona society of the latter half of the nineteenth century, it is possible to overdo the talk of shootings, lynchings, drinking and general carousing. Law and order did generally prevail with some notable exceptions. In all communities the institutions of society soon became evident. Newspapers made their weight felt, generally arrayed on the side of community good. The *Silver Belt* of Globe, the *Citizen* and the *Star* of Tucson, the *Miner* of Prescott and the *Republican* of Phoenix, though they often changed their names and even more often their editors and publishers, were well-known. Thomas F. Weedin, Louis C. Hughes, William (Bucky) O'Neill, Dwight B. Heard and others labored for the welfare of the public as they saw it. Churches also exerted much influence. While the Catholics and the Mormons were active in Arizona first, by the end of the 1870's the various Protestant groups began to arrive. It is generally said that a Presbyterian mission built in Tucson in 1878 was the first Protestant church in Arizona while the small Episcopal church in Tombstone is the oldest presently standing.

Schools were laboriously built and staffed. There were schools in Prescott and elsewhere following the founding of the territory and Governor Safford in the early 1870's got the legislature to begin the first comprehensive public school program. Most communities had social organizations of one sort or another. Fraternal groups existed from the start of many settlements and ladies organizations, cultural societies, and the like were also formed. Culture, in the form of the arts, was not unknown and travelling companies of actors and singers performed in all parts of the territory. For example, in 1897, Phoenix then a very small town was treated to a full production of Verdi's *Othello*. Then too the local Chautauqua was an important thing in the lives of several generations of Arizonans.

For many years in this state there was a general feeling that Arizona was a separate and distinct, perhaps even isolated place, and to some extent this is true. Far to the south was the Mexican civilization, but it was remote and Mexico too had a frontier to her north. To the west lay California but there was a desert in between Arizona and those largely coastal settlements. To the north was Utah and its Mormon society, but there was a vast and largely unsettled area in between. Sandwiched in between Utah and California was Nevada, in reality a colony of California with its actual seat of affairs in San Francisco. Finally to the east was New Mexico but its principal settlements were centered around Albuquerque and Santa Fe and again a great distance separated that territory from Arizona.

It is generally believed that most settlers who arrived in the territorial period were from the southern United States but this is not really true. It would be more accurate to say that the pioneers were from all the states, as well as several foreign lands. They were interesting and they did their best to build not only for their present but for the future as well. Arizona was a hostile and often uninviting land and these people wrested a new life only with work, courage, and hardship. Arizona owes much to the memory of these pioneers who have now largely passed from the scene. Groups such as the Arizona Historical Society at Tucson, plus county and local organizations are today dedicated to keeping alive memories of those who brought Arizona into being.

Ever since the pioneering historical work of Frederick Jackson Turner in the 1890's, students of the American civilization have been concerned with the significance of the frontier and the west as a factor in American history. Some have seen the west as the "safety valve" whereby the pressures of society were released by the fact that a man could always go to a new land and get a new start in life. Others have viewed the frontier as a force for democracy. However much argued are these points, it must be evident to all that the west really did not have a civilization of its own, at least one that lasted for any length of time. As soon as the trappings of the American society and its institutions arrived on the frontier, then the most important single factor of life was the desire of the newly-settled area to emulate the more established parts of the United States. Hence the civilization found in Arizona by the late nineteenth century was virtually a carbon copy of that in Ohio, or California, or Virginia. There were, of course, the regional variations but the fundamental similarity is obvious to all. □

Territorial Prison at Yuma
Termed 'Hellhole of Arizona'

9

PATTERNS of TERRITORIAL GOVERNMENT

FROM 1863 UNTIL 1912, Arizona was an organized territory of the United States and as such it was governed by a system devised in the 1780's for the administration of areas of the United States not yet ready for full statehood within the Federal union. Since the old territorial form of government has now disappeared from the scene it is difficult to visualize that arrangement. In essence, as a territory, Arizona was more or less under the direct control of the Federal government. Territories were thought of as being not yet ready to assume full political responsibility and hence were under the tutelage of the older and presumably wiser sections of the nation.

Various agencies of the Washington government were involved in the day-to-day operations of the political organization of far-away Arizona. Article IV, Section 3, of the United States Constitution states that the Congress shall make "all needful Rules and Regulations respecting the Territory and other Property belonging to the United States," and therefore it was that legislative body which enacted the Organic Act of 1863, thus creating Arizona. That act, borrowed from and patterned after earlier laws, particularly the one for New Mexico in 1850, served to outline the basic structure of government but it was amended and changed many times before it ceased operation in 1912. One item, however, remained in effect throughout the half-century prior to statehood and that was the provision that all laws passed by Arizona's legislatures were subject to Congressional review and if disallowed then the law would be void. Obviously this is one marked difference between lawmaking in a state and in a territory. Also the fact that the form and structure of territorial government could be changed or altered by act of Congress is another radical departure from the system utilized in the states where such power to change rests in the state government itself or in the hands of the people directly.

The President of the United States was more or less involved in the governing of the territories although the interest taken in such matters usually varied from one chief executive to another. In the period 1863 to

1912 few presidents ever visited Arizona and with the possible exception of Theodore Roosevelt none had any real interest in the area. Nevertheless the chief executive appointed the Federal officials who were to operate the government of Arizona.

Four of the executive departments of the Federal government likewise had a direct hand in the territorial system. Prior to 1873, the State Department had a vague administrative jurisdiction over territories which consisted mainly of receiving letters of application from those who wanted jobs "out West," and collecting the necessary reports submitted annually by Arizona officials. This task was then assigned to the Interior Department for the next several decades, and that agency also came to have charge of Indian affairs. The War Department became involved in Arizona during that period when Indian wars were the rule of the day and a very small army tried to police a vast western empire. The Treasury Department was responsible for the supervision and administration of the financial affairs of the territory of Arizona, almost down to the last penny. Spending was particularly watched by the Federal authorities for there was a tendency in the West to go in for some questionable projects which now and then even enriched the lives of local politicians. In addition, from time to time, other agencies of the Washington government had dealings with Arizona and its people. The Attorney General might be asked about the legality of some action, or contemplated action, the Agriculture Department was concerned with that economic activity throughout the whole nation, and the Post Office Department had facilities everywhere as well.

In the face of all this Federal activity, the people of Arizona had only one representative in Washington, the territorial Delegate who sat in the House of Representatives. Elected every two years on partisan political lines, the Delegate was principally a lobbyist, for he had no vote as a Senator or Representative did. His success depended upon persuasion and whatever influence he could manage. Over the years Arizona was represented in Washington by some able men. Charles D. Poston, John N. Goodwin, Richard C. McCormick, Marcus A. Smith and Ralph H. Cameron did their best for the folks back home. For good or ill there was often an intrusion upon Arizona affairs by a member of Congress from some state within the Union. Generally the delegations in Washington from California and Nevada exercised much influence, and the latter state's position constantly upset many Arizonans since it actually should not have been admitted to the Union in 1864 and had less claim to be in the Union than Arizona did.

The chief executive of Arizona was the territorial governor, officially appointed by the President and confirmed by the Senate for a four-year

The second building from the right was built in Prescott to house the Territorial Government's offices.

term, but as a practical matter, subject to dismissal at any time by the will of the President. Sixteen men held the office of governor and considering the low salaries, difficulties, and the bad experiences of other territories, Arizona was most fortunate in those selected for the office. The first three, Goodwin, McCormick and Safford, were influential in the organization and establishment of Arizona. John P. Hoyt, who then served only briefly, was a man of ability who was dislodged in 1878 to make way for John C. Fremont, "the Pathfinder of the West," who had more influence with the President and who needed a job. Fremont at last left in 1881 after being involved in squabbles connected with his alleged absence from the territory, and as a replacement, Frederick A. Tritle became the first Arizona resident to hold the top territorial post. Tritle, a man of considerable ability, was replaced in 1885, by C. Meyer Zulick who had a stormy four years ahead caused, among other things, by his quaint notion that Indians were human beings and were going to be treated as such by the settlers.

In 1889, Lewis Wolfley began a brief tenure to be replaced in 1891 by John N. Irwin of Iowa who had the distinction of being the last of the carpetbaggers, as those appointed from outside Arizona were called. For a year Nathan Oakes Murphy then held office, and in 1893 when Democrat Grover Cleveland became president again, Louis C. Hughes, a Democrat, was appointed governor. Later Hughes, a first-rate personality, was dismissed in a political quarrel with the President, and Benjamin J. Franklin briefly held office until in 1897, when Myron H. McCord was commissioned. McCord, a Wisconsin politician who had lived only a short while in Arizona and was accused of being an outsider, soon resigned to serve in the Spanish American War, but returned to live out his life in Arizona, and then left two widows to fight over his estate which confused things no end.

From 1898 to 1902, former governor Murphy again held office and then in that latter year, Theodore Roosevelt appointed his old Rough Rider comrade, Colonel Alexander O. Brodie, to the governorship. Brodie, a fine man respected by all, returned to active military duty in 1905 and his place in Arizona was taken by Judge Joseph H. Kibbey, another first-rate figure. The last territorial governor, and a very able one, was Richard E. Sloan, lawyer, jurist and scholar. Of the sixteen governors three were Democrats and thirteen were Republicans. Most had extensive political careers either in Arizona or outside before they assumed office. All were fortunately at least reasonably dedicated to their duties as they saw them, and none were outstandingly corrupt or incompetent. Their powers as chief executive were much more extensive and vital than their successors under the state system.

If the people of the territory had no control over their governor, they did over the legislature. The Organic Act provided for an upper house, called the Council, of nine members, and a House of Representatives of eighteen, but this was increased by act of Congress in 1878, to twelve in the Council and twenty-four in the House. The early legislatures met irregularly but from the sixth assembly in 1871 on, they sat every other year in January, until the twenty-fifth and last session convened in 1909. Special sessions were not possible, and the regular sessions could not last over two months. In the early legislatures both houses were roughly apportioned along population lines but later sessions saw the development of Council seats being assigned along county lines and the House adjusted at intervals according to population. There were almost constant squabbles over apportionment and the usual attempts to change the system to suit some political advantage or another. There are no verbatim records of the sessions but the journals and printed acts of the various legislatures (when supplemented with newspaper accounts), give a good idea of what went on.

The President of the Council, and the Speaker of the House, both elected by their respective colleagues, presided over often lively sessions. Frequent complaints were made by the members that they were underpaid but once again salaries were set by Congress and all the legislators could do was to petition Washington for more money. All things considered the members of the legislature usually did a respectable job of enacting laws for their constituents though time was wasted with trivial and unimportant bills. In the early days divorces were granted by the law-making body, persons' names were changed by the group, and one legislature solemnly enacted a statute that no house of prostitution could be located within four hundred yards in any direction from a public school building.

The Organic Act of 1863 provided for a territorial supreme court to consist of a chief justice and two associates, justice of the peace courts, and probate courts. The last mentioned jurists had dealings with wills and estates although other jobs were given to them too, and justices of the peace had the conventional jurisdiction over lesser legal matters. The members of the Supreme Court, which was increased in size by Congress to four judges in 1891 and to five in 1905, actually spent most of their time as district judges, holding trials in their respective areas of the territory and then gathered together at specified times to hear cases on appeal. Some of the justices of the Court over the years were outstanding; Charles G. W. French, Joseph H. Kibbey, Richard E. Sloan, Albert C. Baker and Edward Kent would have graced the bench of any state or nation, but a number of the jurists were obscure political appointees who briefly held office and then vanished from the scene. They were often criticized because they were outsiders who made themselves even more inaccessible by taking long vacations away from Arizona, but once again the problem centered around the fact that salaries were so low that it was difficult to attract good legal talent. At one point the legislature authorized extra compensation from the territorial treasury, but this was found to be in violation of Federal law.

Various other officials labored to keep the territorial system in operation in Arizona. The territorial secretary, appointed by the President, performed the routine work of running executive and often administrative affairs, acted as governor when the chief executive was absent from Arizona, or as was occasionally the case, in between the leaving of one governor and the arrival of a new one. Federal officials also included a United States district attorney, a marshal, a surveyor general, and in the early period a superintendent of Indian affairs. Territorial officials, whose posts were created by the legislature, included an auditor, a treasurer, an adjutant general, an attorney general, a superintendent of public instruction, as well as other posts created or abolished as the legislators desired. Territorial officials were all appointed by the governor and confirmed by the Council.

As time passed and the territorial system became more established, it was necessary to pay more attention to the matter of administration. As institutions such as a university, a normal school, a prison, an asylum and the like were created boards and commissions were necessarily established to manage them. During the territorial period Arizona had such agencies as a Board of Equalization, a Board of Education for the territory, a Live Stock Sanitary Commission, a Railroad Commission, a Board of Medical Examiners and even a board for the Chicago World's Fair of 1893, and one for the St. Louis Fair in 1904. All such agencies were created by the legislature and their members were then appointed by the governor, with of course the approval of the Council.

When Arizona began its existence as a political entity, it was necessary to also provide for local government. Counties were created by the legislature and their boundaries, officials and finances were regulated by the Council and the House. Laws to provide for the incorporation of cities and towns were likewise passed and municipal government in general fell under the scrutiny of the territorial government.

Starting with a brief Organic Act in the midst of the Civil War, the territorial government had by 1912 grown into a full and complete system, which though sometimes resented by the people it served, it was nevertheless relatively efficient and successful. In many ways it was a better government than the state government which replaced it. On the day Arizona joined the Union the whole structure vanished and ceased to operate, but its influence remains in Arizona today. Many patterns of government, agencies and institutions were borrowed from the territorial system and incorporated into the state political operations. In future years when many necessary reforms in Arizona state government are undertaken, the new structure which will emerge, will oddly enough, more closely resemble pre-1912 ways than post statehood arrangements. □

10

CREATION of the STATE OF ARIZONA

THE DESIRE OF THE PEOPLE of Arizona territory for statehood in the Union was a natural one for several reasons, and indeed the only unnatural thing about the situation was that it seemed to take so long to achieve this status. So long as the area remained in a territorial position, its people did not vote for president, they had no real representation in Congress, many of their officials of government were appointed rather than elected, and there was always the matter of Congress limiting the actions of the government in general and the legislature in particular. Although it is difficult to put into concrete terms, there was also a psychological reason for pressing toward statehood. In the 1890's a legislative resolution begged Congress to end the then nearly thirty years of "territorial vassalage."

The first discussion of entering the Union came in the early 1870's but there was little real hope of immediate success, since the area had a small population, and a reputation, especially in the eastern United States, for being remote, inaccessable and a wild uncivilized place. The 1880's brought more people and more talk of winning a new status. Arizona's neighbor California had once gone ahead and written a state constitution without first receiving the customary permission of Congress and in 1889 the Arizona legislature decided to try the same approach. It called for a consitutional convention, which after some delay, met in Phoenix in the fall of 1891. This gathering in short order brought forth a fundamental document for the proposed state which was then approved by the voters 5,440 to 2,280. In 1892 the United States House of Representatives voted in favor of admitting Arizona but no action was taken by the Senate. Arizona would surely elect two Democratic Senators, a Democratic Representative, and cast three electoral votes for the Democratic candidate for president if granted statehood, and the Republican majority in the then current Senate had no particular desire to see this happen. Arizona also wanted the unlimited coinage of silver as currency, while the eastern power structure in Congress, regardless of party, wanted the gold standard. Thus the Constitution of 1891 would have only historical significance for when the 1910 document was being written the convention members did not even have a copy of the old document on hand.

In 1893 and then in the succeeding years until the early twentieth century other attempts were made to win statehood, but all were to no avail. A real crisis developed in 1904, 1905, and 1906, when Congress nearly combined Arizona and New Mexico into a single state. Arizona, which was very much opposed to the idea, was saved only by a last minute provision that joint-statehood must be approved by the voters of both territories involved. New Mexico gave its approval; Arizona did not. In 1908 both major political parties favored statehood for the two remaining continental territories and in the fall of 1909, President Taft, passing through Arizona on a tour, expressed his sympathy with the desire of the people to be admitted to the Union.

At last in June of 1910 an enabling act was passed for Arizona and now a constitution could be written subject to approval by the President of the United States and the Congress. Governor Richard E. Sloan scheduled an election for September 12, 1910 to select delegates to the constitutional convention, and at that time forty-one Democrats and eleven Republicans were chosen. The group met in the Phoenix capitol at noon October 10, 1910. George W. P. Hunt, Globe businessman, legislator, and an advocate of social, political, and economic reforms, was chosen president of the meeting which contained a number of able and interesting personalities. Hunt, Benjamin B. Moeur and Sidney P. Osborn, would among themselves occupy the governor's chair in the new state for a total of over twenty-six years. Morris Goldwater, a staunch Democrat, (who was also an uncle of Barry M. Goldwater), Everett E. Ellinwood, a Grover Cleveland type Democrat, and Alfred Franklin, later chief justice of the state, were all prominent in the proceedings. Other highly useful members of the group were Fred T. Colter, Mulford Winsor, Jacob Weinberger, and Edmund W. Wells. To Michael G. Cunniff, Harvard graduate and former eastern editor and journalist who came to Arizona in search of better health, goes the credit for the final style and wording of the completed constitution.

The Arizona constitution of 1910 was written at the peak of the so-called Progressive movement of the early twentieth century, an epoch characterized by many hopeful and optimistic attempts to reform society and its institutions. The crusaders of that day sought to renew the democratic traditions of America which they felt were being lost in the materialistic society developing around the large corporation, with concentration of wealth and power in the hands of a few, and the corresponding problems of poverty, social and political ills. That there were problems in our society could not be denied but how best to solve them was open to debate. Governor Sloan felt that this was a "wave of radicalism, in the form of constitution tinkering," which would produce many undesirable results. Time has demonstrated that although the Progressives, both Democrats and Republicans, were men of good will and sincerity, some of their reforms were not awfully successful in the long run. For example, they were great believers in the initiative, referendum and recall, while a half century later these devices of direct democracy, stand almost universally condemned as impractical, useless and often unwise. On the positive side the Progressives brought forth reforms which are the basis of our economic and political society today. The idea of government as a referee in economic affairs so as to protect the consumer, the programs for the conservation of natural resources, and the graduated income tax were, if not originated, popularized by these middle-class urban reformers of the days of Theodore Roosevelt.

There exists no verbatim account of the work of the Arizona constitutional convention but various sources provide a good general idea of what went on and what was said in the meetings. President Hunt appointed the members of the two dozen committees which functioned within the group. Whereas the Federal constitution was written by a committee of the whole with all members sitting around the room and working together, the Arizona document was put together in committee sessions. There was, for example, a committee on "Legislative Distribution of Powers and Apportionment," one titled "Executive, Impeachment, and Removal from Office," another on "Railroads," and one on "Labor." An almost endless number of proposals were made by the delegates for inclusion in the new document and they were referred to the appropriate committee for consideration. The committee would then make a recommendation to the full convention. Next, sessions of the whole would be held and everyone would have a chance to express his views. Since Arizona was one of the last states to be admitted to the Union there were opportunities to draw upon the experiences of those states which had gone before. Jacob Weinberger, probably the last survivor of the group, recalled many years later that the delegates investigated the constitutions of the "Progressive states," meaning Wisconsin, Oklahoma, California, Oregon and some others.

In reading over the accounts of the proceedings it almost seems that the Arizona constitution was put together with scissors and paste which is not quite true although there was a good deal of borrowing done. By mid-November the group was holding morning, afternoon and evening sessions and still the work seemed to be going forward at a slow pace. At last on

Delegates to the Constitutional Convention in 1910.

the night of December 5, the convention started over the semi-finished document for a last look and a few days later the work was finished. The major hassle of the entire session was over the provision for the recall of judges but when the last battle had been fought that provision remained intact and the constitution of Arizona was adopted with five Democrats and eleven Republicans voting against it. However, only one Democrat and ten of the Republicans ultimately refused to sign it.

To many the Constitution seemed too radical. Especially did the recall of judges notion seem dangerous, while others were just as vehement in their defense of the idea. Then too there were those who thought that organized labor had had too great an influence on the convention. As one looks back from more than a half century later it becomes evident that the constitution was not radical at all but typical of state documents of the time when it was written. In some ways it was a backward, reactionary step for it used the decentralized executive system with its host of elected officials and little power placed in the hands of the governor.

A state constitution contains an outline of the features of state government. There is generally a bill of rights included which will roughly parallel the Federal Bill of Rights. There is also found a plan for the structure of government, state offices and officials, a discussion of state powers and responsibilities, provision for local government, and some method provided for amending the constitution. The Arizona constitution conforms to this pattern. The state boundaries are set forth, there is a declaration of rights, and articles dealing with the three customary branches of government. The electoral process is spelled out and mention is made of education, counties, administrative agencies, and water, as well as labor.

Today's state constitutions have many problems built into them. Most are too long—the Federal constitution of about six thousand words is adequate to govern a nation of over two hundred million, while some states require over one hundred thousand words to accomplish the same task for a much smaller number of people. Arizona's constitution is fortunately relatively short as state charters go. Around 1850 people in the states developed a distrust of state legislatures in general and so there began a tendency to plan for any possible eventuality and this resulted in excessive detail in the constitutions. Once this was done the documents became rigid, inflexible, and in need of constant change. Generally today almost all state charters need a general overhauling but there is little desire in most places to undertake the task. Special interest groups are fearful of upsetting their hard won *status quo* apple cart. In the last half century fewer than a dozen states have faced up to the matter and in Arizona there has been little serious discussion of a complete revising of the 1910 fundamental law. Instead limited and piece-metal changes have been made by amendments.

When the 1910 convention adjourned there remained the task of winning approval for the handiwork of the Arizona founding fathers. A general closing of ranks among the people of the territory took place in an effort to win statehood. Those who did not like the constitution thought it best to nevertheless get into the Union and to then attempt to make needed changes. In February 1911, an overwhelming majority of voters approved the constitution but almost immediately the United States Senate rejected a statehood resolution and there was much gloom in Arizona. At last in August another try was made to pass the needed authorization and this time the "Flood Resolution," named for the Virginia Congressman who authored it, secured approval. Now, however, the White House stalled the long sought admission to the Union. President Taft, whose background and temperament were fundamentally those of a jurist, was opposed to the idea of the recall of judges. This troublesome question could have been avoided by a wiser handling of the problem. An embryo state must submit its institutions and political process to the scrutiny of the Federal government, but once in the Union, has much more latitude in managing its own affairs.

When the constitution was being written it was understood that the recall of judges idea would not be approved in Washington but Arizona was at last going to be the master of its own destiny, and Arizonans were most eager to throw their weight around—a little too eager as it developed. There was no doubt but that the President had the upper hand and Arizona was forced to bow to his authority. The offending recall was stricken by an election in late 1911, and on February 14, 1912, Arizona was formally admitted as the forty-eighth state in the Federal Union. The following November the recall of judges was once again placed into the constitution, where the provision has been peacefully gathering dust ever since. Arizona voters got even with Taft, however. In the first presidential election held in the new state, Woodrow Wilson, the Democratic nominee, carried Arizona, Theodore Roosevelt, Progressive, came in second, while William Howard Taft, Republican, ran fourth even behind Eugene V. Debs, the Socialist, who was third. □

11

POLITICS and POLITICAL PARTIES

UNFORTUNATELY SOME PEOPLE have the notion that politics and political parties involve things not quite respectable but rather things which are to be tolerated as necessary. Indeed parties are necessary, for without the art of politics and the politician our democratic system could not function. In the early days of the republic the political figure and his work were respected, but in the age of Jacksonian democracy a cloud came over this aspect of life and even today the cloud cannot be fully dispelled. The old tradition. "I vote for the man and not the party," is often customary and probably always will be in the United States. Though there are at times certain unfortunate things to be found within our political system, hopefully most politicians are honorable men and women operating within the rules of the game. To believe otherwise is to have little faith in our entire democratic system. Today Arizonans for one reason or another seem to have relatively little interest in politics which is most unfortunate for the welfare of our state government. Arizonans of past generations were fortunately more concerned with the workings of the political process and perhaps future generations will emulate them.

In the national scheme of things Arizona is politically a small and relatively unimportant state, yet it has produced a presidential nominee, Barry M. Goldwater, an Associate Justice of the Supreme Court of the United States, William H. Rehnquist, an Attorney General, Richard G. Kleindienst, a Secretary of the Interior, Stewart L. Udall, and an Ambassador to Great Britain, Lewis W. Douglas.

Those from the politically older and more important states such as New York or Ohio may have given the nation a larger group of leaders, but it may be noted in rejoinder that Arizona has exerted greater influence in one very important area—that of the Congress of the United States and the Senate in particular. In 1912, Arizona sent to the upper house Marcus Aurelius (or just plain "Mark") Smith who served well until 1921 and Henry Fountain Ashurst, or "Five Syllable Henry," as he was called. Ashurst who served not only ably but colorfully until 1941, was one of the last of the old-fashioned spread eagle orators and a Washington institution. When he died in 1962, the *New York Times* noted that no Senator then serving was as much fun to have around the halls of Congress as Ashurst had been in his time. The Senator was a character. On one occasion when he changed his mind on an issue a colleague remarked, "Well, Henry, I see you have seen the light," to which the Arizonan retorted, "No, I have merely felt the heat."

From 1921 to 1927, Ralph H. Cameron, a Republican Senator, represented Arizona in Washington and was then replaced by Carl Hayden, in many ways a unique figure. Hayden and Ashurst soon became the Arizona team and as the latter once put it, "Arizona is fortunate to have a show-horse and a work-horse," and there was never any doubt but that Hayden was the quiet, hard working unassuming member of the Senatorial team. Senator Hayden, an Arizona native, was the state's original Congressman in 1912 and served in the House until he moved over to the Senate. When he retired in 1969 he had served nearly fifty-seven years in the national legislature, and in influence and ability few Senators have ever outranked Carl Hayden. Self-effacing and almost never known to make a speech, the gentleman from Arizona had a mastery of the workings of the Senate far beyond that of the average member of the Congress.

During the years 1941 to 1953, Senator Hayden's Democratic colleague in the upper chamber was Ernest W. McFarland, later governor and a justice of the state supreme court. An indication of McFarland's importance in Washington was the fact that he was the Senate majority leader during the latter part of the administration of President Harry S. Truman. In 1953, the well-known Barry M. Goldwater went to Washington and whatever one's personal politics it must be admitted that Senator Goldwater brought fame and notice to his state, and also probably he fairly represented the prevailing political thought of Arizonans in the mid-twentieth century. In 1965, Paul J. Fannin, a former Republican governor, became a Senator from Arizona, and in 1969 Barry Goldwater began another period of service in the upper chamber. Thus in over six decades, Arizona has sent but seven different men to the United States Senate.

In the House of Representatives, Arizona's strength is not great in numbers. Originally entitled to only one member, that number was doubled in the 1940's, grew to three in the 1960's and to four after the census of 1970. Since 1912, our Congressmen and Congresswoman have included Carl Hayden, Lewis W. Douglas, Mrs. Isabella S. Greenway, John R. Murdock, John J. Rhodes (who in December of 1973 was elected by his colleagues to the important post of Republican leader of the House)

Two of Arizona's residents have been Republican Party nominees for the Presidency of the United States. They are Territorial Governor John C. Fremont (left) in 1856, and Senator Barry M. Goldwater in 1964.

and the Udall brothers. When there was only one Representative there was no problem in selecting him; he was chosen at large by all voters. Then two districts were made out of the state and in 1948 a most interesting law quietly slipped through the Arizona legislature which was responsible for drawing Congressional boundaries. It provided what should take place when a third Congressman should be added as the population grew, and partly because of this law and partly because of population changes, the census of 1960 showed the districts of Arizona to be inhabited as follows:

FIRST ....663,510 SECOND ....440,415 THIRD 198,236

Not long after, the United States Supreme Court decided that all Congressional districts must be of approximately equal population and so the Arizona legislature was faced with remedying the situation. Though it struggled in its customary fashion, it never could quite seem to reach a decision and the United States courts drew the new boundary lines. District I was to be composed of the bulk of Maricopa County, District II comprised the southern part of the state, and District III was made up of western Maricopa County and the northern counties. In voting District I was considered Republican, District II was Democratic and District III was about evenly divided (it was thought) although it went Republican in the first two elections after its creation.

During the special legislative session of January 1970 the lawmakers while reapportioning the legislature also redrew the Congressional boundaries. The following May a panel of United States judges ruled the plan invalid but allowed the election of 1970 to be held according to its provisions. The theory was that the 1970 redistricting was more current than the earlier court-announced boundaries due to shifting population and the rapid growth of some areas. However the legislature was instructed to utilize the 1970 census figures in producing new Congressional districts for the future. At that time it seemed likely Arizona would receive a fourth member of the United States House of Representatives. Such was the case and the legislature divided the state into four districts of approximately equal population. This plan was acceptable to the Federal court which retains the power to enforce the "one-man, one vote" rule.

Many Democrats complained that the state had been gerrymandered by the Republicans and there was probably some truth to the charge. However, strange as it may seem, there is no great perfect model for drawing political districts. Although only contiguous territory may be included, otherwise the creators of districts may add a few voters from here and there to form a final combination.

At the present time District I is a part of Phoenix, some of Scottsdale, Mesa, and Tempe. District II is the southwestern corner of Maricopa County and the southern counties. Western Maricopa County, the western and northwestern counties form District III, while District IV is northern Phoenix and Scottsdale plus the northeastern and eastern counties.

The two major political parties, the Democratic and the Republican, were imported to Arizona territory in the years following its organization.

For years the former was considered the majority group. In reality Arizona usually had three parties with the Democrats split into two warring factions. One group tended to regard Grover Cleveland as its logical patron saint, while the other was sympathetic with the national administrations of Roosevelt, Truman, Kennedy and Johnson. The problem was further clouded by the time-honored tradition of the pinto Democrat, a Republican who registered Democratic so as to vote in the primary, and then went back to his or her own group for the general election.

The role of the pinto has been greatly lessened in recent years. The complete purging of the voter rolls by act of the legislature required everyone to reregister and many were seemingly stricken by an attack of intellectual honesty. Then too there is a lot more going on in the Republican fold than there used to be. When but a small minority group—Senator Goldwater has said he can remember when the Arizona party could hold its convention in a telephone booth—there was a feeling that everyone must hang together and avoid factional troubles. Now with growth the Republicans have shown they can have the same bruising fights which the Democrats have so long enjoyed.

On the national level, until the election of 1960, Arizona had the distinction of being always on the winning side. Up to that time the successful presidential candidate, regardless of party, gained the electoral votes of Arizona. Since then, however, Arizona has twice been on the losing side of the campaign and twice with the winner.

Since World War II, the Republican party has been on the upswing in the state. There are many reasons for this, not the least of which is the Democratic in-party feuding, and their often (or at least occasional) tendency to go into battle with something less than a presentable first-rate candidate. On the other hand, the Republicans have come forth with at least articulate, vocal and acceptable nominees. Within the past two decades Arizona has received substantial numbers of retired people who tend to be Republican or in sympathy with Republican policies. In certain areas the newspapers tend to be of a Republican persuasion which is of great value to that group. It ought not to be forgotten that new arrivals into Arizona often come from areas where the Republican party predominates, and they bring their politics with them. The mid-west is the case in point here, but California which contributes many new arrivals, is really made up of people from somewhere else and here again the mid-west often furnishes the temporary Californians.

Political parties serve several functions. They narrow issues and compromise views so as to obtain a working majority and most importantly they serve as brokers to furnish the public with candidates. These parties need funds on which to operate for radio and television time, posters, printed circulars and letters, transportation, and the other costs of a campaign involving many expenses. Funds are sought from all sources and spent for many things. Laws on campaign expenditures are virtually non-existent and almost never enforced. As a result a way to spend all money obtained can usually be found. The costs of campaigning for an office, particularly a state-wide one in a big area like Arizona, are so troublesome to raise that the state is often times denied some able would-be public officials who simply have not the resources with which to conduct a campaign and do not wish to be beholden to those few who could provide the funds.

In the 1970 race for United States Senate the winner reported spending $261,282 on his campaign while the loser reported his expenses as $180,777. Similarly the incumbent governor that year spent $122,918 while his challenger spent $63,530. Two years later in the race for Congressman from the new fourth district the winner spent $85,123 while his opponent listed expenditures of $101,801. Even the losing candidate in one of the state supreme court races reported spending $28,492 while the victor's total was $22,516. In a hotly contested race for the State Tax Commission the winner spent $6,968 while his challenger reported expenditures of $15,077. Thus it can be seen that to participate in the race for political office is no inexpensive proposition.

Throughout the nation the political parties are finding it difficult to enlist popular support, particularly of a monetary nature, from the general public. Especially in Arizona is the party organization weak and the problem is compounded by the arrival of so many new people trying to get established in a new community and who have not yet decided to take an active role in party affairs. There is, however, a very great need for all Arizona voters, newcomers or old settlers, to take an interest in political affairs and to work for the party of their choice. Now that both parties within the state are of approximately equal strength, Republicans and Democrats must attempt to harmonize philosophical differences and avoid factional disputes. Both groups must also try and hold to their cause the groups they presently have supporting them in the state while at the same time attempt to win over converts from the other party and the independents.

For the citizen interested in the details of party work, and hopefully in participating in it, a visit or a telephone call to local party headquarters should bring forth a response from those in charge. Party workers are ever in demand and there is always much to be done by way of labor in the political vineyards. Once upon a time in the United States, notably before the Civil War, a good citizen was expected to not only vote but to hold office as well. In this era of spectator sports and spectator politics we might well hark back to that age for a more vital political life. Perhaps that government is best which is not necessarily the most efficient and most expert, but that which involves the broadest possible participation.

The statutes of Arizona provide for the organization of the present political parties and for the possible creation of new ones although the latter is difficult to achieve under Arizona law. Hence there is a reinforcement of the traditional two-party system. The idea of two and only two principal parties is already deeply ingrained in our political fabric but often results in different wings of a party unable to totally agree on party principles and programs.

The basic unit of party organization, not only in Arizona but throughout the nation, is the precinct. The precinct is a relatively small area wherein all those voting go to the same place to vote. Arizona presently has almost nine hundred precincts. Each political party has at least one committeeperson from each precinct unless there is no party organization within the precinct. It may have more than one committeeperson because extra representation for that precinct is based upon the number of votes cast for governor in the last election. Often it is relatively easy to become a committeeman or committeewoman; one can be elected with a few votes, or if no one runs, the county chairman appoints someone to fill the vacancy.

By custom the parties have legislative district committees although these are not required by law as are the county committees. All precinct committeepersons are members of their county committees. The county committees meet after each primary election is held and select their officials. An active, capable county chairman is a great asset to a party. He or she has many assigned duties such as recommending to the county board of supervisors those who will serve as election officials. The county chairman serves on the state party committee which is supplemented by members chosen in proportion to the votes cast for governor in the last election. Since the state committee is a sizeable group it has an executive committee which does much of the work of operating the party and a state party chairman, chosen by the state committee, who presides over the party.

Each party holds a state convention every two years and customarily adopts the party platform, a rather meaningless document which is a statement of alleged principles framed in language so broad as to allow everyone in the party to nod in agreement just before the matter is forgotten. Through the state party organizations, members of the Democratic and Republican national committees, the delegates to the national conventions and presidential electors are chosen.

Every four years Arizonans join in helping to nominate candidates for the office of president and vice president of the United States by selecting delegates to the national nominating conventions. Traditionally these delegates and an equal number of alternates were selected through party committees and meetings. Most often long-time party workers and officials were chosen. In recent years the presidential primary has become popular but Arizona has not seen fit to adopt this procedure in its pure form. The Republicans still choose their delegates through party meetings with those who sit on the various committees of the group having to make the ultimate decisions. However, the Democrats, since 1972, use a system whereby the rank and file members of the party on a given day vote for individuals who will in turn make the final choices of those who will attend the nominating convention. The numerical strength of our state's delegations is not great when compared to states like California. Typically, in 1976 the Arizona Republican delegation to the Kansas City convention totaled 29, but each state plays a role in selecting presidential and vice presidential nominees in proportion to its population. The system by which we select national party nominees is often criticized but until better arrangements are devised the current procedures do work. In recent years attempts have been made to involve more voters in the process, certainly an admirable ida.

In addition to their formal party structures the Republicans and Democrats have what are called extra-legal or informal groupings. These include fund-raising committees, Young Democrats and Young Republicans and the like. Since the goal of political parties is to involve as many persons as possible political organizations can be very inventive in the creation of clubs and committees. These are also highly useful for spending money on party candidates since generally laws on campaign finances limit a party or a candidate but do not apply to what outside organizations can spend on behalf of one who is seeking office. □

12

SUFFRAGE, NOMINATIONS and ELECTIONS

RATHER OBVIOUSLY, THE KEY to the workings of a political system based on democratic principles is the involvement of the citizenry in the selection process of persons who will govern the nation, state or community. In the United States we tend to think of universal suffrage as the rule, and perhaps remember that this is a far cry from the colonial period when only free men who met property or religious qualifications participated. Yet even today there are some restrictions on the suffrage. In Arizona full involvement in things political is conferred on those who are citizens of the United States, eighteen years of age or older, those who are not insane within the legal meaning of the word, who are not serving a prison sentence for having committed a felony, and who have met the necessary residence requirements. Even as late as February 1912, when Arizona became a state, women did not vote though the suffrage was extended to them that same November. Not until 1948 did the Arizona Supreme Court rule that Indians, either men or women, living on the reservations had the right to vote. Until 1969, in bond elections there was the requirement that only owners of real property would be allowed to cast a ballot.

Under the Federal system most laws regarding the suffrage were traditionally made by the states. However in recent years a number of Congressional acts have involved the Washington government more and more in voting matters. For a long time Arizona required one year's residence in the state in order to vote. In 1964 it allowed those who had been here less than a year nevertheless to cast ballots for president and vice president. Arizona law always required a minimum age of twenty-one years to vote. After a Congressional law extended the franchise to eighteen year olds in voting for Federal officials an amendment to the United States Constitution was proposed which provided for a minimum age of eighteen for voting in state elections as well. Arizona approved the amendment in May of 1971 and by the end of the next month the Twenty-sixth Amendment to the Federal charter was in force.

Arizona long had a literacy test for voters which was never really used to any extent except for occasional attempts to keep some people away from the polls. By Federal action the literacy test is not presently used. The requirement of United States citizenship remains a universal requirement throughout all states.

If the election machinery is to work in a smooth fashion some system of organization of the voting process must be in existence. It would of course be possible simply to allow people to show up at any polling place on election day, but it is said that this would be an open invitation to fraud and corruption. Arizona, like many other states, utilizes a semi-permanent registration arrangement for voters. One may register with the office of the county recorder, a justice of the peace or with a deputy registrar of voters. There are a great number of the latter so that it is not really difficult to find someone to register a potential voter. In the early 1970's a controversy arose not only over how long one must be a resident to vote in a state but also over how close in time to an election one may be allowed to register. The one year's residence was voided and any resident can register until the time is reached when the state needs to begin to prepare the final voter registration lists. That is currently fifty days before an election. In general this is a part of the trend toward making it easier for people to register and to vote.

In 1970 the Arizona legislature adopted an "election reform law," much opposed by Democrats. It purged the registration rolls and made everyone reregister. Originally this was to be done every decade but in 1972 the legislature changed its mind and abandoned the notion of re-registration every ten years. Instead once a person is registered then re-registration is necessary only if there is a change in residence, a change in name, a change in party affiliation, or a failure to vote in a general election. (In the case of the latter event, the county recorder will send the non-voter a post card asking if the person wishes to stay registered; if the card is returned then the individual stays on the rolls and can vote at the next election without reregistering.)

An essential part of the political process is the selection of candidates to run for office. In the early days of this nation candidates for office were chosen by the caucus, mass-meeting, or other informal gathering. Then in the second third of the nineteenth century the party convention came into use. That system prevailed in Arizona, as well as most states, until the early twentieth century. On the state level in many places it was charged that the convention system was often corrupt, and not always responsive to the public will. To achieve needed reforms, something called the direct primary was introduced and came to be used almost universally in the states. Although Arizona had not had a bad experience with the convention system, we got on the band wagon and switched to the primary. Under this method, a candidate or his friends will obtain nomination petitions and will seek the signatures of qualified voters to place his name in the running. A small percentage of voters' names is required and hence it is relatively easy to get into the primary election.

The primary election is the contest in which party nominees for office are chosen. It is held in September preceding a November general election and is different from the general election in that if one is registered as a Democrat in Arizona, one votes only for Democratic candidates, or if one is registered as a Republican one votes only for Republican candidates. If one belongs to a minor political party, is an "Independent," or declines to state a party affiliation, he or she might as well stay home on primary day. Thus our state is said to use the "closed" as opposed to the "open" primary. Under Arizona state law the person receiving the highest number of votes in the primary becomes the nominee of his party for the particular office he seeks. There is no "run-off" contest if a candidate fails to receive a majority of the votes cast as is found in many Southern states. Thus in the 1950 Democratic primary with a half-dozen candidates running for governor, the winner polled only thirty percent of the total votes cast, but was nominated nevertheless.

Some now challenge the primary as not being the best possible system obtainable and some states, such as Massachusetts, have effectively combined the best features of the primary and the convention. In that New England state a party convention is held which gives the party faithful a chance to pick not only their best possible and strongest candidate, but the one for whom they will work in the general election. However, if the losing candidate receives a substantial convention vote, he may force the convention winner into a primary which gives all of the voters of the party a chance to make the final decision in the matter. Generally, however, a primary which is costly to hold is avoided and public funds have been saved. Arizona would do well to consider this system and thus avoid some of the difficulties inherent in the primary as it is used here.

Since the primary in Arizona is held at a late date, as compared to many states, the general election race is relatively short which is a good idea for it would seem that a long campaign serves to lessen voter interest rather than the hoped-for opposite. It is difficult in Arizona to get good, competent, effective and interested candidates to run for office and seemingly even more difficult to get the same sort of voter to turn out and exercise the franchise. Usually when one omits the deep South states which have traditionally limited voter action by less than legal means, Arizona has the lowest percentage of qualified potential voters who do bother to vote of any state in the Union. An extreme case, and one admittedly complicated by a high Indian population, is Apache County. Here out of an estimated population of more than thirty-five thousand, only twenty-five hundred voted for governor in 1958. A better showing was made by Arizona in the 1964 presidential election, where the normal picture was somewhat altered by a native son running for president, but where less than fifty-five percent of those of voting age cast their vote. Nevertheless, thirty-five states including all of our surrounding neighbor states, had better records.

A truly amazing thing occurred in the election of 1972. While in the presidential race of that year there was generally a considerable decline in the number of voters across the nation, Arizona had the distinction of being the only state to increase its voting performance. It was estimated that 52.7% of the total potential voters actually cast ballots as compared to 51.4% in 1968. This compared to national figures of 61% in 1968 and 54.5% in 1972. Thus even with our increase in voter turnout we were still somewhat below the national average.

Considering that the United States as a whole has a low percentage of voters who vote, this is something of a national as well as a state disgrace. Not to excuse the Arizona citizens, but it must be admitted that we have a peculiar problem or two. It is axiomatic that most everyone now in Arizona is from somewhere else, and hence we have many people who have not yet become familiar with Arizona or who have not been introduced to the Arizona political process. Then too, many people are so busy earning a living, raising a family, or watching the latest pseudo-western or murder mystery or soap opera on the television, that they have little time or inclination to pay attention as to how they are governed. Further, our political process throughout the nation, but especially in Arizona, tends to frighten voters away from the polls. In a national election in Great Britain, for instance, one votes by making one choice from two or three candidates. Here the voter is confronted with choices regarding the President of the United States every other general election, usually a Senator, always a Representative, and a whole host of state and county officials. Also on the ballot are the governor and the other executive officials, members of the elective commissions, members of the legislature, several judges and so on down to the superior court clerk for the county, not to mention the amending of the state constitution by popular vote which is practiced here. Many officials who are now elected should be chosen in some other fashion, and some, such as court clerk, should be chosen on a permanent civil service basis.

In both the primary and November general elections it is possible to cast an absentee vote in Arizona. The Australian, or secret, ballot has long been in use in Arizona, and for many years voting machines were usually used. Then in the primaries of 1970 all but two counties introduced punch card voting. It was said that these cards could be counted very rapidly by computers and the new system would be more speedy and efficient. These shining hopes have frequently not been realized for there are delays in getting the process started. Once the cards are fed into the computers the process seems to go well but preliminary problems have often resulted in longer delays than were the case with the old systems.

The November general election, held every two years, is of course the one at which office holders are finally chosen. Arizona long used the party column ballot, as opposed to the office bloc system, because it worked to the advantage of the Democrats who created it. In the former arrangement the names of all Democrats running for office were arranged in one column while all Republicans' names were listed in the same order on the opposite side of the ballot. Thus by punching out one place on a card, or making a single mark, one could vote a "straight party ticket." Republicans in Arizona generally did not like this arrangement and in 1974 it was abolished. Now Arizona ballots are of the office bloc arrangement, and the voter makes one choice from between or among candidates running for each office. Unlike the primary where there is a party limitation in voting, at the general election one may vote for anyone on the ballot regardless of party affiliation. Some offices are filled on a non-partisan basis. It is still possible to vote for all Democrats or all Republicans but now all offices are voted on individually.

For a long time in Arizona, municipal, school board and special elections were held at times other than at the November general election. This is still true of two of the three categories but a 1972 law changed school board elections to coincide with the general. Over the years few people had actually voted in school board races but under the new schedule more people will vote since they are already at the polls for other voting.

Once successful at the polls an officeholder is given a specific term during which he or she holds office. The legislature may impeach an Arizona official, thus ending his term before it expires. Or the voters themselves may in this state use the recall. Under the recall, a petition is circulated and a special election may be held to determine if the official goes or stays. Considering the great uproar over the recall in the years 1910 to 1912, it is curious that since statehood it has almost never been used on other than the local level. Any official in the state holding an elective office is subject to it, and except for members of the legislature, the officer must have served six months of his present term before proceedings can be initiated. A petition signed by a number of voters equal to twenty-five percent of those who voted in the last previous race for the office under challenge is obtained and filed. Unless the official then resigns a recall election will shortly be held. At that time others who may want the office are listed on the ballot as well as the incumbent and the voters settle the matter. It takes only five percent of the voters to nominate someone to run against the incumbent in a recall elecion.

In the 1920's a superior court judge was removed by the recall and there was talk of possibly recalling Governor Hunt before World War I. When some threatened to recall Governor Moeur the chief executive, having had a bad day, stormed out of his office and offered to sign the petition. In 1972 and 1973 a more serious attempt was made to recall Governor Williams. He signed a controversial farm labor law passed by the legislature and opponents circulated recall petitions. They thought they had sufficient signatures to bring about a recall but the attorney general decided that those petitions circulated by deputy registrars of voters were invalid. Hence the number of those requesting a recall was not enough.

It is said that in order to attract good independent officeholders adequate salaries must be paid. The matter of providing adequate sums for this purpose was long a problem. Generally salaries lagged well behind the inflationary trends of our time. It was often politically unpopular to give the necessary approval for raises. At last in 1970 an amendment to the constitution provided for the creation of the Commission on Salaries for Elected State Officials. Except for legislative salaries which must still be approved by the voters, the Commission recommends to the governor what salaries should be paid for the principal officeholders of the state. The governor in turn recommends to the legislature the sum he believes should be paid and unless either house vetoes the proposal by a majority vote it becomes the salary of the officeholder. In 1971 elected state officials were paid an annual total of $2,230,500; in its first set of recommendations the Commission increased that total sum by 45% to $3,236,000.

In Arizona of the past, a state with a small population, voters were contacted by candidates through a largely personal approach. Now newer procedures are used while not entirely ignoring intimate contact. Public relations techniques and methods are more and more a part of our political life. So too is something else we are not sure we like—the work of the pressure group. Somehow we do not like to admit that these blocs, be they economic, social or religious, exist, but they do and they are necessary. A pressure group is in its simplest form a collection of like-minded persons who have banded together to obtain a mutually desired end. They wish to influence the course of action in our political socitey.

Arizona has the usual collection of pressure groups operating within the state. Business corporations and business organizations are very important to the Arizona political process. So too are the professional groups such as physicians, lawyers and even teachers. Farmers and unions form pressure groups and ideally they exert pressure on the political process, and thus influence the course of government, in relation to their numerical strength within the state. An ideal political society is one in which the various groups are fairly competing among themselves with no one dominant. These blocs carry on lobbying activities and are active in election campaigns. The day is gone when one person acting alone can exert very much influence on the political society. Now he joins with his fellows and together they work to gain their ends which are hopefully legitimate and worked toward in an honest fashion. □

13

The EXECUTIVE BRANCH

THE EXECUTIVE ARM of state government does, or in some cases should, center around the person of the governor, just as the chief executive of the Federal government is the President of the United States. It is common to think of the governor as a junior president, but in most states he is very junior indeed. In Arizona he is little more than a glorified figurehead. The governor of this state, or of any of the other states, holds an office which is descended from the powerful governors of the colonial period in our national history. However, with the coming of the troubles of 1776, our ancestors, blaming those difficulties in part on the executives, determined to cut them down in size. In the state constitutions written in the Revolutionary War period, the governor had few real powers and his office was very largely of a ceremonial nature. In some cases he was even elected by the legislators.

In time, the governor made something of a comeback, but in Arizona two things worked against his reaching even the level of power to be found in many states. One was the fact that some of the members of the Constitutional Convention of 1910 were from the Southern states where the Radical Republican executives of the Reconstruction period had gotten too much power and had it taken away from them later. The unpleasant memories lingered in the minds of the reconstructed rebels. The other factor in the powers of the Arizona governors was that the non-elective territorial governor had had considerable power and hence the state's founding fathers wanted to transfer as much power as possible from that official.

At a time when some of the really progressive states were moving toward the centralized executive system in the early 1900's, Arizona moved backward and has never recovered from those actions. The centralized executive system involves the election of a governor and possibly a lieutenant governor, and then the appointment of the other executive officials. This centralizes responsibility in state government and if voters feel that the state administration is not doing well, they know who to blame—namely the governor who appointed the offending people—and they may vote him out of office. With the Arizona decentralized arrangement it is impossible to fix responsibility. We may blame the governor for whatever goes wrong, but with his responsibilities, we do not give him power sufficient to control the situation. Almost without exception, the Arizona governors since statehood have felt that the office carried with it powers too limited to effectively be the chief executive of the state. The President of the United States would be a very weak official indeed if the voters elected his cabinet as well as the members of the many administrative agencies in Washington, gave him no control over money matters and made him not the chief executive but merely one of many co-equal executives.

The governors of the several states are now chosen directly by the people. The term of office in a majority of states is four years, and Arizona recently switched to this instead of the old two-year arrangement. If the term is but two years it means that the official is barely launched in office before he must start a campaign for reelection. Some states forbid reelection of the governor, but Arizona allows as many terms as one can manage. The average governor has had some prior political experience before arriving at his present post, but along this line a curious trend has been unfolding lately. Some call it the decline of the governorship, for seemingly the more able and ambitious politicians seek a Federal office, say a Senatorship, rather than running for the top state office. There seems to be some connection between this and the fact that a half century ago, ideal presidential candidates were governors, while now they are Senators. With the decline of the states in relative importance in the scheme of government, corresponding decline in the quality of officials has taken place. There is generally a constitutional requirement regarding a minimum age and residence factor for a governor and Arizona asks for an age of twenty-five years, ten years citizenship and a residency in Arizona for at least five years. Once in office the governor is generally not well paid. Arizona is about average in providing financial rewards to the executive, and since 1975 he has been provided with an official residence which was donated to the state by a Phoenix resident.

A brief look at the state governors of Arizona will reveal that unofficial qualifications are more important than constitutional requirements. In the first sixty years after the state was admitted to the Union, Arizona has had thirteen different men in office. Most were in their 40's or 50's when they first entered upon their duties, and while only two were natives of the state, all had lived here the bulk of their lives. About half could really be classified as college trained with the institutions represented ranging from Harvard to Phoenix College. The governors have included several lawyers, a physician, engineers, a newspaperman, two radio personalities, as well as some businessmen. Some combined two or more careers, and most had had prior political experience before entering the governor's office. Tenure lasted from two years to a total of almost fifteen.

George W. P. Hunt, the first of the list, managed to win election seven times and to dominate Arizona politics on the state level for some twenty years. In between Hunt's terms were two Republicans, Thomas E. Campbell and John C. Phillips. Dr. Benjamin B. Moeur, a Democrat, who served two terms in the 1930's finally ended Hunt's career, but was himself defeated in a third term attempt by R. C. Stanford, another Democrat. Stanford soon saw that the office was a hopeless one and declined to run for reelection. Next Robert T. Jones, a last minute Democratic substitute for the regular nominee who was killed in an air crash, served one term, and then was replaced by Sidney P. Osborn. Osborn, a Democrat and probably the best of all the governors, promised to become a perennial chief executive but died in office in 1948 after serving only seven years. The only "accidental" governor of the lot, Dan E. Garvey, filled out Osborn's term and one of his own. In the early 1950's the Republicans managed to capture the governorship for the first time since 1928, and J. Howard Pyle served two terms. He was followed by Ernest W. McFarland, another Democrat and two-time winner. Paul J. Fannin, a popular Republican, then won three terms in office, to be followed by Democrat Samuel P. Goddard in 1965. Defeated after one term Goddard was replaced in 1967, by John R., "Jack" Williams, Republican and a Phoenix columnist and radio personality. The current governor is Raul H. Castro, a native of Mexico, and a Tucson attorney and judge who formerly was ambassador to two foreign nations. The governors have served the state to the best of their abilities. None has been corrupt, bad or incompetent, and some were very able and outstanding.

Like the governors of other states, the Arizona official has several categories of powers and responsibilities delegated to him. First of all he is the ceremonial head of state, and as such appears at all sorts of functions to make speeches, perform rituals, and to be the representative of his state and its people. However, when he goes travelling outside of Arizona, his powers as governor do not go with him and the secretary of state becomes acting governor.

The power of appointment given to the governor of Arizona means that he nominates to office a sizeable group of state officials, mainly those serving on the dozens of state boards and commissions. Unfortunately, there is no corresponding power of removal, and considering that the appointed officials generally serve a six year term while the governor has but four, it can be suspected that the executive has little control over appointees unless he is at least reelected and can thus outlast his predecessors' appointees. One governor who is said to have solved this problem was Osborn with his "little black box." He is reported to have required each appointee to give him in advance, a signed, undated letter of resignation which could be trotted out if the governor felt it necessary to do so. Curiously, the governor sits as an ex-officio member of many of the agencies which he staffs by appointment.

Another block of powers of the governor involves the legislative process. The governor may call special sessions of the legislature at any time, and the stronger governors have on occasion kept the legislatures at work until they actually produced some worthwhile results. Laws may be urged and recommended by the governor, but whether or not the legislature acts is quite another matter. Then finally the governor of Arizona may veto laws, either entirely or in the case of financial expenditures, may disallow only a part of a bill. The latter arrangement is called the item veto.

Until recently the governor of Arizona had no power over budget matters at all, but then in the middle 1960's Arizona became the last state in the Union to adopt some sort of executive budget system. Still, however, the executive will propose and the legislature will dispose. Originally the governor had complete pardon and parole powers, but the voters took them away, and now he may act only upon the recommendation of the state board concerned with such matters. The governor is also the commander-in-chief of the state national guard, when it is not in Federal service, and as "chief executive," he also sees to the best of his powers that the laws are executed and enforced. Finally, he is the leader of his political party and his success in that role often determines his success in his other areas of activity.

Under Arizona's present executive system, in addition to the governor, there are four other officials elected in the same manner, at the same time, and for the same term as the governor. (Some classify the members of the one elective state commission as executive officials but for purposes here they will be included among administrative officials for discussion.) Arizona has no lieutenant governor and the second ranking official, the one next in line for the governorship if there is a sudden vacancy, is the secretary of state. The secretary's office is the principal record keeping agency of the state, and various tasks such as witnessing the governor's signature and applying the state seal, as well as publishing actions of the legislature, constitute his daily duties. It is utterly absurd to elect this official, and rather than have the office an appointive one, it would be better to have it covered by civil service. The duties are purely routine and clerical in nature and do not involve policy making in any way.

George W. P. Hunt astride burro in a Flagstaff parade, 1926.

If the secretary of state is the number two person in rank in the executive branch, the number two officer in importance (and some would say he is even more powerful than the governor), is the attorney general of Arizona. This person, as head of the Department of Law, must have practiced his profession in the state for five years immediately preceding his election. Once in office, he advises the state agencies and officials on matters of a legal nature, represents personally and through assistants, the State of Arizona in legal disputes in which it is involved, and may also render advisory opinions. It is the latter power which in a way makes the attorney general a little legislature in himself. Someone asks a ruling on a point of law: "Are kindergartens included within the legal meaning of the phrase 'public schools,' and hence entitled to state money for their maintenance?" The attorney general of the state once ruled they were not and therefore for many years until the legislature acted no money was spent on kindergartens. There are many of these advisory opinions, and they are as binding as a law or judicial decision though they receive little publicity.

An area of activity on the part of the Department of Law which has lately received much attention is related to consumer protection. Arizona is not exactly noted as the national center of protectionism but some good work is being done. For example, stores in northern Arizona had been told to stop selling Hong Kong manufactured Indian Jewelry as the genuine item. In the early 1970's there was an interesting intra-departmental difference of opinion as to how and to what degree consumer protection matters should be handled.

With the possible exception of the superintendent of public instruction, (there is no expert opinion as to how he should be named to office), the remaining executive officials should all hold jobs covered by civil service, possibly appointed by the governor, but certainly not elected as is the fashion at the present time. The superintendent of public instruction, whose duties like those of the other executive officers are spelled out in state statutes, serves to apportion state educational money for the various counties as required by law, and as the chief administrator of educational matters within Arizona. Included in the latter area is the certification of those who will teach in the public schools. The superintendent's office serves as the channel through which many Federal funds and programs are brought to Arizona.

The office of the state treasurer collects, keeps and pays out state funds. For years Arizona funds were kept in local banks where they earned little interest for the state. In recent years, however, due to changes in the laws the state treasurer has been allowed to invest temporarily unneeded funds so as to receive much greater returns. The state treasurer is subject to two unusual restrictions: he cannot be immediately reelected to the office, and while in office he cannot legally leave the state without the permission of the governor or the legislature.

For many years these executive officials all had a term of office of two years but this has now been changed to four. The qualifications for the office are the same as those of the office of governor, plus any additional items which the laws may specify. As originally written the state constitution restricted the executive offices to males. Every now and then someone will read Article V and find the language still there. Instead of getting upset they should go on to Article VII which says that the right to hold office in Arizona shall not be so restricted.

Those who wrote the state constitution provided that there should be a state mine inspector and allowed the legislature to later decide on the duties of the office. This official still has a two year term of office, must be at least thirty years of age and have had at least seven years experience in underground mining. Again as in the case of several of the other executive officials this post is really an administrative one wherein policy is not formulated but duties are routinely prescribed. Appointment or civil service status could well suffice for staffing the job.

14

The LEGISLATIVE PROCESS

THE LAW-MAKING PROCESS is in many ways the key to the operation of state government, or indeed any type of government. Laws are the rules by which a society lives, and they are usually thought of as being based on merely formalized custom. If a democracy of the direct type existed, then each voter would gather in an assembly with his fellows and help to write the laws. Obviously this is impossible and therefore most lawmaking is based on the functioning of a representative democracy. Legislators in Arizona are chosen to serve in either the Senate or House of Representatives, a system common to all but one of the states in the Union. Nebraska is presently the only place where a unicameral arrangement operates. However, now that representation in both houses of the legislature is to be based roughly on population, it is possible that there may be a trend in this direction since an argument for the bicameral system was a different basis of representation in each house. Oddly enough, although George W. P. Hunt as president of the constitutional convention failed to push the idea, a few years later as governor, he argued for the unicameral legislative branch. In the nineteenth century it developed that state senates should be based on geographical consideration while the house reflected population distribution, or as in the Arizona situation, the membership of the house was based on actual voters rather than population.

Until 1953, Arizona gave two senators to the more populous counties, while the lesser areas had but one. Then by constitutional amendment a Senate composed of two members from each county came into being, and a House of eighty members reapportioned at intervals was established. The issue of representation in the state legislatures in general came to the fore when in 1964 the United States Supreme Court ruled that both houses must be arranged along the "one man, one vote" principle. To allow one house to be apportioned on other than population, the Court said, would be to make a vote in a rural area worth more than one cast in an urban center. While there is no doubt but that in most states the rural interests

THREE ARIZONA SEALS — On the left is the State seal. Seal in the center was originally suggested by Richard C. McCormick, while the seal at the right was used during almost all of the Territorial period.

effectively dominated the legislature to the detriment of the cities, one may inquire if now the opposite situation may not prevail.

Regardless of the merit of the issues involved in the reapportionment question, the Arizona legislature faced up to the matter and with its characteristic statesmanship, did absolutely nothing. Then in early 1966, the Federal courts revamped the legislature for the time being with the understanding that the lawmakers may alter the new system so long as it conforms to the Supreme Court rule. For the time being there was to be an Arizona Senate of thirty members, and a House of double that number. The state was divided into eight districts, each with a prescribed delegation in the two houses. Under this new system the counties with few voters lost heavily in membership in the Senate, while Maricopa County which has roughly half of the state's population now has half of the Senators instead of one-fourteenth of the total as before.

The 1967 regular session of the legislature tried its hand at a new reapportionment measure. This law sought to establish a Senate of 32 members and a House of 64, but it was not the number of legislators to which some objected, but rather the Democrats cried that the Republicans had gerrymandered the state to their advantage. The Democrats then circulated petitions so as to force a referendum on the issue. In December of 1967, the Federal judges who have general supervisory power over enforcement of the "one man, one vote" principle ruled that the referendum should take place as scheduled in November 1968, and at least until after that election, members of the legislature should be chosen under the previous court established system. The voters approved the new proposal but the trio of judges held that it was not valid. A special session of the legislature in January of 1970 enacted another proposal. It featured the creation of thirty districts from each of which would be elected one senator and two representatives. Although once again the Federal court ruled that the plan violated "one man, one vote" it was decided to hold the election of 1970 under the plan's provisions. Then the legislature would have to try again which it did, this time basing its apportionment on the figures from the 1970 census. By then it seemed a custom to continue the idea of thirty districts with each entitled to one senator and two representatives. On the basis of the 1970 population of Arizona each district contained just under 60,000 people. As usual there were also the customary complaints from the opposition party that the majority had yielded to temptation and had drawn the district boundaries on the old principle of "Do unto others, before they get to you." Nevertheless the new apportionment went into effect.

At one time it was customary to hold sessions of the state legislature every two years, but now there is a trend toward annual sessions and Arizona is in line with this. The sessions of the Arizona legislature commence in January and the legislatures have been numbered since statehood. Thus the Twenty-Fifth Legislature held its first regular session in 1961 and its second in 1962. Until 1969 the job of a legislator was not a full-time one but by constitutional amendment an annual salary of $6,000 has been provided and no mention was made of how long the annual sessions of the Senate and House of Representatives should last. They have averaged five to six months in duration in recent years and in addition the governor may at any time call a special session which may last thirty days. In his call the governor specifies what subjects shall be discussed by the lawmakers and only these matters may be officially considered. The Arizona Constitution provides for another method of calling a special session. Although never used to date, two-thirds of the members of the Senate and House of Representatives may petition the governor to hold a special session which must then be assembled. In this situation the lawmakers themselves decide the subjects to be considered by the meeting. The record for special sessions to date is the 1947 to 1949 legislature where there were seven. Ideally a legislative session should be bifurcated so that it would open and the members be given an opportunity to introduce laws. Then a recess would be taken for a month so proposals could be studied, and finally the legislators would return to do the actual enacting of the laws.

Presiding over the Arizona legislature are the President of the Senate and the Speaker of the House, both elected from the membership of the chambers. The Legislative Council, composed of the two presiding officers and five others from each house, functions as an interim group when the legislature is not in session and also provides a legislative counsel for the members, particularly helping to draft proposed laws. The writing of a law is a technical matter and expert advice is often necessary to avoid costly mistakes.

Arizona legislators serve a two year term although a four year plan would give them more of a chance to perform once in office, and lessen the number of costly and frequent elections and election campaigns. There has been some sentiment for changing the term of at least the members of the upper house to four years but as yet no action has been taken. It was quite a struggle to provide annual salaries for the lawmakers and some feel the current salary is still inadequate even considering that Senators and Representatives receive some extra money for travel expenses and subsistence when performing duties other than their regular work. All in all it cannot be considered a lucrative post.

Little study has really been made of legislators from a biographical point of view, but from information available, it appears that anyone and everyone serves. Truly the legislature of Arizona is a cross-section of the total population. Professional people, the retired, the housewife, the young, the old, the new resident and the native all get elected. Generally there is a high rate of turnover and many serve one term and then vanish from the scene. All over the nation the quality of state legislators often leaves something to be desired. One develops a feeling that not all are statesmen of highest rank. Fortunately for the states there are the dedicated, the hard-working, and the at least moderately able Senators and Representatives. There must be many good potential nominees for the legislature since almost everyone in Arizona is in theory a possible candidate due to the fact that a law-maker needs to be only twenty-five years of age, a resident of Arizona for three years and of the county for only one year.

The operations of the Arizona legislature are those largely common to any lawmaking body in the United States. Each house judges its own affairs and its actions, may seat or expel a member, grants to those duly admitted certain privileges such as free speech, and keeps a journal of its own proceedings. The Arizona lawmakers use the committee system to transact business and in this situation, the arrangement is used with a vengeance. A member of the House or Senate will try to get on as many important committees as possible and hope he may win a chairmanship since these posts are not based strictly on seniority as found in the United States Congress. Until 1967 there were nearly two dozen committees in each house but then there started a wise movement to cut down on the number.

A member may introduce almost any bill, but the important factor is how well that proposal does in committee. A proposal will be considered by more than one committee and its passage will ultimately depend largely on how hard the committee chairman and the leaders of the majority party in each house will fight for it. Political party lines are tightly drawn in the legislature, and often the majority will have agreed in advance just which bills they wished passed. Although there have been occasional squabbles among the members as to what ought to be done on a given issue, generally party discipline, at least among the Republicans, has been maintained. Although there is always room for improvement it is almost universally agreed that the quality of legislation and legislators has improved remarkably in recent years. In 1966 for the first time since statehood the Republicans captured control of both the Senate and the House of Representatives, holding their majorities until 1974 when the Democrats took control of the Senate.

There is activity in the legislative field the year round now. During those months when the lawmakers are not in formal session the interim committees meet, study and lay plans for future sessions. Then from January until late May or June the holding of the regular session will heighten activity. Between six and seven hundred bills are introduced each year of which not over two hundred will usually pass. From statehood until 1973 there was a constitutional requirement that each bill go through three readings on three different days before its final passage. The proposal was actually read out loud when introduced, when it received committee approval and again just prior to its being voted upon. This was an old tradition, dating far back into the history of legislatures, and in 1972 the voters approved a constitutional amendment which modified it. Now a bill is read aloud when introduced and on one other occasion before it is approved. Laws are enacted in the Senate and House by a majority vote, but in this instance it must be an "absolute majority," meaning one more than half of the total membership as opposed to a majority of the members present. When a law has been enacted in this manner, it does not take effect until ninety days after the end of the session of the legislature. This gives time for the invoking of the referendum provisions of the Constitution in case there is a challenge to the bill by the people. The Constitution does, however, also provide for what are called emergency enactments. If a proposal states it is necessary for it to take effect at once because of some critical situation and it is passed by a two-thirds vote in both houses, then with the signature of the governor it will become law at once. As a practical matter anything which can muster the two-thirds vote is considered an emergency act. Should the governor veto an emergency bill instead of the usual two-thirds vote to override a veto, a three-fourths majority is required in both the Senate and House of Representatives.

The life of a state legislator can be a busy one, and staff assistance is vital to the task. In Arizona it has not been traditional to provide a Senator or a Representative with clerical, secretarial and other help as has been the rule in other states. Not even adequate office space was furnished although a remodeling project in 1974 and 1975 brought about some improvement in the problem. A 1971 study by the Citizens Conference on State Legislatures ranked Arizona forty-third out of the fifty legislative bodies in overall effectiveness. While our state was commended for such matters as the legislature being free from executive or judicial domination it was criticized in other areas such as a lack of staff assistance and low salaries paid to legislators. (The study sponsored by the Ford Foundation did not influence the Arizona voters for in 1972 they rejected a proposal to increase lawmakers' pay to ten thousand dollars per year.)

Most legislative enactments are bills which when formally voted and signed into effect by the executive, become laws or statutes. However, there are also joint resolutions which are expressions of sentiment on a subject passed by both houses and signed by the governor; concurrent resolutons by which Federal constitutional amendments are approved or referendum proposals are submitted to the voters (and these require no action by the governor); a simple resolution passed by one house or the other; and memorials by one or both houses directed toward someone or something. The lawmaking process is a serious one, and most bills are solemnly enacted. However occasionally there are lighter moments. In 1971 the Arizona legislature formally adopted the bola tie as the state's official neckwear but declined to go along with a proposal to make the margarita the official drink, the mountain lion the official mascot, and black the official state color. (The latter proposal came from the only Black member of the Senate, a man with a good sense of humor.) Resolutions and memorials likewise can cover many subject areas. The legislature in 1972 paid tribute to the memory of Carl Hayden, asked Congress to call a constitutional convention for the purpose of enacting an amendment to the Federal charter which would allow prayer in the public schools, and implored the Congress to allow states to fix residence requirements for persons receiving public welfare.

Within the framework of the American constitutional system the legislature has broad power to act. Laws will be declared unconstitutional if vague, and must not of course conflict with the United States Constitution or acts of Congress when they are applicable. A very important matter for a state is the police power, not found on the Federal level, by which it is possible to protect the health, safety, welfare or morals of the citizens. Considering the broad possible range of operations, it is sad indeed to consider the quality and wisdom of so many laws passed by the Arizona legislature, and to also note the need of the laws which fail of passage. One of the supposed advantages of the Federal system is the so-called "test tube" aspect of this plan of government. In theory a state may experiment with new ideas and if it discovers something which will work it may be applied to the other states and to the Federal scheme of things. If it fails, the whole system has not been disrupted, and hence the states serve as a test tube for trying out novel ideas. The only trouble with the theory is that most states have not had many constructive ideas in decades.

Now and then the Arizona legislature is called upon to act as an agency for the impeachment of a state official, something quite different from its lawmaking functions. The House may vote the impeachment of a state official by a simple majority, and if two-thirds of the Senators vote to convict the person at an impeachment trial conducted by the upper house, then that official is removed from his post. The impeachment process is rarely used and is not awfully significant in the governmental process. Still it remains a useful thing if there is a dire need for it, and the checks and balances arrangement of government may depend upon it.

A vital aspect of the work of the legislature is its relationship with the governor. It is traditional in Arizona that the governor proposes and the legislature disposes. Because of his weak position, the executive can rarely have his way in a fight, and perhaps the best that can be hoped for is the arrangement followed by some governors under which they completely abdicated executive leadership in the sense used by Governor Osborn, let the lawmakers guide policy, and gratefully signed any laws deemed necessary by the two houses. Of course this does something to the concept of executive leadership.

Ordinarily when one thinks of the legislative process one immediately also thinks of a congress, a council, a parliament, or on the state level, a legislature. As a major part of our representative democracy, the legislature brings into being many of our laws. However Arizona also has some features of a direct democracy. Mention has already been made of the recall which involves the citizens directly in the governing process. Two other forms of direct democracy are also available to the Arizona voters. One is the initiative by which an individual or a group may propose a law and have it voted upon, provided of course enough who want the law will sign a petition circulated by its authors. The trouble with the initiative is that it often results in poorly worded laws, and is overworked by special interest groups to gain an end not approved by the people's lawmaking representatives.

There has been some discussion recently about the ease with which an initiative proposal can be made. Only the signatures of ten percent of the qualified voters are required to propose a law and any fifteen percent can propose an amendment to the constitution. Sentiment has been building in the legislature to raise these figures and thus lessen the total number of attempts at direct lawmaking. The other aspect of the people's legislative power is the referendum. Two approaches are available here. The legislature may specifically refer a matter to the voters; often this is done when the matter is especially vital or controversial. This is also the method by which constitutional amendments originating in the legislature are approved. Otherwise, any five percent of the qualified voters may invoke the referendum against a matter enacted by the legislature unless it is a so-called "emergency act" which has been passed by a two-thirds vote of the members of both the Senate and the House of Representatives. Here again some feel that the low five percent required to bring about a referendum should be raised.

□

15

The JUDICIARY

COURTS EXIST TO SETTLE DISPUTES and to enforce the laws which are duly enacted. For the most part the judiciary is the least well-known branch of our government. The courts and their officials go quietly on their way generally attracting little attention. In a way, this is a part of the concept of the independent judiciary in the American political system. We are fond of saying that we are a government of laws and not of men. Although men do make, enforce and administer the laws, the thought is that the judges are to be kept free from partisan influence and secure in their positions so as to attend to their duties fearlessly. The American legal system is all in all a very complicated one, and mainly the difficulty is caused by the dual system of one Federal and fifty different state court systems. The average citizen has a hard time indeed knowing whether a particular matter should go before a Federal or local court. In general, the Arizona courts are concerned with the state constitution, the statutes of the legislature, executive and administrative acts, as well as local governmental ordinances. The laws of the state are to be found in the *Arizona Revised Statutes,* a code which is periodically modernized and brought up to date.

The legal system of this state is like all but one of the other states, based on the old common law system of England as supplemented by later court decisions and legislative enactments. It also utilizes the *stare decisis* principle by which judges are guided in the present by decisions based on similar circumstances in the past. Since the statutes and precedents of the several states differ, there is a further problem with our legal systems in that they are often quite different from one state to another. Considering how much people move about it becomes obvious that the average citizen, newly arrived in an area, may find himself in difficulty because he does not know the variations found in the law of his new residence. In order to alleviate this problem, attempts have been made in recent decades to create model or uniform codes of laws on different subjects which may then be adopted by as many states as are willing to do so. Although progress has been made in this area, there has often been a feeling in

Arizona, and other states, that outsiders ought not to tell us what to put in our state laws. However in 1967 the legislature adopted the Uniform Commercial Code designed to cover many business transactions and in 1973 the lawmakers added the Uniform Residential Landlord and Tenant Act to the statutes of Arizona.

The legal profession, governed in Arizona by the State Bar Act of 1933, is represented by the Arizona Bar Association, which regulates lawyers, admits new practitioners, and polices its own members. The profession in turn provides the judiciary with not only its judges, but those who argue the cases before them. On the Federal level, judges are appointed to office but in most states the judicial posts are elective. From state to state, court organization is similar but there are minor variations in places.

The higher courts are termed courts of record which means simply that decisions are written and a full transcript of court proceedings is kept. Traditionally the courts of the states are decentralized. That is, new courts were created as a need arose and no one really exercises supervision over the various courts or sees to it that they operate in a uniform manner. Arizona now has the centralized judicial system so that the highest state court has general supervision over lower courts, sets forth the rules and procedures within which the courts operate, and generally sees to it that the judiciary is properly functioning. In the matter of court procedures Arizona is also fortunate in that the state has adopted rules based on the Federal Rules of Civil Procedure, a relatively clear and uncomplicated system when compared to the rules in force in most states. In 1973 a set of revised, well-reasoned and modern criminal rules went into effect.

A very important aspect of the state judiciary is the method whereby judges obtain their offices and the arrangement for continuing them in office. Until 1975 Arizona used a system of electing all judges, unless there was a vacancy in an office or a new court was created, whereupon the governor filled the post by appointment. Then the voters by a relatively narrow margin approved a major change in the state constitution. An eight member non-partisan appellate court commission appointed by the governor and presided over by the chief justice of Arizona came into being which receives applications from those individuals who wish to serve as justices of the supreme court or judges of the court of appeals. From among the applicants at least three are chosen and their names given to the governor. The chief executive then names someone to fill the vacancy on the basis of merit. In order to serve as a justice of the supreme court one must be of "good moral character" and have been a resident of Arizona admitted to practice law for at least ten years prior to taking office. To serve on the court of appeals one must be at least thirty years of age, "of good moral character," an Arizona resident and a practicing attorney for at least five years prior to entering office and a resident of the county over which the court has geographical jurisdiction.

At the next general election after a new justice or judge is in office two years the voters are asked whether he or she shall be retained in office. If the answer is yes then the person continues in office; if no then the person is out and the process starts over again. After an initial term the justice or judge holds office for a period of six years before going back to the voters to be retained or rejected. One may serve as long as the voters approve but no one sixty five years or older may initially be appointed to office on the appellate courts.

Under the constitutional changes of 1974 those counties having populations under one hundred fifty thousand may, unless they choose the merit system, go on electing their superior court judges as they always have. Judges must meet the same requirements as those serving on the court of appeals. They are nominated in the party primaries and in the general election run for four year terms on a non-partisan basis. If there is a vacancy or a new court the governor appoints someone to office. In those counties having populations in excess of one hundred fifty thousand, which means Maricopa and Pima counties, the process for the selection of superior court judges is similar to the selection of appellate court judges. There are commissions on trial court appointments which meet in Phoenix and Tucson and which are composed of eight persons named by the governor. Each group is presided over by the chief justice. On the basis of merit the names of at least three individuals who meet the requirements for an appeals court judge are submitted to the governor. Someone is then named to office.

After a judge of the superior court in Maricopa or Pima county has been in office two years, at the next general election the voters are asked whether he or she shall be retained in office. If the answer is yes then the person continues in office; if no then that person is out and the process starts over again. After an initial term then the judge of the superior court holds office for four years before going back to the voters to be retained or rejected. One may serve as long as the voters approve but no one sixty five years or older may initially be appointed to office.

The state of Missouri originally pioneered the plan which Arizona now uses. The idea behind the "Missouri plan" or "merit selection" is that the voters often do not know much about those running for judgeships and therefore there should be a screening group which would consider their qualifications. However the voter should retain the final authority after someone has been in office for a while to say whether he or she is performing in a satisfactory manner. In its initial stages the new system seems to be working well.

Now and then, but fortunately not very often, there are problems with a judge who is not functioning well in office. One may be ill and not realize it, have other personal problems, or simply not carry out the duties of the office. A 1970 amendment to the state constitution provided for the creation of a nine member state commission on judicial qualifications. This group, composed of judges, attorneys and laypersons, is responsible for investigating the possibility that a judge may not be performing in a satisfactory manner. The commission may recommend to the Arizona Supreme Court that someone should be removed. The supreme court has the final responsibility for removal or non-removal. There are times when merely the fact that the commission is concerned with a problem will be enough to help resolve the issue.

In all states there is a high tribunal, the highest appellate court, which is generally called the supreme court. There are usually five or seven judges sitting together although there may be as few as three jurists or as many as nine or more. Originally after statehood the Arizona Supreme Court had three members, but in 1948 the number was increased to five. The work of the court largely centers around appeals from lower courts but occasionally a trial might be held, if for example, one county were to sue another. The court also issues certain writs which are court orders directed toward someone or something. Writs often have Latin names such as *mandamus* or *quo warranto,* but now all such matters are in Arizona called "special actions." In the course of its work the supreme court is often called upon to interpret the meaning of the laws of Arizona including the provisions of the state constitution. The high tribunal sits at Phoenix but it can hold sessions anywhere in the state.

From among their number the justices elect a chief justice and a vice chief justice who serve for five years. One can resign as chief justice or vice chief justice at any time and stlll remain a member of the supreme court. Especially does the chief justice have many extra work assignments not the responsibility of the other justices. At specified times the supreme court hears oral arguments in its courtroom in the capitol and many matters are submitted to it in writing. Generally one member of the court will author what is called the opinion of the court. Any member can then add something to it. Disagreements with the majority opinion are called dissents. Unlike the United States Supreme Court where dissenting opinions are an important part of its procedure, the Arizona Supreme Court has more of a tradition of attempting to resolve differences of opinion and thus presenting a united front of common agreement. All court opinions are printed in volumes known as *Arizona Reports* — and they can also be found in another source called the *Pacific Reporter*. Justices are not overly well paid considering what good lawyers can earn and in the past supreme court members were often underpaid. Fortunately some individuals were willing to make the financial sacrifice necessary to serve on the supreme court and other tribunals, and for the most part Arizona judges have traditionally been adequate to their task. A few have been outstanding.

As the state of Arizona grew in population, the work load of the high court increased and it fell behind in the performance of its duties. By 1964, there was a delay of two and one-half to three years in hearing appeals, and it became necessary to revamp the judiciary. Instead of enlarging the membership of the Supreme Court, the legislature created the new Arizona Court of Appeals. This level of the judiciary is commonly found in the more populated states and exists to reduce the work load of the high state court. Commonly there are three to nine judges and usually those serving meet the same qualifications as the state supreme court justices. In Arizona the legislature originally created two courts with Division 1 sitting at Phoenix and Division 2 at Tucson although each might hold court anywhere within its geographical area of jurisdiction. Within a few years, however, the work load of Division 1 became so heavy that an additional court had to be authorized to operate at Phoenix. A few years later still a third court was added.

Each court is composed of three members. The work of the court of appeals is mainly centered on cases tried in the lower courts and then affirmed, reversed or modified on appeal. In most instances cases stop here and do not go to the supreme court unless there is a constitutional issue involved or other special situation which makes it necessary to appeal further. The three tribunals which are designated Departments A, B and C of Division 1 hears cases from Apache, Coconino, Maricopa, Mohave, Yavapai and Yuma counties while the one tribunal designated Division 2 has jurisdiction over the rest of the state. In time it will become necessary to create a Division 3 which should serve the northern counties and set at either Prescott or Flagstaff. The opinions rendered by the Arizona Court of Appeals are found in *Arizona Appeals Reports* and the *Pacific Reporter*.

The main trial court in Arizona is called the superior court, a name borrowed from California. In other states this tribunal is often styled the county court, district court or circuit court. Here there is at least one superior court in every county, and there is supposed to be another judge in addition to the original one for each 30,000 inhabitants over the minimum population figure. There are counties which have one superior court judge while in 1976 Maricopa had 33. The superior courts hear a few appeals from lower courts, but mainly they try cases. Their work includes the more serious criminal matters, larger civil suits, divorces, child care cases and probate matters. They also hear all cases affecting the title to real estate.

All civil cases where the amount in controversy is at least one thousand dollars must be heard in the superior court. If the suit involves an amount between five hundred and one thousand dollars it may be heard either in the superior court or in the justice of the peace court. If the amount is under five hundred dollars it must be heard in the justice of the peace court. In the criminal area the superior court is concerned with all felony matters and misdemeanors where the possible fine is more than three hundred dollars and/or there is a possible jail sentence of more than six months. Lesser matters are heard in the justice of the peace or city courts. In those counties where there are only one or two superior court judges each man or woman will try many different types of cases. However in the more populous counties there is a trend toward specialization among the jurists. Someone will be assigned to handle juvenile matters, one or more will conduct criminal trials, and still another may be concerned with another particular area of the law.

There are also certain minor courts presently in operation in Arizona. The justice of the peace court, commonly called the "j.p.court," is said by wits to mean that the letters "j.p." stand for "justice for the plaintiff." These tribunals are often, it is said, a problem in Arizona. J.p.'s, and there are just under one hundred presently serving, must only manage to get themselves elected by the voters to be in business. They hold office for four years and preside over districts drawn by the county board of supervisors. All too often these courts are staffed by persons unaware of the technicalities of the law and now and then evidence of corruption is revealed. The more progressive states have in modern times changed these lower courts so as to require a degree of training in law for the justice of the peace. Urgent reform along this line is needed in Arizona. There are about fifty other minor court judges serving within the state, often as ill equipped as the justices of the peace. These are the police magistrates, traffic judges and the like, provided for in city charters, and hence their selection and tenure will be determined by the charter. Finally there are dozens of court officials, clerks, stenographers, bailiffs and the like, who in some instances actually hold their posts by election or appointment, when they should all be covered by civil service. In the final analysis the clerk of a superior court has remarkably little to do with the formulation of great legal policies.

There are some needed reforms evident within the Arizona judiciary. Often the creation of new courts lags behind the population needs and overburdens the workloads of those courts already functioning. Care should be paid to insure that the disposition of cases is swift, for "justice delayed is justice denied." A more pressing problem is the matter of the minor courts. The average citizen rarely has dealings with the two highest Arizona state courts, and only infrequent association with the superior courts. It is therefore the justice of the peace or the city traffic court where most contacts with the judiciary take place, and it is here that one is most apt to get an unfortunate view of the court system. Trained, capable and efficient jurists must replace many of those who now hold lower court posts.

The general public enters upon the scene often in the role of a juror. The grand jury is a body of citizens who hold preliminary hearings and determine if the evidence warrants the bringing of someone or something to trial. The petit, or trial jury, then determines the facts which are in dispute, while a judge applies the law once those facts are determined. The idea of the jury has often come under attack in recent years, but there is really nothing wrong with the institution except the people who serve. If the good citizen finds excuses so as to avoid jury duty then the system is weakened to a dangerous point. Service on a jury is little enough to ask of a person in performing his proper duties as a citizen.

During territorial days in Arizona the grand jury system was extensively used but after statehood was practically abandoned. During the 1970's it has made a comeback and now again plays an important role in the judicial process. At the trial level an interesting matter is the size of the petit jury and by what vote it must reach a verdict. Traditionally Arizona has used twelve persons whose vote must be unanimous in criminal cases and in civil cases at least nine must agree. A constitutional amendment effective in 1973 continued the status quo in criminal cases where there is a possible death sentence or imprisonment for thirty years or more. However, in lesser criminal cases and civil matters the legislature now has the power to enact laws changing the composition and vote required of Arizona juries. However in no case can a jury of fewer than six persons be used.

Much has been said of late of the lack of respect for law in this nation. Sad to say, this is probably a true observation and it should be of serious concern to all. Those charged with law enforcement while not always themselves perfect humans or above temptation are still to be given their just respect if our democratic system is to survive. Laws are the rules upon which a society operates, and it cannot long endure if the average responsible citizen of the society openly disobeys these rules or looks the other way when other persons do the same. □

16

ADMINISTRATION

IT IS COMMONLY SAID THAT there are three branches to most American governments, but there is also the so-called fourth branch. Public administration is that aspect of government which brings the workings of the other three branches down to the level of the governed. It is not as exciting and dramatic as the others but is absolutely essential. Once again it is the level of government where the people have the most contact with their state. The term bureaucracy is a perfectly good one to describe this area of government although the phrase has become loaded in meaning. In the early days of state government there were few administrative agencies but as populations grew, and the society became more complex, the bureaucracy also grew. Think of how many agencies of government are needed simply because of the invention of the automobile. The licensing activity of state government accounts for many agencies, and then as the idea of regulation of the economic activities of people developed, so did bureaus, commissions and the like to handle this work.

Unfortunately, state administration often just grew and not much planning was exerted in the process. When a new agency or department or board was needed it was created by the legislature or by the voters, and then it was in business. Duplication and often waste were by-products. Today the problem is that many of the states have administrative bodies in operation which in total number exceed one hundred, and some states are approaching or even passing the one hundred fifty mark.

Many jokes are made about governmental bureaucracies and their inefficiency. Actually, there is little evidence to prove that a governmental bureaucracy is any more or less efficient than a private bureaucracy of roughly the same size. It seems that the larger any organization is, the less efficient the bureaucracy will be. On the governmental level the citizen has a right to demand as much efficiency and competency as can possibly be managed. More and better supervision is often needed for a state bureaucracy, but the legislature, which is the only agency in many cases with the power to supervise, is generally busy with something else.

With a minimum of effort all states could condense their many agencies, bureaus, boards, departments and commissions into fewer agencies than now exist. Certain units of administration are essential, but ideally a dozen to twenty at the most will do the job and more efficiently than it is presently being done. In most states there is little interest in reforming the bureaucracy, and those who hold administrative jobs are usually the most vigorous opponents of reform out of fear for their own little empires so carefully constructed over the years. Suggestions are made that there should be agencies on the state level concerned with budget, taxes and spending matters, public instruction, military affairs, agriculture and the land in general, especially conservation, health both mental and physical, highways and roads which would include motor vehicle regulation and licensing, justice, welfare of all types, and others as the peculiar needs of the state may demand. After the second World War, when the Hoover Commission studied the reorganization of the Federal bureaucracy, the states often created similar study groups, but then promptly forgot about the matter and continued to cling to old ways. Arizona was long a good case in point to show the need for administrative reorganization throughout the government.

The Arizona founding fathers of 1910 seemingly had great faith in government by administration, and over the years the legislature and the voters have added to the sum total so that there are now nearly one hundred twenty-five agencies which can be counted as a part of the administrative process. To explore the workings and operations of all such units would be impossible for our purposes here. Even before looking at a few of the more important administrative agencies it might be well to look at some general statements about the subject. The great bulk of those who direct state administration in Arizona win their posts by appointment although some are directly elected. A long term of office is usually granted, and although some attempt is made to insure nonpartisanship in some places, this generally is not said to be a great success. Politics is involved in public administration as much as in any other aspect of Arizona state government. In 1968 the legislature at last took notice of the fact that a state civil service system was badly needed. Not only were individuals being paid at different rates for the same work performed but there was no standardization of working conditions. Vacation periods for workers showed great variety. Changes were needed in order to obtain better qualified personnel and also to justify higher salaries for permanent professional employees. By statute the State Personnel Commission was created with five members appointed for 5 year staggered terms. No more than three members of the group could be from the same party and certain professional experience was required. In turn the commission would hire a director and together they would supervise the new system of job classification. Although the new program caused some controversy and some state workers resented it, it represented a necessary step.

Traditionally in Arizona salaries paid to state employees were far too low. An example of this type of false economy was represented by a state agency which employed many accountants. As a result of the inadequate salaries those who worked there were recently graduated and in need of some on-the-job training. As soon as that was obtained the bulk of the accountants went on to higher paying jobs, and the state had to train a new group. Another traditional problem with the bureaucracy was that no one supervised its work. In theory this was the responsibility of the legislature but they were often occupied with other matters. As a result there was a tendency to ignore problems until a scandal occurred or conditions had become so hopeless that the matter could no longer be ignored. No one will ever know how much money Arizona wasted by not having a central purchasing agency, but not until the middle 1960's were there any serious attempts to do something about the problem.

In the early 1970's a plan was announced by the leaders of the legislature and the governor to consolidate most of the state's administrative agencies into twelve departments, mostly headed by directors to be appointed by the chief executive with the approval of the state senate. The plan would, it was said, bring about more efficiency and economy in operations. Some departments such as Public Safety and Corrections were already both in existence; some such as Agriculture were obviously illustrations of logical new agencies; others seemed not to fit into readily understandable combinations. However the legislature created the Department of Administration which compressed the Department of Finance, the Department of Library and Archives, the Department of Public Buildings Maintenance, the Surplus Property Agency and the State Personnel Commission into one new super agency. Critics of the new program charged that it was a paper reorganization only, something to be shown on an organizational chart, but hopefully out of it all will come a new and better system of state public administration. All during the decade of the 1970's Arizonans will be occupied with these problems. Both the legislature and the voters will need to keep an eye on what is happening. Some portions of the reorganizational proposals met with defeat within the first few years after they were unveiled while others were changed or modified. Some ideas required only changes in the statutes while others necessitated constitutional change.

The voters themselves have a little control and responsibility for the one state commission whose members are popularly elected. The Corporation Commission is an agency with three members elected for six year staggered terms. Sadly there are virtually no qualifications of a professional nature needed to hold the post of commissioner. In 1968 an attempt was made to amend the constitution of Arizona so as to revamp this important agency but the proposal failed at the polls. The voters did at that time, however, remove from the commission the power to regulate insurance companies and brought into existence a Department of Insurance with an appointed director. The Corporation Commission was left with the significant functions of issuing articles of incorporation to new Arizona corporations and licenses to out-of-state corporations which wish to do business in our state. It has the power to regulate the sale of stocks and other securities, control over common carriers in the transportation field (such as airlines, buses, ambulances and taxis), and the regulation of public utilities which are privately owned. Thus if the telephone, gas or electric company wishes to change its rates it must get permission of the Corporation Commission. It must be remembered, however, that this state agency has power only over intra-state matters as the Federal government controls and regulates interstate commerce. There are frequently times when the workings of the Corporation Commission demonstrate one of the fundamental problems in administrative law. Over a period of time the regulator becomes so familiar with the problems and viewpoints of the regulated that he tends to identify with this group and forgets the problems and difficulties of the public at large.

Approximately two dozen state agencies are concerned with the regulation of professions or trades. Each one is generally staffed by that particular occupation for only teachers are forced to submit to lay regulation of their trade. Imagine, if you can, what would happen if someone suggested that physicians or lawyers should have their trade regulated by the general public! Even the notion that there should be one central licensing agency, with actual power to license remaining in advisory boards from the occupations, caused some vocal consternation just before the matter was dropped.

Agriculture accounts for some important agencies of an administrative nature as there are groups concerned with the livestock industry, poultry raising and the use of pesticides in Arizona. The Game and Fish Commission is concerned with the state's live natural resources and sometimes with its recently deceased ones as witness the recent annual controversies over buffalo hunting and how it should be conducted. The State Land Commissioner administers the almost thirteen percent of Arizona land area which is owned by the state. The Arizona Racing Commission is responsible for the conduct of horse and dog races. It decides the number of days the tracks will be open, who may own and work the establishments and supervises the animals which provide the entertainment. The State Superintendent of Banking has many responsibilities in this important field of economic activity while the Arizona State Retirement System invests and manages funds paid into accounts by state employees who will one day retire and withdraw their contributions and those monies contributed by the state. Hopefully the managers of these accounts will have made wise and prudent investments. The State Fire Marshal has responsibilities of a serious nature as does the Arizona Civil Rights Commission. Some agencies work closely with corresponding Federal groups. Typical examples are the Arizona Atomic Energy Commission and the Arizona Commission of Indian Affairs.

In Arizona there were traditionally several agencies concerned with health and welfare. In 1973 three administrative units were combined into a new Health Services Department which became operational in 1974. In 1972 the lawmakers combined the Department of Public Welfare, as well as the Employment Security Commission and several other agencies into the new giant Department of Economic Security. The units of administration concerned with education will be discussed under that heading. In 1972 the national guard and civil defense departments were merged into the Department of Emergency and Military Affairs headed by the adjutant general of the state. The State Highway Commission, which operated the Arizona Highway Department, as a result of the administrative reorganization program became the Department of Transportation. Earlier in 1969 a Department of Public Safety was established and at that time the highway patrol was transferred from the Highway Department to the new agency which had as one of its purposes the centralization of all state law enforcement activities in one administrative unit.

The Industrial Commission of Arizona, a five member group appointed by the governor, administers workmen's compensation, first adopted in 1925. The main agency handles claims while a special three member board invests the money paid into a fund by those who participate in the program. In effect this is an insurance program paid by employers to provide benefits for their workers who may be injured on the job. The State Fair Commission which in 1967 was renamed the Arizona Coliseum and Exposition Center Board, holds that annual event which goes back in time to the territorial period. Usually attracting little attention are such agencies as the Apprenticeship Council, State Athletic Commission, Arizona Beef Council and on through the list one may go until in alphabetical order one reaches the Water Quality Control Council or the Western Interstate Commission for High Education.

For many years *ex officio* boards and commissions were popular in Arizona. In this arrangement officials who hold particular posts would by virtue of their office and state law join others to form a new group. For example, the attorney general and the superintendent of public instruction comprised two thirds of the old board of pardons and paroles. Together they selected a third member. The role of *ex officio* agencies has now been lessened. When the new Department of Corrections came into existence in 1969 a new State Board of Pardons and Paroles was created. It now has five members appointed to office by the governor and members work only at the tasks connected with pardons and paroles. An example of a surviving *ex officio* group is composed of the governor, the director of the Department of Administration, and the state treasurer who are by law designated as the State Loan Commissioners. This body is charged with the responsibility of paying state indebtedness. The governor also sits in an *ex officio* capacity as a member of various groups including the board of regents of the universities while the superintendent of public instruction is an *ex officio* member of the State Board of Education and the State Board of Directors for Community Colleges.

In choosing men and women to serve on the various state boards and commissions it is important to insure that all geographical areas of the state have fair representation. This is particularly essential now that the "one man one vote" principle in the state legislature has reduced the influence of many areas on Arizona government and also since most executive officials come from the more populous counties. All Arizonans must feel that they are a part of the governmental process. Fortunately for the financial health of Arizona many of the members of the various administrative boards and commissions are not paid a salary, and no money is advanced to them beyond certain expenses which they are allowed while actually on duty. Thus in effect they donate their time and services to the state.

Bearing in mind that the average citizen has most contact with the administrative arm of government, those who are a part of the bureaucracy should always be aware that they are the servants of the people instead of things being the other way around. For the average citizen association with the bureaucracy is often frustrating and troublesome. Red tape, living up to the letter of the law and the rule, and the production of paper forms in at least a triplicate state are all at times unfortunately a part of the bureaucratic mind. In order to provide the citizen with a knight in shining armor to protect him from the troubles of administration, the Scandinavian nations long ago created the post of ombudsman. The idea of having an official responsible for going to bat for the citizen in the clutches of the bureaucracy is in this nation a new and novel one, but some states are already considering the possibility of establishing such an office. □

17

The ARIZONA ECONOMY

THE SALT RIVER PROJECT of Arizona uses as its slogan the statement "Arizona grows where water flows." No truer statement can be found to describe the relationship between water and the growth and future growth of the Arizona economy. Some areas of the state are blessed with an abundance of water, but most of Arizona is not so fortunate. The land has a limited rainfall, and as things have developed within Arizona, the water supply is not always near the population centers. Therefore the matter of effectively using water resources occupies much of the story of Arizona's past. Almost from the very beginning of the territory the old common law doctrine of riparian water rights was rejected and through the Howell Code, the Kibbey decision which dealt with the relationship between land and water, and various other laws and judicial decisions, there has been the development of the idea that water must be conserved as much as possible and utilized in an effective manner so as to avoid waste.

In the late nineteenth century, dams and canals were constructed, often in a crude and inadequate manner, so as to bring needed water. Irrigation has always been the obvious answer to problems of this nature, but there was never enough capital within Arizona to adequately finance water projects. In 1902 Congress passed the Newlands Act which put the Federal government into the area of irrigation and water. The first major project to be completed under this act was the construction of Theodore Roosevelt Dam, the first link in the chain of dams and lakes built as a part of the Salt River Project. Over the years other such projects as the Coolidge Dam, Laguna Dam and the like helped to trap and conserve the waters of the rivers of Arizona. By the end of the 1920's all available water within the state excepting that in the Colorado River had been brought into use.

The history of the Colorado, greatest of all the Arizona rivers, is intertwined with the whole history of the territory and state. Unfortunately, from the standpoint of Arizona's association with the river, it also involves six other states plus the Republic of Mexico. After World War I an attempt was made to apportion the river waters. The seven states sent delegations to a meeting chaired by Secretary of Commerce Herbert Hoover at Santa Fe, New Mexico, and the result was the Santa Fe Compact which divided the waters between the upper basin states and the lower basin group made up of Arizona, California and Nevada. It was then the responsibility of the states within the two divisions to further divide the water among themselves. The upper states achieved a settlement, but the lower basin states spent the next several decades feuding among themselves. Governor Hunt of Arizona led the fight in opposition to the Compact with the result that Arizona was soon the sole state which refused to approve it. Not until 1944 did Governor Osborn force the legislature to approve the 1922 agreement. Thereafter there still remained issues to be settled, and in the early 1960's the United States Supreme Court decided important questions in favor of Arizona. This brought great joy and hope to Arizona, but it was soon evident that it was one thing to have the water and quite another to successfully utilize it.

At the time of statehood one of the dreams of the Arizona pioneers was that somehow they could build a dam on the Colorado and generate electricity which would then be sold, and the resulting profits would insure that the state would have few or no taxes. Sad to say this did not work out for while it was possible to anchor one half of the dam to Arizona, the project would also have to touch some other state which would involve not only the other state but the Federal government as well. There was also the small matter of Arizona being a poor state without sufficient capital ever to finance such a project. In 1928, the United States Congress enacted the Swing-Johnson Act which resulted in the erection of Hoover Dam, a giant completed several years later. The passage of this law was over the vigorous protests of Arizona's delegation in Congress. Some years later Arizona objected even more mightily to the construction of the diversion dam at Parker, and on this occasion even called up the National Guard to show its opposition. By the early 1960's the state was in a more cooperative mood. After the United States Supreme Court quieted Arizona's title to additional water, the state's delegation in Congress endeavored to induce the Federal government to finance projects which would allow Arizona to make use of the water thus obtained, and also to insure the continued water supply of the area. These hopes and needs are embodied in the proposal long called the Central Arizona Project. The idea is to bring water from the Colorado River through a series of canals and aqueducts to the centers of Arizona population. After many defeats in Congress the authorization for the Central Arizona Project passed the Senate and the House and was signed into law by the President in 1968. There yet remained, however, the fact that money must be appropriated in order to actually undertake construction of the project. With Carl Hayden no longer in the Senate to push the matter funds were not immediately forthcoming. Largely in an effort to prod Congress into action there was talk of the state itself financing the project, one of the most genuinely absurd suggestions ever heard in Arizona. By the end of 1971 the first dirt had been turned and early in 1973 the first substantial funds, more than eleven million dollars, became available to seriously begin the actual construction. In a way the battle over the Colorado is at best a comic opera, for while the struggle rages, few seem to understand that there really is not enough water in the river to meet the needs of the contending parties. For the moment the purification of salt water seems not to be commercially profitable, and therefore eyes now turn toward the north and the possible tapping of the Columbia River system. This in turn upsets the good people of Washington, Oregon, and the surrounding states who are interested in their own future development.

There is an intimate relationship between water and land, and in Arizona both seem to present problems for the state. In looking at the land area of Arizona one must immediately note that there is the peculiar fact that only fifteen percent of the total area is privately owned. Just under thirteen percent is state owned, and the remainder is under Federal title. Included within the Federal lands are the large Indian reservations which comprise one-fourth of the area of Arizona, certain military installations, as well as the seven major national forests. While the size of the government land is somewhat unusual, not all of these areas are noncontributory to the Arizona economy. The Arizona state lands are primarily grazing lands and leased to private persons who pay for the privilege of using the land. The Indians on the reservation enter both the buying and selling markets of Arizona. The state derives income from the Federal forests since Washington and Phoenix share in the revenues thus obtained. Finally, military bases mean jobs and payrolls, and indeed government in general is a major employer within the state of Arizona.

The traditional Arizona economy was said to involve the "three C's, copper, cotton and cattle." Of the three copper was the earliest and greatest aspect of the total picture. It, however, contributed to a problem insofar as the people of Arizona were concerned. The machinery needed to exploit copper in its natural state was very expensive, and therefore Eastern capital was invested in Arizona with the resulting absentee ownership of the economy. For decades criticizing the "Eastern big interests," was a popular Arizona sport. It must not be forgotten that fundamentally Arizona was long an area which was never able to fully control its own destiny and to a degree was manipulated from the outside.

During the 1920's some of the great Arizona mines began to be depleted, and with the coming of the depression of 1929, the mining industry generally fell on hard times. Fortunately it recovered, and copper today is a major Arizona product although the producers are often forced to utilize raw ore with a very low percent of pure copper, an amazing feat of engineering and technology. Presently this state alone accounts for fifteen percent of the copper produced in the non-Communist world. On the other hand the mining industry is not now as important in the total economic picture as it was during the early period of Arizona's statehood.

The cattle industry has always been and still is important to the state, as is also the raising of sheep. Here the main problem seems to be occasional difficulty in competing with the importation of foreign animals, and the matter of overgrazing on the range lands. The area will simply hold only a limited number of animals especially when rainfall is less than adequate. The third C, cotton now presents a special difficulty for it is really suffering from a shrinking market. Were it not for the Federal government's subsidies the cotton farmers would probably be driven out of business. The difficulty is that the so-called miracle fabrics, the synthetic fibres, have cut heavily into the cotton market. For example, the cords used in automobile tires were once cotton, but are now made of synthetics. The clothing industry is another obvious instance where markets once open to cotton are now narrowed. Clearly some additional use of the product must be found through scientific research much as Dr. George Washington Carver found other uses for the once lowly peanut. Truck farming, the raising of fruits and vegetables, is often called the brightest aspect of the Arizona agricultural economy. In many parts of the state there are rich soils already in use, and others waiting to be utilized, dependent of course upon the availability of more water. Recently it has been noticed that the state is following the national trend toward fewer but larger farm units. The old-style family farm is rapidly being replaced by the agricultural business enterprise.

The "fourth C" in the Arizona economy is climate which means the tourist business. Around the turn of the century, the more adventuresome wealthy Easterners "discovered" Tucson as a vacation spot or winter home, and later the slightly less fashionable began to come to Phoenix and other spots. Out of this grew an important aspect of the Arizona economy. Unfortunately at times all is not well in this business. There are many places throughout the nation catering to the tourist and Arizona has some rough competition for the tourist's dollar. Other problems have appeared to make the serene sky now cloudy. One of the local talking points was the beautiful pure air, now somewhat polluted by the growing population, the automobile and the factory.

Clearly, if the Arizona economy is to continue to grow and to prosper, it must share in the industrial revolution which has been underway in many parts of the nation for nearly a century and a half now. Not all areas of the United States have developed at the same pace, and therefore it was not until after World War II that Arizona began haltingly to turn toward industrialization. Most manufacturing and related fields were amost unknown in the state until the late 1940's. Then a campaign was undertaken to bring more factories to Arizona, but the idea has not been without its built-in difficulties.

Some areas of the United States are natural centers of industry. For instance, southern Michigan is the most logical location for the automobile industry as present, or readily available, are raw materials, capital, a labor supply and markets for the products once they are finished. Arizona, on the other hand, must create an artificial economy if it is to industrialize. Raw materials must be shipped in from great distances, and the resulting products must then be shipped to the population centers of the nation. All this cuts into the manufacturer's margin of profits. Yet another problem is that for the most part industry must be lured into Arizona from some other part of the nation. This is done by offering low taxes as well as offering good accommodations to industry and its personnel. When a plant does move into Arizona, often the company brings many of its own staff with it, and then whether native or newly-arrived, the people connected with the business want schools, highways, recreation areas, and a whole host of governmental services, all of which cost money. The problem is then how to raise the necessary funds without driving industry out of the state. Not long ago when there was talk of raising state taxes, a major industry in Phoenix delivered an ultimatum: "Raise taxes and we will move out of the state."

The Arizona economy in the 1950's and 1960's had usually been described as a booming one for most. Rapid increases in numbers of jobs available characterized the picture although while some skilled jobs went begging, there was often a surplus of the unskilled or semi-skilled workers. While this situation was true to an extent all over the nation, it was compounded here by the fact that the person most likely to pack up and come out to Arizona in the hope of finding a job was one who had no marketable trade. Some estimated that as many as one out of every three coming to Arizona to seek jobs eventually moved on to some other place. In many areas, wages were low in Arizona as compared to other parts of the nation, while the cost of living was as high or higher than it was in many places. Trade unions, once influential in Arizona, were no longer so and there was a decidedly anti-organized labor atmosphere permeating the area. In 1969 the per capita income of Arizona's residents was $2,750 while the national average was $3,159.

A brief look at the Arizona economic picture at the end of the decade of the 1960's will show conditions as they existed at that time and also what the promise of the future seemed to be. Manufacturing in the state was producing annual goods valued at more than two billion dollars and nearly one hundred thousand people were employed. Almost twenty thousand individuals were working in Arizona mines and production, 85% of which was copper, had an annual value of eight hundred million dollars. Other important products included gold, silver, molybdenum, lead, sand, gravel, stone and lime. The tourist industry which included not only the winter visitor but those who came to see Arizona's many parks, monuments and recreation areas brought over five hundred million dollars to the state's economy. Some agricultural crops such as cotton seemed to be declining but sugar beets and vegetable production were up. In 1968 some 443 Arizona farmers received in excess of twenty-five thousand dollars each in Federal farm subsidies and one corporate farm received in excess of a half million dollars. Federal government spending in all forms amounted to somewhat over one and a half billion dollars annually. The number of unemployed individuals was one of the lowest in the nation except that in these statistics Indians living on the reservation were not counted; if they had been the rate would have been quite high. Retail sales throughout Arizona in the late 1960's amounted to about three and one half million dollars.

Industrialization will not be accomplished in Arizona overnight, nor without difficulties, but clearly the process must continue if for no other reason than to provide jobs for the increased population. Some Arizona old-timers like the state the way it once was and take the attitude, "If they can't find jobs let them stay at home." It is not possible, however, to go back to the Arizona of 1912 or thereabouts, and in all probability the area will continue to grow and hopefully to enjoy an expanding economy.

The decade of the 1970's dawned with much hope for a continued bright economic future for Arizona in many areas. While there was some indication that some copper mines, especially in Cochise County, might be closed because they were no longer profitable, the state remained a major copper producer. In 1971 gold production, mostly a byproduct of copper mining, totaled 89,930 ounces which were worth $3,687,000. Silver production totaled 6,338,000 ounces which were worth $9,818.000. 97% of the silver mined also came as a byproduct to copper mining. In 1972 agricultural crops worth more than 870 million dollars were produced, an increase of twelve percent over the year before. Cattle was the state's leading farm product, with cotton ranking second. The total production of the latter decreased but prices in 1973 were up which proved a benefit to farmers. In 1972 retail sales topped five billion dollars for the first time. At the end of the year more than three-quarter of a million Arizonans held jobs and the economy seemed to hold promise of continued growth. It was estimated at the time that 33,000 new jobs are needed each year. About 22,000 people in the state finish their education each year and 11,000 new job seekers arrive from other places. A possibly serious trouble spot appeared at the end of 1973 in the form of the "energy crisis." In Phoenix and Tucson the year closed with long lines of motorists at gasoline stations seeking fuel so that they might drive to work in an area where public transportation was practically unavailable. Some large users of natural gas found their supplies curtailed. The impact of all this on Arizona was being widely discussed and wondered about. □

Rep. John J. Rhodes in 1973 was elected Minority Leader by congressional Republicans

18

FINANCES

IT HAS BEEN SAID that governments were not expressly created to spend money but once they came into existence the raising and distributing money became two of their major operations. Here a fair number of individuals spend their working hours performing tasks connected with public money. This is a vital area of activity since citizens are asked to pay the levies made and we should all make certain that we are receiving maximum value for what we give over to government. Mention has already been made of some of the individuals who have responsibilities here. The state treasurer is, for example, the custodian of state funds. At least two other parts of the government should also come to mind, the governor and the legislature.

Each year at the opening of the session of the legislature in January, the governor is required to submit a budget for the state to cover the next fiscal year, July 1 to June 30. The tradition in Arizona is for the legislature to totally ignore the governor's recommedations and to do as it pleases. The problem was long compounded by the fact that until 1966 Arizona had the dubious distinction of being the only state in the Union without some sort of state budget agency. Then the legislature created one in part in an attempt to coordinate money requests from the various state agencies instead of each governmental unit going directly to the lawmakers.

The legislature itself must vote actual state expenditures in most cases and here the Joint Legislative Budget Committee is the vital group. Composed of both senators and representatives, and including the chairmen of the appropriation committees of both houses, these men and women are largely responsible for deciding how state funds shall be spent. Individual lawmakers in their respective houses may later propose changes in the appropriation bills but most of the budget work is done in the joint committee. The task of checking to see that money is properly and correctly spent is assigned to the auditor general who holds office at the pleasure of the Joint Legislative Budget Committee.

Two administrative agencies much involved in state finances are the Department of Administration and the Department of Revenue. In the former there is a division of finance which was once itself a separate department. Among its past interests were the creation of a uniform state accounting system and the bringing of Arizona into the age of the computer. Now the tasks performed here include the preparation of the budget, planning for the long-range viewing of state finances, and a central purchasing office. Within the Department, but organized as a separate division are those who handle the disposal of surplus property. The Department of Revenue upon its creation took over many of the functions of the old state tax commission. It is best known to most Arizonans as the place where one pays one's state income tax; it is also the agency to which businessmen submit their monthly sales tax reports together with the money collected. In short most state taxes are collected by the Department. It is as well responsible for such things as delinquent taxes and the keeping of tax records.

There is a general axiom in matters pertaining to taxation that anything that can be taxed will be taxed. On the state level the power to tax is broad and there are few limitations or restrictions placed on it. It is not possible for Arizona to tax the operations of the Federal government, or even to collect a state sales tax on the Indian reservations, but otherwise it is generally free to levy assessments as it pleases. Taxes are considered to be the traditional form of raising revenue, for such things as a lottery or the state engaging in business to make money will be considered unholy or unethical, or both. Over the years economists and politicians have devised many types of taxes and today the state of Arizona uses most of them. One of the most troublesome is the state property tax, now being depended upon less and less in most states. The trouble with this tax is that it is difficult to correctly assess properties for the purpose of taxation, and hence the taxpayer does a good bit of squawking about the unfairness of the entire matter. Unfortunately Arizona has had one of the highest property taxes in the nation and one of the most unfairly administered. Agricultural interests, the businessman, and the land speculator all have had friends in state government who saw to it that they escaped the worst aspects of the property tax, but it was for the most part the owner of residential property who paid much more than his fair share.

Compared to many states, business in its various operations is lightly taxed in Arizona. The state taxes the operations of public utilities and transportation companies based in Arizona. There are also taxes to be collected on financial institutions and assessments in the form of license fees on trades and professions ranging from physicians to peddlers. The various places of amusement are likewise subject to taxes. In the early 1960's the inventory tax, so hated by merchants, was repealed by the voters thus eliminating one area of revenue income for the state. Arizona collects luxury taxes which means principally levies on liquor and tobacco. These are about average as compared to other states. There are gasoline and auto license taxes, unemployment taxes, as well as estate taxes. In the early twentieth century the states began to levy income taxes, and ultimately Arizona jumped on the band wagon. Now the rates of this tax are average as compared to other states. For a long time there was some objection to the general sales tax on the grounds that it was regressive. That is, the person with a lower income pays proportionately more of his money out in sales tax than the person with the larger income. However, during the depression years of the 1930's, Arizona adopted the tax as a necessity, and now there is a general feeling that it is a relatively painless way of raising revenue.

The tax laws of a state are generally the result of many years of additions and amendments to the various revenue raising statutes. Arizona's experience has certainly been a good illustration of this, and several legislatures have refused to face up to the problem of making a comprehensive revision of the state's tax laws. However, aided by a ruling of the state supreme court which made it necessary to set classes of property for assessment purposes, a special session of the 1967 legislature in December of that year attempted a complete overhauling of the Arizona tax structure. The result was a series of laws which attempted not only to settle the matter of the classes of property for the purpose of assessment but also to win some tax relief for the owner of residential property. Different types of property are assessed at different rates. Homes, farms and vacant lands are assessed at 18 percent of their full cash value, commercial property including rentals at 25 percent, utilities at 40 percent and mines and railroads at 60 percent. Another modification in the tax laws was the exemption of household goods from the property tax and also the limitations on veterans' and widows' exemptions approved by the voters in 1968. Between 1963 and 1967 a comprehensive program of revaluation of all real property within the state was undertaken.

The year 1967 saw major changes in almost every matter connected with state finances. The legislature not only reorganized the administration of finances but also created a new system of financing schools with more emphasis on state participation rather than local backing, the state income tax was raised and various tax loopholes were theoretically eliminated. The results of the activities of the twenty-eighth legislature were controversial as might be expected. Democrats were critical and contended that many of the new laws were little more than a shifting of money paid from one fund to another. They argued that in the end the average taxpayer would pay about the same amount in total taxes by merely finding reduction in one area only to face an increase somewhere else. Republicans were hopeful that their work had benefitted the state and could at least take comfort from the fact that they had tried to accomplish something whereas the previous legislature had steadfastly refused to act at all. The battle still continues. In 1972 a prominent Democratic legislator charged that the end result of the changes in the tax laws had been to give corporations "an unjustified tax break" and insisted that while income taxes paid by corporations had remained about the same over the years those paid by individuals had greatly increased. Another special legislative session convened in October of 1973 to wrestle again with many of the same old issues. At that gathering the state sales tax was raised from three to four percent, changes were made in the income tax laws, and school districts were allowed to henceforth calculate the state funds they obtain on a new formula. In technical terms the change was from average daily attendance of a school to average daily membership, an arrangement somewhat more favorable to obtaining support.

To one with a sense of history the controversy over taxes sounds vaguely familiar. Since the territorial legislature in the 1860's enacted the very first Arizona tax laws there have been controversies over who shall pay and how much. At no time is everyone pleased and this is an area where pressure groups are ever at work. In some cases it is possible to legally avoid taxes in one way or another; there are times when some merely ignore the laws. When in 1969 the state purchased from the Federal government a computer tape which contained the names and addresses of Arizonans who paid a Federal income tax it was discovered that some 60,000 of those individuals were not filing an Arizona state income tax return. Those persons were contacted by the state.

It sometimes comes as a surprise to a person to note that taxation provides the state of Arizona with only a minor part of its total income. In addition to taxes, funds are derived from the lease of state lands, the funds shared by the Federal government coming from national forests and mineral lands, tuition charged university students, and a number of miscellaneous sources. For example, the United States pays Arizona $300,000 per year as its share of the money due from the Boulder

GOVERNMENT FINANCES, 1970-1971

Sources of Income

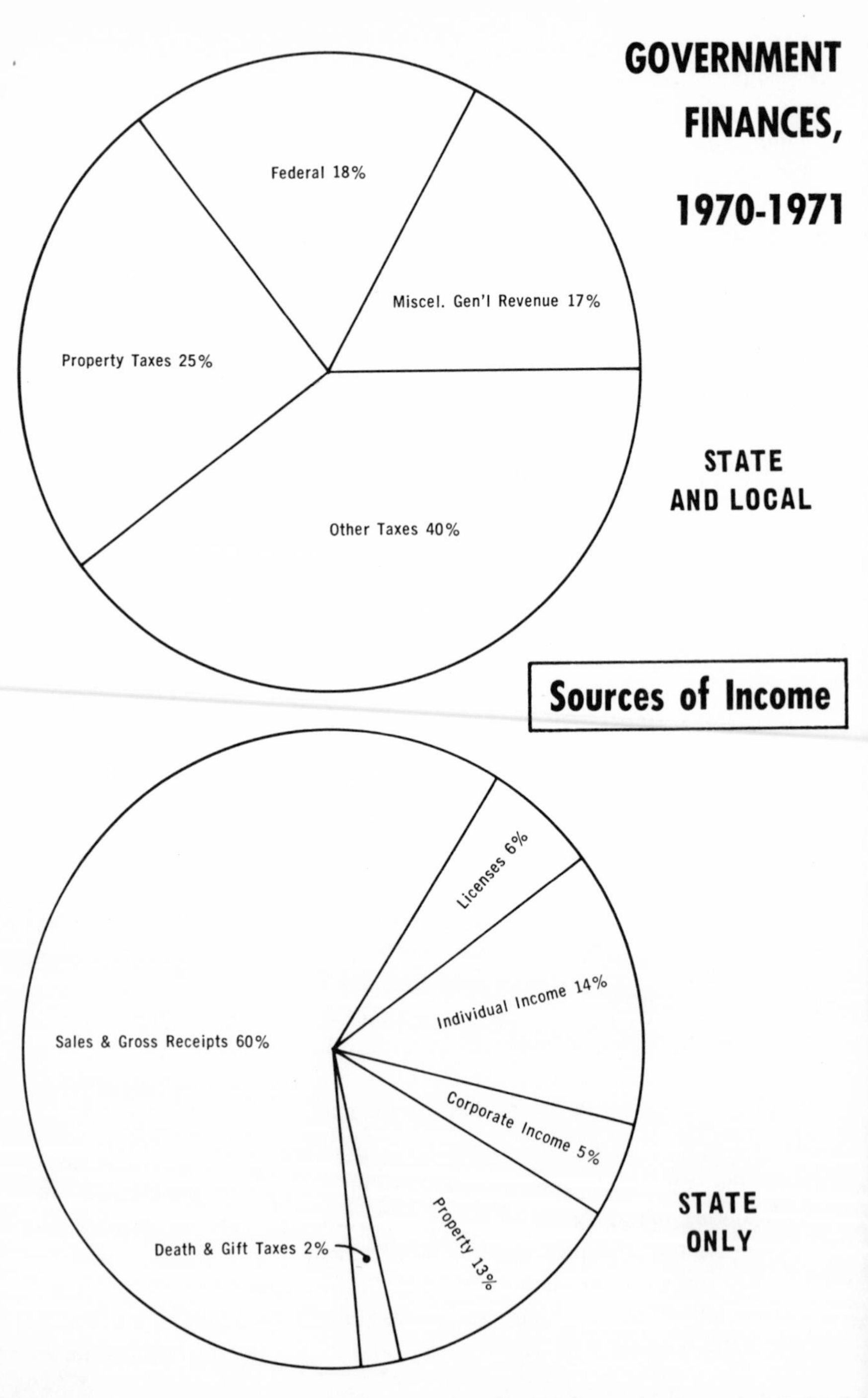

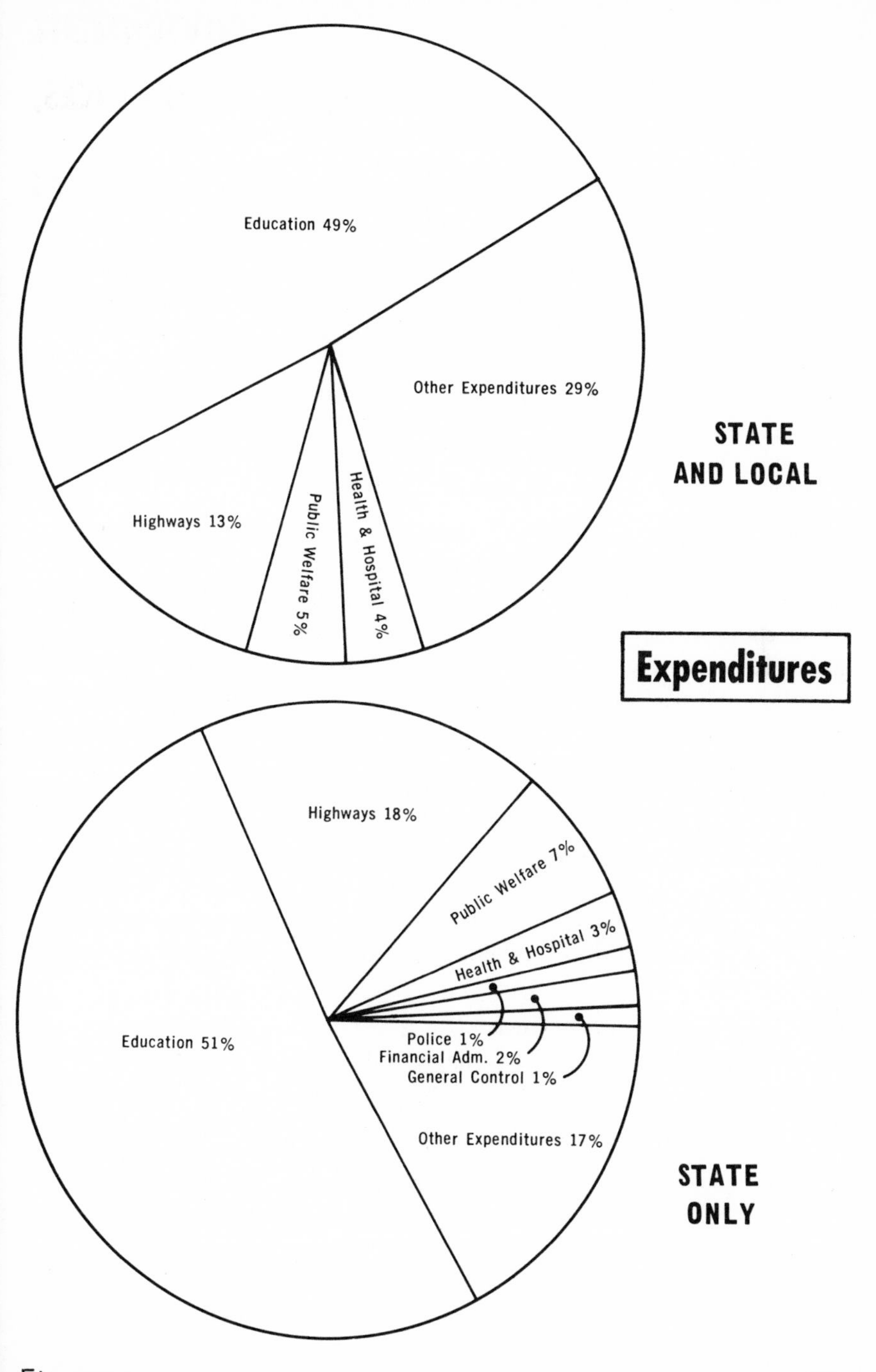
Education 49%
Other Expenditures 29%
Highways 13%
Public Welfare 5%
Health & Hospital 4%
STATE
AND LOCAL
Expenditures
Highways 18%
Public Welfare 7%
Health & Hospital 3%
Education 51%
Police 1%
Financial Adm. 2%
General Control 1%
Other Expenditures 17%
STATE
ONLY

Canyon project. Very importantly there is the matter of the revenue granted Arizona in the form of the grant-in-aid programs. By 1960, over one-fourth of the state budget was met by Federal grants and since then the trend has been steadily upward. A report made by the state's budget director to the governor, based on the fiscal year 1974-1975, showed the total of all Federal funds spent within the state equalled almost half of the money spent by the state of Arizona. Eighty million dollars from Washington went to the Department of Education, with slightly smaller amounts to the Department of Transportation and the Economic Security Department. These figures represented a gain of several million dollars over the year before but continued the trend that most of such Federal funds are spent on schools, highways and welfare programs. In addition Arizona has been receiving twenty five million dollars per year through the Federal revenue sharing program. These funds may be spent by the legislature without the Federal supervision required with the grant-in-aid programs.

On the Federal level most income received by the government is placed in one common pot in the Treasury and is drawn upon as needed. On the Arizona state level, however, certain tax monies are ear-marked for special purposes and may not be spent for any other matter. Fuel tax money goes for highways, for instance, and certain special excises for education. Theoretically the tax burden should be evenly distributed and equated to a person's ability to pay, but such is not always the case. In addition to certain property being lightly taxed, others receive special benefits. Widows and veterans get consideration in the form of exemptions and thus escape taxes to a degree. There is the potentially explosive issue of the taxation of the property of charities and religious institutions. In 1969 the assessor of Maricopa County attempted to place on the tax rolls some five million dollars worth of church lands previously not taxed, thus setting off a minor furor and setting the stage for some interesting legal controversies.

There are occasions when state expenditures outstrip income and the result is debt. Arizona is strongly imbued with a "pay as you go" philosophy of government, and the state constitution even limits the state from incurring obligations of more than $350,000 except to repulse a foreign invasion. By the middle of 1973 it was estimated that the state debt was actually close to ninety million dollars with the seeming inconsistency resulting from the fact that state agencies may take on debts in the form of bonds issued without this amount being charged to the total state debt. An example of this would be bonds issued by a university which will then be repaid from money derived from future income in the form of tuition and fees. Arizona's total debt is fairly low compared to many states. The annual budget of the state of Arizona in 1969-1970 was over three hundred eleven million dollars and this did not include funds spent by state agencies which were derived from other sources. It was estimated that these amounts would raise spending by all state agencies to more than five hundred seventeen million dollars. Since that time budgets have increased to a considerable degree. Early in 1973 the governor recommended to the legislature that the budget for the following fiscal year be five hundred forty five million dollars and that state revenues alone would total nearly six hundred million dollars without many Federal grants being included in that total. Where do these funds go?

In its expenditures Arizona is fairly typical of most states. Just a few years ago about one-third of all state funds went for education but currently this figure has risen to about one-half. Not only are there more people attending schools but the average student is remaining in school longer. In 1969 Arizona ranked thirty-third in ability to pay for schools based on per capita income. Yet its people contributed 6.5% of their total income to schools, probably the highest percentage of any state in the union. During the fiscal year 1969-1970 the per capita state expenditure for education was $310.89. Traditionally the state spent another third of its money on highways but this percentage has declined in recent years. Highway problems remain but simply have not received as much in the way of funds as before. Now there is more and more clamor for public transportation systems, which will cost large sums of money. In 1969-1970 the per capita spending for highways in Arizona was $83.19, a figure slightly higher than the average for all states.

In its public welfare expenditures, which have actually declined as a percentage of the total of state spending recently, Arizona ranks below the national average. In 1969-1970 the per capita expenditure here was $29.51 with another $28.08 spent on health and hospitals financed by state and local agencies. Traditionally about one-fourth of the budget went to the public welfare areas. Since Arizona has a growing population and one which is not settled and stable there will doubtless be more needs here for the future. Once long ago many matters included in this area were considered to be the responsibility of the private family but are now being more and more shifted to the public sector of life. Some critics say that the state is simply not meeting its problems while others say the state cannot do more. In 1969 4.4% of the Arizona population were on welfare and these 75,000 individuals caused the state to spend

A page from the state executive budget

THE LIVESTOCK SANITARY BOARD

AGENCY SUMMARY	Actual 1967-1968	Actual 1968-1969	Actual 1969-1970	Estimated 1970-1971	Requested 1971-1972	Recommended 1971-1972
THE BOARD	694,498	729,522	811,483	975,993	1,153,152	1,035,100
THE STATE VETERINARIAN	71,950	87,140	80,393	100,180	109,708	106,800
CHIEF VETERINARY MEAT INSPECTOR	125,606	145,835	240,656	311,973	388,934	340,100
POULTRY INSPECTION				25,000	25,508	21,300
	892,054	962,497	1,132,532	1,413,146	1,677,302	1,503,300
PERSONAL SERVICES						
Number of positions	112	119	125	133	146	140
Personal Services	642,565	691,940	834,738	1,031,361	1,188,562	1,092,600
Employee Related Expenditures	534	408	357	115,351	134,428	126,300
OPERATING EXPENDITURES						
Professional & Outside Services	23,302	30,024	24,739	29,300	29,300	27,300
Travel - State	139,231	139,591	119,381	100,250	137,650	128,900
Travel - Out-of-State	1,272	2,168	11,885	12,225	11,925	6,400
Other Operating Expenditures	27,592	28,874	34,905	38,458	47,504	42,800
CAPITAL OUTLAY						
Equipment	374	11,869	56,878	55,201	74,933	48,000
OTHER						
Predatory Animal and Rodent Control	39,789	42,623	40,274	25,000	47,000	25,000
Payment of Bounties	15,820	9,350	8,900			
Indemnities for Reactor Animals	1,275	5,650	475	6,000	6,000	6,000
	892,054	962,497	1,132,532	1,413,146	1,677,302	1,503,300

over forty million dollars per year. It was estimated that as of the end of 1973 sixteen per cent, or roughly 335,000 Arizonans were living at or below the poverty level. Finally the budget supports the costs of general government including the salaries of officials, the various expenditures of the many governmental agencies and the like. Suffice it to say that for every dollar available for spending there are many agencies and programs in competition for it. The likelihood that taxes and expenditures will go down seems a remote prospect indeed.

In so many areas the costs of government go steadily upward because people demand more and more in the way of governmental services. Therefore government becomes a bigger and bigger business, and under the circumstances the best which can be hoped for is to make certain that every cent spent is wisely used, and that waste, duplication and inefficiency in state government are avoided. There can often be a considerable difference between true economy in government and false economy. The cheapest item is not always adequate to the purpose. In a state which hopes to gain industry to prosper, it will eventually be discovered that an enlightened corporation, thinking of relocating in a state, will inquire not only about tax rates, but be concerned with the quality of state services offered to potential employees.

Justice William T. Howell, author of Arizona's first set of laws, The Howell Code.

As of 1973 eight states in the union have turned, rather in desperation, to the use of a lottery as a way to help finance state government. There has been some discussion in Arizona of such a scheme from time to time. However in 1970, the last time the voters had occasion to express their views on a lottery the notion was soundly rejected.

Americans in our contemporary age seem to object to taxes in general and Arizonans are especially vocal in their denunciations of all forms of revenue raising. While the scope of this discussion does not directly involve the tax program of the Washington government, still the matter figures in the Arizona story to such an extent as to be inescapable. There is no doubt but that taxes in the state and nation are at an all time high, but there are reasons for this. During all of the 1950's and 1960's, a twenty year period, there were the almost staggering costs of military expenditures, the usual yearly outgo amounting to about half of all Federal spending, with another sizeable amount being used to pay for past wars. Clearly the enormous national debt we now have is attributable to our involvement in wars both hot and cold.

Then there are the increasing costs of the various public welfare programs carried on by government at one level or another. It is not possible to get something for nothing, and therefore if people want these services then they must pay for them. Many people seem to forget in the midst of this new affluent society we have that tax paying is a necessary thing. As Mr. Justice Holmes once remarked taxes are the means by which we buy civilization. □

19

ARIZONA SOCIETY

In many ways it is very difficult to generalize on the subject of the social aspects of life in Arizona because there are in actuality several different Arizonas. Some of the state's inhabitants reside on remote Indian reservations, some in small or medium sized towns, while others make their homes in one of the larger metropolitan areas of the entire nation. To each group the styles of living, customs and mores are different. In ranching and rural areas the traditions of the "Old West" still exist while in the cities all of the problems and difficulties of the modern order are to be found. Especially as one chronicles the almost endless list of social problems, frictions and troubles it must be remembered that not all problems are equally found in the different types of communities; in some places all seems tranquil and orderly. Of course one of the main reasons for using the Phoenix metropolitan area as an example in this subject area is that statistics are more readily available for the state's largest city.

One of the most striking characteristics of the Arizona population is the fact that seemingly almost everyone has come to the state from somewhere else. The number of adult natives is rather small but gradually growing. Community leaders have generally risen to prominence rather recently. Unlike some states where some old families are influential generation after generation, Arizona is too recently settled to have this factor operate. Technically our neighboring state of California contributes the largest number of families who move to the Phoenix area but evidence indicates most of those people actually originated in another state. Nearly ten percent of the new arrivals are from Illinois, over six percent from Ohio and almost as many come from New York. Texas furnishes over five percent but far and away the greatest numbers come from some Midwestern states. In 1969 there were just over fifty thousand non-citizens of the United States who were residents of Arizona. Unfortunately there were many thousands more who did not regard themselves as Arizonans but rather still as New Yorkers, Alabamians or Kansans.

The most numerous racial group in Arizona is "white." However it is estimated that one-third of the population is of some racial minority group, a figure higher than the national average. The state has the largest Indian population to be found anywhere in the nation. Currently the issue of "red power" is receiving some attention. Since the Indians for the most part live in areas somewhat remote from view they have often been ignored. Now there is much discussion as to whether or not the time has arrived for the Federal government to end its paternalistic policy toward the original inhabitants of our land and allow them control over their own destiny. Everyone is aware of the important Negro or Black "rights revolution" of the contemporary period. Black men and women have resided in Arizona for generations and were often subjected to prejudice and discrimination. Until the 1950's schools were often segregated, public accommodations were denied to Negroes and jobs were often reserved for whites only. In 1919 the first Arizona chapter of the National Association for the Advancement of Colored People was formed in Phoenix and in 1944 the Urban League began its work in the state. Census figures indicate that the Black population of Arizona is under five percent of the state total and well over half of this group reside in Maricopa County. While some areas of the nation were troubled by outbreaks of violence in the decade of the 1960's Arizona was largely spared. There were some peaceful demonstrations demanding equal rights which took place at the capitol and in 1967 some violence erupted in Phoenix. For the most part the leaders of the Arizona Black community are integrationists seeking equal rights and opportunities for all.

During the decade of the 1960's those people who had previously been called Latin Americans came to be known as Chicanos. In the late 1960's one study indicated that just under fifteen percent of the state's population had Spanish surnames. The 1970 census concluded that one-fifth of Arizona's population was of the Spanish heritage. This was determined on the basis of including those who either had Spanish surnames or reported that they lived in a household where Spanish was the mother tongue. In our contemporary age the Chicanos too are demanding their full equal rights. Stereotypes and prejudices are resented and all Arizonans should remember how important the Spanish and Mexican influence on us has been. Traditional concepts of ranching, mining and water rights sprang from the Latin heritage. Such legal doctrines as community property rights between husband and wife also had their source there. Between four and five percent of the state population is of Chinese or Japanese ancestry, two other minority groups who have contributed much to the building of modern day Arizona.

To many people, especially those of an older generation, it seems as though today the world is falling apart. Problems of all sorts abound and Arizona often seems to have more than its share of social problems. Again the fact of our new population compounds our difficulties. While some areas of Arizona have grown slowly and in a planned, orderly fashion, the urban areas have not. Housing for all is a problem whether the dwelling is located in a remote agricultural area or in a metropolitan slum. Increasingly in cities where land is expensive the apartment unit is replacing the single family dwelling. Some of the state's builders and contractors are experimenting with low cost housing units while others are wrestling generally with urban renewal. Tucson participated in the Federal model cities program but Phoenix was barred because it did not have a housing code. Several cities and towns in the state are suffering from blight in the downtown centers and Phoenix has been the hardest hit. The inner city has been in trouble for some years; businesses have moved out and into decentralized shopping centers scattered around the metropolitan area. Now serious efforts are being made to rebuild the inner city and once again make it a productive part of the total picture. Unfortunately the problem was long ignored in the hope that somehow it would vanish of its own accord.

Arizona is known nationally as a good place in which to retire, and therefore many senior citizens come seeking sun, quiet and tranquility. Actually the state's over age sixty-five group is less than ten percent of the total population and while growing rapidly is not as large as most people think. Such retirement communities as Sun City and Youngtown have received much attention and many people hope one day to retire there or to a similar settlement; others feel that they do not wish to be segregated by age and wish to continue residing among younger people. In 1973 it was estimated that a retired couple in Phoenix would need an annual income of about five thousand dollars to live comfortably, a figure just about average for the metropolitan areas of the nation. In common with most of the nation today the stability of the family unit in Arizona seems on the decline. The Maricopa County divorce rate is one of the highest in the nation and is supplemented by the "poor man's divorce," where the head of the household merely departs for an unknown new residence. The Arizona birth rate is relatively high and just under fifty percent of the population is under the age of twenty-one years.

In 1964 New York City suffered serious outbreaks of crime and violence and the good citizens of Phoenix looked askance at those happenings. Calm and mostly untroubled they failed to note Federal Bureau of Investigation figures which pointed out that New York had the thirty-fifth highest crime rate in the nation while Phoenix had the fourth highest! During the decade of the 1960's crime in Arizona increased five times as fast as the population growth and in 1967 the Phoenix crime rate was double the national average. Particularly a cause of concern to many is the drug problem and narcotics addiction. It is estimated that almost half of the high school students in Maricopa County have experimented with drugs in one form or another.

Alcoholism is a problem all over the nation and one from which Arizona certainly does not escape. Currently it is estimated that this disease costs the state's employers ten million dollars annually in lost production and employee absenteeism. A 1973 study concluded that 180,000 Arizonans could be classified as heavy drinkers in that they regularly consume at least five or six drinks per day. About three-fourths of the state's population over the age of fourteen years drank alcoholic beverages at some time. Approximately a half of all highway fatalities can be attributed to the abuse of alcohol. The state's traffic toll is high; since 1960 at least five hundred people have been slaughtered on the state's roads and highways each year. By the end of the decade that figure had gone above the six hundred mark annually and was still climbing. One small step taken to attempt to do something about this problem was the passage in 1969 of an implied consent law. It provides for either the taking of a test to determine the presence of alcohol in the blood stream in excessive quantities or otherwise certain legal presumptions may be drawn from a refusal to take the test. It has been suggested that Arizona needs to utilize unmarked patrol cars to police traffic and more strict laws for reckless drivers who repeatedly endanger the lives and property of their fellow citizens. Statistics indicate that drunk or sober Arizonans are miserable drivers and the state's accident rate is one of the highest in the nation. Had a shortage of gasoline not interferred with our activities in late 1973 the state's motorists were within range of achieving the distinction for the first time of killing one thousand people in a year's span.

Exactly what to do for and with the alcoholic in society has long been a debated matter. There is considerable agreement that utilization of the criminal law against those who were merely drunk has not worked so Arizona at the outset of 1974 tried something new. Henceforth a person publically drunk would be taken to a local alcoholism reception center, a LARC for short, or if such facility does not exist, to another social service agency or to the person's home. In time it is planned to have counseling

The oldest Protestant church building in Arizona, St. Paul's Episcopal Church of Tombstone.

and referral for further treatment. The alcoholic is involved with what is called victimless crime. There are other examples of this type of activity within our society. If the alcoholic is to be protected against himself then what ought society to do with others who need to be protected regarding other activities? A few years ago there was much controversy over whether or not motorcycle riders ought to be compelled to wear helmets. Does the state have a sufficient interest in the matter to force a person to wear something against his or her will? If evidence continues to show that tobacco smokers need "protection" against themselves should the criminal law be invoked? In the early 1970's Arizona began to enact laws which severely limited places where tobacco could legally be smoked. Is this a step in that direction or merely recognition that non-smokers have rights which protect them from being forced to breathe second-hand tobacco smoke? These matters present interesting problems for future debate and action.

A look at the amounts expended by state and local government on welfare problems will show the difficulties found in this area. Families pack their belongings and head for the west without promises of a job or without adequate resources. Families disintegrate for one reason or another and dependent children frequently need help. In 1969 there were 45,000 mentally retarded individuals in Arizona and substantial numbers who needed psychological help and counselling. Given the pressures of modern life we must accustom ourselves to the fact that at one time or another many individuals need help in this area.

Most of the state of Arizona enjoys a fine climate and therefore with the trend toward more and more leisure time there is much to do. Hunting, fishing, camping and skiing are all fine recreations. Hikers and other outdoor devotees abound. In 1969 there were over 36,000 boats registered in Arizona. In recent years there has been discussion nationally of more gun control laws, something much opposed by many Arizonans. This is even the land of the "true Old West" fast-draw artist. Now and then the newspapers chronicle the fact that one has inadvertently shot a hole in his own foot.

To those who come to the state from older settled areas it sometimes is a shock to note that some business establishments do not survive decade after decade. Arizona has a very high bankruptcy rate and many firms are here today and gone tomorrow. This problem is compounded by the fact that many new arrivals attempt to go into business with limited resources and little knowledge of the problems of owning and operating a small business. Currently the Arizona legislature has been considering and now and then enacting laws to protect the consumer. There is little doubt but that some useful steps have been taken in the direction of protecting the customer from some of the evils of the marketplace. People who buy from door-to-door salesmen have a time period in which they can change their minds and cancel the contract. However at times needed legislation does not win approval in Arizona. In 1973 a proposal to license auto repair shops was rejected and prior to a Federal law which outlawed the turning back of odometers on used cars a similar proposal was voted down in Arizona. A leading lawmaker insisted at the time that to make this illegal would be an undue burden on commerce. The sad part about this is that the great bulk of Arizona's businessmen and businesswomen are being, and will continue to be, hurt by the activities of a few. Unless something is done to remedy problems public pressure can build up to a point where harsh legislation will be enacted which will hurt the business community. Like most people in other parts of the country large numbers of Arizonans run afoul of the credit system. Buying with cash seems passé and all too often the only question one asks is not what the total price will be, but how much down and how much per month.

The role of religion and the church in late twentieth century America is the subject of debate and disagreement. Arizona has many lovely church buildings and some would say that some congregations suffer from an "edifice complex," paying more attention to the structure than with matters within and without. Statewide religious statistics are difficult to compile accurately. A survey in the Phoenix area indicates that 66% of the population is Protestant, 25% Roman Catholic, 6% Mormon, 2% Jewish, 5% belong to some other group, while 2% have no religion. (These figures equal more than one hundred percent for some households have members of two or more groups.) It is rather evident that there are more than 2% of the people who do not attend church even now and then and yet consider themselves to be of a particular faith. Mention has been made of the decline of the downtown areas of cities and in Phoenix, for example, many once inner city congregations have moved out to more suburban surroundings.

There is much to criticize and to worry about in Arizona society. There is also some room for hope. The very newness of the state creates opportunities. There is no stifling tradition or stagnation, but rather still the opportunity to create new traditions. Not all areas of the nation or the world progress and develop at the same rate, and in many ways Arizona is passing through the same period lived through by many other states in the 1880's and 1890's. We can profit from their past mistakes and avoid them if we are willing to learn. While it will probably take a few generations to accomplish it, a new and grander society can be created here. Based upon the principle of a maximum of individual freedom and true individuality, it must rest on the principle that unless we make Arizona a reasonably good place for all, it will not remain a decent place for any of us. The building process will take the effort and the cooperation of all. It will require enlightenment and a realistic appraisal of the good life and what it means to each and every Arizonan. Many seem to assume that Arizona must follow in the footsteps of the southern half of California but let us hope not. Rather Arizona has the opportunity to become a model for others to follow. The choice will be made by present and future generations.

□

20

CULTURAL AFFAIRS

CULTURE IS OFTEN broadly defined as being the sum total of the ways of living built up by a group. Although these ways may change over the years the total is stable enough to be transmitted from one generation to another. For our purposes we will consider largely the non-material aspects of our civilization. The fact that culture is something that involves a heritage built up over a lengthy time tends to influence matters in Arizona. Except for certain Indian cultures the other influences found in the state have been rather recently imported. The very newness of the society results in the fact that we have not yet produced giants of literature, artists or musical figures as have some of the older areas of the nation. There has not been the time nor the financial resources available to build famous art museums, centers for the performing arts, resident opera and ballet companies and the like.

Cultural affairs properly involve many areas of human endeavor. Literature, for instance, involves not only books but newspapers as well. Arizona literary figures have included Zane Grey who wrote absurd fiction and Ross Santee, less well known, but one who handled the same themes with honesty as well as literary quality. Dick Wick Hall was an Arizona humorist of local note who achieved popularity. Some prominent writers have spent time living in Arizona and such a list would include J. B. Priestly, Harold Bell Wright, Owen Wister, Joseph Wood Krutch and Clare Boothe Luce. One great writer had an imagined residence in Arizona for Samuel L. Clemens, on occasion, signed himself: "Mark Twain, M.A., Professor of Belles Letters in the Veterinary College of Arizona." In the area of the press, Arizona has had a few fine newspapers, some mediocre ones, and some not worth mentioning at all. About the year 1908, American newspapers in general reached a peak in per capita circulation and since that time have steadily declined. It is often difficult now to keep a newspaper going, much less to start a new one. A city can certainly benefit from good newspapers as the record of Tucson will show, for its press has doubtless contributed to its reputation as "Arizona's most civilized city."

The newspapers have lost ground in part to the radio and to the television set. Radio came to Arizona in the early 1920's and rapidly became a popular thing in an area with so many wide open spaces and one which was thinly populated. The first television station in Arizona, KPHO in Phoenix, was in operation by the end of 1949, and it and the several others in the state play an important part in the lives of people. Radio also still survives and thrives. The motion picture is another cultural force in the lives of many, and in Arizona there is a great variety of offerings. In the Phoenix metropolitan area, for example, if something is shown in Scottsdale it is labeled an "art film," while if the same screening takes place on East Washington in downtown Phoenix it is pornography. The motion picture coincidentally even brought refrigeration for general use on the Arizona desert for it was a theatre which was the first public building in the state to be so equipped.

This state has at least one magazine of which all people can be proud, the world-famous *Arizona Highways,* which has become the model for similar publications. Beginning in the 1920's as a mimeographed sheet it was soon producing fine black and white photographic work which in the late 1940's blossomed into full color. Arizona has a number of individuals in painting and sculpture whose works enjoy a degree of local popularity and others who produce items for their own enjoyment only. Since the 1920's both Phoenix and Tucson have had symphony orchestras and in the last two decades similar groups have appeared in other cities. The universities produce not only musical works but also have legitimate theatres. The "Little Theatre" movement got its start in Arizona in our two largest cities and there are now many other amateur groups performing. Cartooning is an art form too, and the well-known Bill Mauldin got his start in Arizona before he moved on to other things, while Reg Manning seems more suited to local tastes. Arizona's greatest architect was a part-time resident of the state for many years, the late Frank Lloyd Wright. Today his disciples continue his work at Taliesin West which the master established several decades ago.

Although Arizona towns have had "library societies," the forerunners of public libraries since the late 1870's, the state still suffers from a shortage of library resources. Again it takes many years and much money to build up great libraries. Meanwhile the book resources to be found here are not generally adequate. Since universities are judged by the library facilities they possess Arizona's three schools have been actively interested in building up their stature. In rural areas the extensive use of bookmobiles

Grady Gammage Auditorium at Arizona State University was the work of Frank Lloyd Wright.

has been useful in bringing reading materials to all those who desire them.

Unfortunately given the great number of new arrivals among the population there has not been very much interest in the Arizona past. Arizona history presents a fascinating story which needs to be told in more detail. Hubert Howe Bancroft, James McClintock and Thomas E. Farish have all written extensive histories of Arizona, while Rufus K. Wyllys did a creditable shorter one. There are still many opportunities, however, for one to do extensive original research in this field.

In 1967 the Arizona legislature created the Arizona Commission on the Arts and Humanities, a fifteen member group composed of persons appointed by the governor for a three year term of office. Officially its purpose is to "stimulate and encourage throughout the state the study and presentation of the performing arts, fine arts, the humanities and public interest and participation therein." Aside from its broad responsibilities in bringing culture to what some might consider a needy land, its practical role was in dispensing the Federal money granted to it each year by the Congress of the United States through the National Endowment for the Humanities. In 1974-1975 that sum amounted to almost a half million dollars. Despite its good works and relatively small cost to the state a determined but unsuccessful attempt was made in the legislature in 1976 to end its existence. Obviously there are those who feel that government ought not to be involved in dispensing culture.

Science and its ally, technology, play an important role in our lives. Due to the once beautifully clear atmosphere Arizona early became a center for astronomers. The Lowell Observatory at Flagstaff dates from the 1890's and here the planet Pluto was discovered by observers in 1930. Following World War II with the great expansion in scientific research the Federal government first planned and then starting in 1958 built Kitt Peak National Observatory in the southern part of the state. However in other areas of science the picture is not so bright. Indeed one national magazine reported that Phoenix was one of the few industrial areas of the nation to be without a nearby first-rate educational and scientific center. The state, like many others, does benefit from the ideas generated in the "think-factories" located mainly on the east and west coasts of the United States. Our neighbor, New Mexico, profited greatly from the atomic installations placed within its boundaries, but Arizona was not so fortunate as to receive similar centers of scientific activity.

Presumably as Arizona becomes an older and more settled society, cultural matters will come increasingly to the fore. In future years people will have more leisure time with which to enjoy these aspects of life. Everything points to an increasingly short work week and people must be retrained to enjoy free time and to use it profitably. New ideas are not always welcome, especially in Arizona, but some radical changes are taking place in regard to people and their culture. □

21

EDUCATION

IN ALL PROBABILITY the United States can truly lay claim to being the home of public education in the Western world and indeed throughout the world. Starting in Puritan New England, the concept of schooling for all the population at public expense has spread out all over the nation. Ironically the American goal seems to be some education for everyone but not too much for anyone, because in addition to their being champions of education, the citizens of this nation also tend to be decidedly anti-intellectual. At the outset of the organization of the territory of Arizona an attempt was made to establish some public schools, but due to a lack of money, a shortage of teachers and the primitive conditions existing, the task was a difficult one. The "Father of Public Education in Arizona" was Governor Safford, who in the 1870's really gave the territory its first school system. Even then there was some opposition to the program for in the mid 1870's, Chief Justice Edmund F. Dunne went about the confines of the territory demanding that Catholics have their own schools and thus be exempt from paying school taxes. Dunne was sacked by President Grant for his efforts.

For some years to come it was difficult to obtain and keep teachers, especially young women, for they tended to get married almost upon arrival and to later exchange the public's children for a collection of their own. Young men who found their way into teaching in those days generally remained just long enough to learn a sufficient amount of law to be admitted to practice, and then they too left the schools for more worldly endeavors. In the nineteenth century school often meant simply the traditional grammar school, often one room, but by the start of the twentieth century the high schools and better facilities for higher education had arrived to complete the picture. Some unfortunate features arrived also in the early 1900's when the legislature segregated the schools according to race over the vigorous veto of Governor Kibbey, a Republican of the Abraham Lincoln type.

For many years the governor of the territory was the superintendent of schools as well, but in 1879 a separate office was created and then carried on over into the period of statehood. Another agency of the schools was, and is, the State Board of Education composed of three lay members, plus several professional educators or educationists, all appointed by the governor. This board functions to establish general educational policies, select textbooks and set educational requirements for all areas of the Arizona school system. It also has official jurisdiction over the qualifications of teachers and in quite another area, prescribes a uniform record keeping system for schools, both financial and educational. In each of the state's fourteen counties there exists a county school superintendent who is something of a deputy to carry out the policies formulated at the state level, and who is elected by the voters, of his county.

During the territorial period school districts came into being rather at random, and they were carried over after statehood. At the present time there are some three hundred school districts, and the trend toward consolidation of schools found in many parts of the nation has made little headway in Arizona. These school districts are legal entities presided over by a board directly elected. Some boards have three members while those in larger districts have five members. Regardless of the number of board members one person comes up for reelection each year. The school board is an old agency in Arizona and the nation as well, and its members have charge of buildings, personnel and finances plus general policy matters. Districts may be changed as to boundaries, which is generally of concern to the residents of the district, the county school superintendent and sometimes the county board of supervisors. The concept of the junior high school is not well developed in Arizona so that an elementary school has domain over children until they pass through the eighth grade, and then they go to the high school. A high school district may be regular (boundaries co-equal with an elementary district), county (boundaries the same as county lines), or union (which joins two or more elementary districts).

Since education amounts to a major part of the state's financial budget it is obvious that money is an important area of educational matters. Originally the idea was that local districts managed their own affairs and raised most of their own taxes, but eventually the state began to also provide money. Unfortunately not all school districts are of equal wealth and therefore occasionally there are schools with adequate or even surplus funds, while others are desperately poor. During the last two decades, the Arizona legislature has changed the school laws so as to provide a degree of equalization of funds. Still the general rule in Arizona is that districts are almost always in need of more financial help especially in urban areas where there are great "bedroom communities," with few items of wealth in the form of property to be taxed. In late 1973 a special session of the legislature convened to consider the matter of financing Arizona's school system. It continued the established trend of shifting more of the burden of supporting the schools from local taxation to the state, thus furthering the cause of equalization. It also attempted to encourage the consolidation of school districts so as to achieve more economy in operation. The school districts did not evidence any later interest in the matter.

There has been much reluctance in Arizona to accept Federal aid for schools, but the battle now seems over, and, if for no other reason than desperation, most school districts have overcome their hesitation in accepting money from Washington. While the school board is given general control over finances, if a school budget takes a major jump, which is over six percent as compared to the preceeding year, this must be approved by the district registered voters. Now and then school districts must issue bonds to meet money needs, especially for buildings, but there are limitations on the amount of debts to be incurred, and of course such matters must be approved by the district registered voters. Year in and year out all school budgets are submitted to the county and state superintendents of education so that the state and its agencies, including the counties, have the ultimate responsibility for supervision of school matters.

In 1885 the territory of Arizona embarked upon a program of providing higher educational facilities for its citizens. At roughly the same time, a normal school was established at Tempe, and the University of Arizona was created at Tucson. Then in the late 1890's the legislature found itself with a building at Flagstaff which was of no use, and another normal school was authorized. The schools at Tempe and Flagstaff have undergone many name changes, and by the middle 1960's, all three Arizona state institutions of higher learning had the status of a university. While good salaries do not necessarily insure a good school they do generally help, and in this area Arizona has always lagged behind many states. During the 1950's and 1960's in the East the three universities were called the "landing strip," meaning that they were places to come to for a year or so while negotiating for a job in one of the California institutions of higher learning where salaries, working conditions and academic programs seemed more rewarding than what was found in Arizona. By the early 1970's for varied reasons this practice had largely come to an end. Presiding over the universities is a Board of Regents composed of eight members appointed by the governor. Private colleges in Arizona are rare. For a time Grand Canyon College at Phoenix, a Southern Baptist institution, was joined by Prescott College, a liberal arts institution under Congregational auspices but by the middle 1970's the latter was bankrupt and was no longer in operation.

In 1960, faced with growing enrollments and the need for more colleges the legislature passed a junior college law which would enable a county, (or two counties joined together in the instance of those with limited finances) to establish this level of education. At the time of the passage of the law Arizona had two junior colleges: Phoenix College in Maricopa County and Eastern Arizona College in Graham County. By 1974 a majority of the counties had junior colleges in operation and the Maricopa County system with its five schools was by far the largest.

Some claim that junior colleges are cheaper to operate than traditional colleges or universities and that being located around the state they make it possible for more people to attend school than would be able to do so otherwise. However, there is a danger that they might be weak academically and at worst no better than glorified high schools. Some say that the junior colleges should be more concerned with vocational and technical education than with traditional subject areas, but most junior college students, at the outset of their college careers at least, seek regular college courses. Above all else the junior college has a prime responsibility to guarantee that their college parallel courses are of standard college calibre but are otherwise free to sponsor such course offerings as are demanded by the community.

That area of education designated usually as "special education," involves the blind, the deaf, the mentally retarded and those needing social correction. This topic will be dealt with under the heading of public institutions. All states have problems currently with their educational systems, and Arizona is no exception to the rule. Probably the most obvious difficulty here is that the state is growing so fast in population that it is difficult to keep adequate facilities, especially as students are now going on for more years of schooling than was previously the case. Some of those in the field of education say that there should be more of a trend toward consolidation of school districts, but there is no uniform thought on this subject. It is, however, a fact that Phoenix is today the largest city in the United States, and indeed the only relatively large one, that does not have a consolidated city school system.

Recently much attention has been paid to the subject of kindergarten in Arizona. While the founding fathers of Arizona intended kindergarten to be supported out of state funds, for a long time an attorney general's opinion prevented it. Probably the person deserving the most credit for finally persuading the legislature to bring state-wide kindergartens into existence was Sarah Folsom, state superintendent of public instruction in the 1960's. Although she did not live to see many of her dreams realized Arizona now has a kindergarten program comparable to most states. Many of the state's founders, especially Governor Hunt, also wanted free textbooks for all students through high school. To date that has not been realized although the notion has considerable support. The financial problems of Arizona schools are widespread and range from day to day operations and budgets to the fact that the teacher retirement program in the state is bad from the standpoint of most neighboring states and downright unbelievable when compared to such states as California. For the most part elementary and high school salaries for teachers have been reasonable, but higher education has had inadequate funds. Some trends toward raising college salaries and other budget items have been observed of late, and hopefully they will continue. Unfortunately below the college level salaries are now dropping when compared to other states.

It seems that in many areas of Arizona everyone in the community is an expert on school matters, and many districts have been troubled by some monumental feuds involving school boards and local pressure groups. This is one area where the recall has been important, but ironically in several of these, after all the uproar was over and the smoke had cleared the situation was exactly what it was before the fighting started. Arizona seems to be a haven for every notion on education in existence, and these squabbles tend to weaken the educational program and to interfere with its normal functioning. Also some people seem to believe that the best education for all is that which keeps the tax rate at its lowest possible point.

This nation has always been sympathetic to the notion that the prime need of the country was to have an educated and enlighted citizenry. Therefore the goal of public education has been to give the young an education whereby they would be aware of the world and its many facets. Along the line the idea developed that the schools should provide the student with training which would prepare him for a job. This latter trend is probably too well established by now to be reversed, but today one may question whether or not general education is about to suffer at the expense of vocational matters. The sum total of human knowledge is increasing at an amazing rate, and yet there is a danger that the average citizen, once poured through the educational system, will actually know little more, or worse, less than did the generations before him. We suffer seriously from what is called cultural lag. Our material civilization is far advanced when compared to our nonmaterial society, our intellectual development and our ability to deal successfully with other human beings. □

Gov. Anson P. K. Safford is considered as 'Father of Public Education' in Arizona

22

PUBLIC INSTITUTIONS

IN THE EARLY DAYS of the American republic the need for public institutions of an eleemosynary nature was quite limited. The thought was that such matters would be the concern of the family and not of the state. Perhaps a county poor farm might finally be needed but not until about a hundred years ago did other institutions become the order of the day. Mental institutions were recognized as being necessary rather early, but thinking had to come a long way from the days when the insane were kept in cages and often put on public view. Actually the humane treatment of the mentally ill is a rather modern idea, and even today many feel such illness is something to be hidden from public view. Only the most emancipated boast of their sessions with the psychiatrist with the same gusto that gallstone operations are recounted. However, given the almost impossible pressures of modern day living one must accept the idea that mental illness is going to be more and more a major problem in our lives.

For some years, Arizona boarded its "insane" in California, and in 1884 a newspaper reported that at Stockton there were 53 people charged to the territory, and they cost the treasury six dollars per week per person for care. Not long afterward an "insane asylum" was built in Phoenix, and ultimately it became the Arizona State Hospital for the Insane. Of recent years the hospital has had more than its share of troubles and problems. In the years following World War II the hospital at last began to place emphasis on rehabilitation rather than merely custodial care. In the 1960's there were disputes caused by the fact that some citizens in the community felt that the hospital's main function was to keep the ill out of sight and not let them escape. Salaries paid staff were often low, and it was difficult to obtain and keep competent personnel. All in all much progress has been made. One of the interesting trends in recent years had been to place mental health facilities in communities other than Phoenix so as to bring treatment to where the people are.

Almost from the time of its founding, Arizona had a reputation as a good place to overcome tuberculosis. Due to this and the high incidence of this ailment among Indian people, the state's disease rate was high. Sunnyslope, north of Phoenix, was originally founded following World War I as a community for what were then called "lungers." During the depression years the Federal government built a sanatorium near Tempe. After World War II ownership was transferred to the state which renamed it the Arizona State Tuberculosis Sanatorium. By the early 1970's advances in medicine resulted in few people being there and so it was converted into the Arizona Childrens Hospital. At Tucson there is the Arizona School for the Deaf and Blind which was once a part of the University of Arizona but which is now a separate institution. The Home for Pioneers located at Prescott, is, except for a similar institution in Alaska, a unique institution. It was opened just prior to statehood. A person sixty years of age who has been a resident of Arizona for the past thirty-five years may apply for admission to the Home and spend his or her retirement among those of similar background. It is most fitting that the state should honor and care for those who contributed to the building of Arizona.

Illustrative of the point that in bygone days there was little need for certain types of state institutions is the fact that the building originally utilized by the normal school at Flagstaff had been built as a reform school for boys, but no potential inmates seemed to exist. Apparently the six-gun or the jail eventually took care of those needing some correction. At about the time of statehood, Arizona opened the State Industrial School at Fort Grant, which functioned for a long time as a corrective institution for boys and young men. In time it became the philosophy of those concerned with these matters that juvenile offenders should be housed as close to their homes as possible rather than in one central location and in 1973 the Fort Grant institution was changed into a part of the state prison to be occupied by first offenders and those not of the hardened criminal type. At one time there was a reform school for girls near Coolidge but during the depression of the 1930's it was abandoned only to be later used as what was known as the Children's Colony, a residence for mentally retarded young people. The institution still exists but has been renamed. In 1969 the legislature created the Arizona Girls School, located north of Phoenix; in 1973 it was renamed the Adobe Mountain School and became coeducational.

Not long after the organization of the territory in 1863, there was discussion of the need for a prison. After many troubles the Territorial Prison at Yuma was opened and existed there until 1909. The Yuma facility, now a museum, was quite horrible even for a prison of its day. Yuma, in pre-refrigeration days, was not the most pleasant place, climate wise, in Arizona, and it was common knowledge that a sentence there for more than a few years was about the same as inflicting the death penalty. Finally the prison was moved to Florence, and here the facilities, now over-taxed for both men and women, include an irrigated farm of several hundred acres which provides food for the inmates. One of the principal problems with the prison is that it is located away from the population centers of Arizona, and apart from the idea that prisoners should be kept within their community and not "put away" somewhere, there has long been the problem of getting people to work at the institution when seemingly so many want to live in the larger metropolitan centers.

Until 1941 there was one state board which had charge of most state institutions, but then the old system was ended and some institutions were placed directly in the charge of the governor while others were given separate boards or commissions. The costs of operating these various state institutions is an ever increasing matter and will continue to be so. Arizona is a growing state and has a new, and often unstable population. A high crime rate and a multitude of social problems are bound to be vexations for many years to come. Many Arizona institutions desperately need more funds for new building facilities and for higher salaries for staff personnel. While there is no denying that considerable progress has been made in the last few years, Arizona has a long way to go before the many troublesome problems existing in these areas are under control, let alone solved.

Currently the Department of Corrections operates seven institutions and has a substantial dollar budget. In addition to those operations already mentioned there is the Arizona Youth Center, a diagnostic facility north of Tucson, a minimum custody facility at Safford where adult felons work outside during the day and return at night, and a school-type institution at Alpine for teenage boys. More than a half dozen half-way houses plus fourteen district parole offices are parts of the Department's operations too. A new prison operation is planned near Phoenix and later a similar institution will be placed near Tucson.

On the lighter side the state fair is an old and honorable Arizona institution. Years ago land was purchased from Phoenix for the fairgrounds, and here have been located several permanent buildings including a new and attractive coliseum named in honor of Arizona's veterans of the wars. Unfortunately, in 1967, there were problems connected with the management of the plant and its operations, but this is merely evidence that vigilance and care must be exercised in supervising the operations of the various state agencies. Another important series of state institutions are the parks developed by Arizona over the years. The State Parks Board currently has eleven facilities under its jurisdiction. Lake Havasu State Park has two parts and offers boating, camping and other forms of recreation for the public. Alamo Lake State Park is a fishing and water sports area on the Bill Williams River. Lyman State Park is for fishing and water sports and is located in the eastern high country. The other parks have some historical significance. Painted Rocks State Park, northwest of Gila Bend, displays Arizona's Indian heritage; while Fort Verde State Park, Jerome State Historic Park, Picacho Peak State Park, Tombstone Courthouse State Historical Monument, Tubac Presidio State Historic Park and the Yuma Territorial Prison State Historic Park all have association with the later story of the territory and state.

Mention has been made of the long struggle Arizona experienced over the location of its capitol. In the 1890's work was begun on the oldest portion of the building in Phoenix, and at the turn of the century the government moved in and occupied what was then the pride of the territory. During the years of World War I the building was somewhat expanded and enlarged, and in the 1930's more area was added. Starting in the late 1920's a series of state office buildings was erected nearby, and in looking at them one may see the development and changes in Arizona architecture over the years. By the 1950's the capitol itself was overcrowded, and more space was needed.

The late Frank Lloyd Wright designed a new capitol complex to be placed in Papago Park on the eastern side of Phoenix. The Wright design seemed to some to be too radical. One legislator told the architect that it looked like "a Siamese house of ill repute," to which the peppery Wright retorted that he was certain the obnoxious solon would know more about that than he did. In the end the Wright proposal was shelved, and a Senate and a House building were constructed in front of the original capitol. As the state grew there was a need for more expansion and starting in the late 1960's several new buildings were constructed in the capitol complex area. At one time there was a threat to the little old capitol building for the rule in Arizona is to preserve nothing of bygone days. The architects of the moment seem to have as their rallying cry, "Tear down the architectural mistakes of the past and put in their places even bigger and better ones for the future!" Rather amazingly though the capitol was saved and a new high rise building was placed behind it.

Between 1968 and the end of 1975 the Arizona legislature appropriated thirty two million dollars to construct ten major buildings in the capitol area. At the beginning of that period it was obvious that new facilities were needed because among other things many agencies of government were housed in rented space. As a matter of fact the state was in 1968 paying one and a half million dollars per year in rents and although the owners of the rental property were happy with the arrangement the thought is that the state should house its operations in its own buildings. Unfortunately in 1976 it was reported that the state was still paying nearly one million seven hundred thousand dollars in rents per year. This was true despite the new buildings and the fact that the 400,000 square feet of building space owned by the state in the capitol area in 1968 had climbed to more than one million square feet in 1976. One of the reasons offered for the situation was the fact that the number of state workers had grown over the years. Some wondered what other factors might have contributed to the situation. It was said that perhaps a lack of good planning and a tendency to make some quarters more extensive than they might be were parts of the overall picture. At any rate additional building projects are still seemingly needed and are in process.

The state of Texas has created in its capital city, Austin, an attractive final resting place for its honored heroes. It is officially known as the State Cemetery, but the Texans proudly call it the "Arlington of the West." Located near the Arizona capitol complex are some old cemeteries used in the pioneer period but lately all but abandoned. Arizona could well take a leaf from the page of Texas' book of memories and turn this area into an Arizona State Cemetery, where in now unused space the honored dead of our state's history could rest. Such forgotten but important men as William F. Turner, first chief justice of the territory, and John J. Gosper, secretary and acting territorial governor currently are buried in unmarked graves in other states. Our state should do something to show its appreciation for the services rendered by once prominent citizens. □

23

COUNTIES and LOCAL GOVERNMENT

THE COUNTY AS A UNIT of government was transplanted into the Southern colonies established by England and ultimately in time spread out all over the nation. When Arizona was created four counties were provided and in 1865 the legislature added a fifth, the legendary lost county of Pah-Ute which was taken from the territory and given to Nevada not long afterward. Starting in 1871 and continuing to 1909, the Council and the House of Representatives established ten new and lasting counties. In this area Arizona shows its Indian heritage for nine counties have names of that origin, while one more honors a great Indian chief. Two others are named for rivers, one for an army surveyor, and one for an early settler in the area.

In the northwest part of Arizona is Mohave County, one of the original four counties, and one which was long thinly populated but one which in the 1960's experienced considerable growth. To the east of Mohave is Coconino County, the second largest in area in the continental United States. Farther to the east are first Navajo and then Apache County, both areas with large Indian populations. In central Arizona is Yavapai County, often referred to as the "Mother of Counties," since so many others were carved from its original boundaries. In the far southwest is Yuma County, a rapidly growing area. Maricopa County in the south central area is the most populous county and indeed roughly half of the people of the state live there. To the northeast of Maricopa County is Gila County, a sizeable but relatively under-populated area; to the southeast of Maricopa is Pinal, another rapidly growing county. In the area to the east are found in Graham and Greenlee counties. Pima County contains the second metropolitan area of Arizona, Tucson. To the south of Pima is little Santa Cruz County, and in the far southeast portion of Arizona is Cochise County.

Each county has a county seat where the business of government is transacted, and the fourteen county seats are:

Apache, *St. Johns*
Cochise, *Bisbee*
Coconino, *Flagstaff*
Gila, *Globe*
Mohave, *Kingman*
Navajo, *Holbrook*
Pima, *Tucson*
Pinal, *Florence*

Graham, *Safford* | Santa Cruz, *Nogales*
Greenlee, *Clifton* | Yavapai, *Prescott*
Maricopa, *Phoenix* | Yuma, *Yuma*

While ordinarily the location of the county seat is of no special issue, on at least one occasion it was. The people of Tombstone were generally very bitter over the 1929 removal of the county seat and county offices to Bisbee.

Since the legislature created the counties it would be also possible for it to form new ones or to change the boundaries now existing. This, however, seems unlikely since there is now a national trend toward the consolidation of numerous small counties in the interests of economy and efficiency. Indeed Arizona is quite fortunate in being a rather large state and having only fourteen counties. Texas on the other hand reaches the height of absurdity in having over 250 small counties, though admittedly it is a large state. In Arizona the lawmaking body found in each county may enact ordinances, which have the effect of law, and the counties also conduct elections, handle public works and welfare matters such as roads and hospitals. Presently two of the counties, Maricopa and Pima, have undertaken the zoning of land within their areas. Counties have the power to tax and also receive income from certain state revenues. The county budget is annually something which runs into a sizeable amount.

The personnel of county governments are provided for in the constitution and laws of Arizona. In each county, excepting Maricopa and Pima where there are five, a three member board of supervisors operates. By law there are over two dozen powers and responsibilities given to this lawmaking arm of county government. The county of Maricopa pioneered the idea of a county manager, a professional trained in the running of county affairs, and responsible to the board of supervisors. Each county has a sheriff, a county attorney, a clerk of the superior court, a treasurer, a recorder, an assessor and a county school superintendent. Generally these officials must be twenty-one years of age, a citizen and a voter who is able to read and write. An exception is of course the attorney who must have special training.

For many years county officials served two year terms, but on a hopeful note the term has been changed to four, a more realistic period. Accompanying county government is a substantial bureaucracy and of course some waste and duplication of services in the case of the cities and the counties. While the need is perhaps not yet pressing in Arizona, in some parts of the nation the idea of consolidation of county and city government is being discussed and in a few instances even being implemented. The city and county of San Francisco in California showed the way in this regard, but usually there is opposition to unification in the outlying areas of the counties.

County government across the nation is often archaic and backward, but it exists largely by weight of tradition and not logic and is often in need of change. Two particular areas of county affairs will serve to show problems found at this level. In the matter of law enforcement it would doubtless be best to have a unified police force instead of the city-county arrangement with its jurisdictional problems and its professionally trained police forces, and its politically inclined sheriff's office. Likewise the schools illustrate how duplication of activities may result as in the case of the operation of the school district bureaucracies and the office of the county school superintendent. Since governmental patterns are slow to change, especially in Arizona, it will probably be a long while before county government is modernized. Fortunately, except for the absurd election of a host of county officials who contribute in a major way to the long ballot, Arizona has been spared the worst features of this area of American political life.

There is an old American adage to the effect that "that government which is closest to the people is best." If this be true then city and town government should be the pride and joy of the American political system, but it is not and no one would ever seriously contend that it is or ever has been. Indeed Lord Bryce in his great study of our government published in the 1880's said that there was one level of public affairs in the United States which was a total failure; namely local government. Conditions have unfortunately changed little since the time of this astute Englishman. Municipal government dates back to the New England colonies where the township became the unit of local government. In time, like the counties this pattern of affairs spread out all over the nation.

In the relationship between the Federal government and the states there is something called "states rights," though what is meant by this term is often not exactly certain. However, in the relationship between the states and local government there is no such thing as "local rights," unless the state deigns to confer something along these lines. The cities are spoken of as the "hand-maidens of the the states," and they are usually rather poorly treated servants at that. A basic trouble is that when most states came into being they had few cities of any size and metropolitan urban areas as we know them today were unknown. In the twentieth century people in the United States began to cram themselves into rather tiny land areas in great numbers, and city government has been hard pressed to keep pace with population trends.

In the time of the Progressive movement of the decade following 1900, there was a movement in this country to establish "home rule." This principle permits a municipality to have a charter granted by the legislature or a government provided for in the laws of the state, and then the municipality is able to govern itself relatively free from outside interference. Since the state of Arizona was formed at the time of the "home rule" discussion, the concept is relatively well developed here. Arizona has about a dozen cities with charters which these places have written for their own self-government, while other municipal units have what is called a "general law" government as it takes its form and structure from the state laws on the subject. Cities of over 3,500 population may take advantage of the charter system. Whether charter or general law is used, an area may incorporate at the wishes of the inhabitants, particularly those who own real property. Once incorporated an area is a town or a city depending upon its size. If an area is unincorporated then its government and governmental services are provided by the county in which it is located.

Cities are said to exist to provide for the needs of their residents, as opposed to the counties which are thought of as agents of the state. Services provided by municipal government include police and fire protection, sanitation needs, and often public transportation. Cities are also concerned with the zoning of land and the protection of the health and welfare of citizens. In some instances the local government may provide and operate utilities which supply water, natural gas, electricity, and even transportation. This government ownership and operation is socialism by almost everyone's definition, but no one seems to object to it. Even the good citizens of such hardly socialist communities as Mesa get along with the arrangement.

An Arizona municipality has a council of five or seven members one of whom is designated as the mayor. The idea of electing a mayor separate from the council, as the city of New York does, is not general in this state. Serving under the town or city council will be a variety of persons. Some two dozen municipalities have adopted the city manager system whereby a professional manager is hired to operate the city under the supervision of the council. His tenure depends upon the council and the keeping of its good will. Cities usually also have a clerk, a treasurer, an attorney, a chief of police, a fire chief, a health officer, and such other officials as are needed. The existence of these offices depends upon how extensive the city government is for obviously the city of Phoenix, an urban area of considerable size, needs a more elaborate governmental structure than would a municipality of 3,500 population.

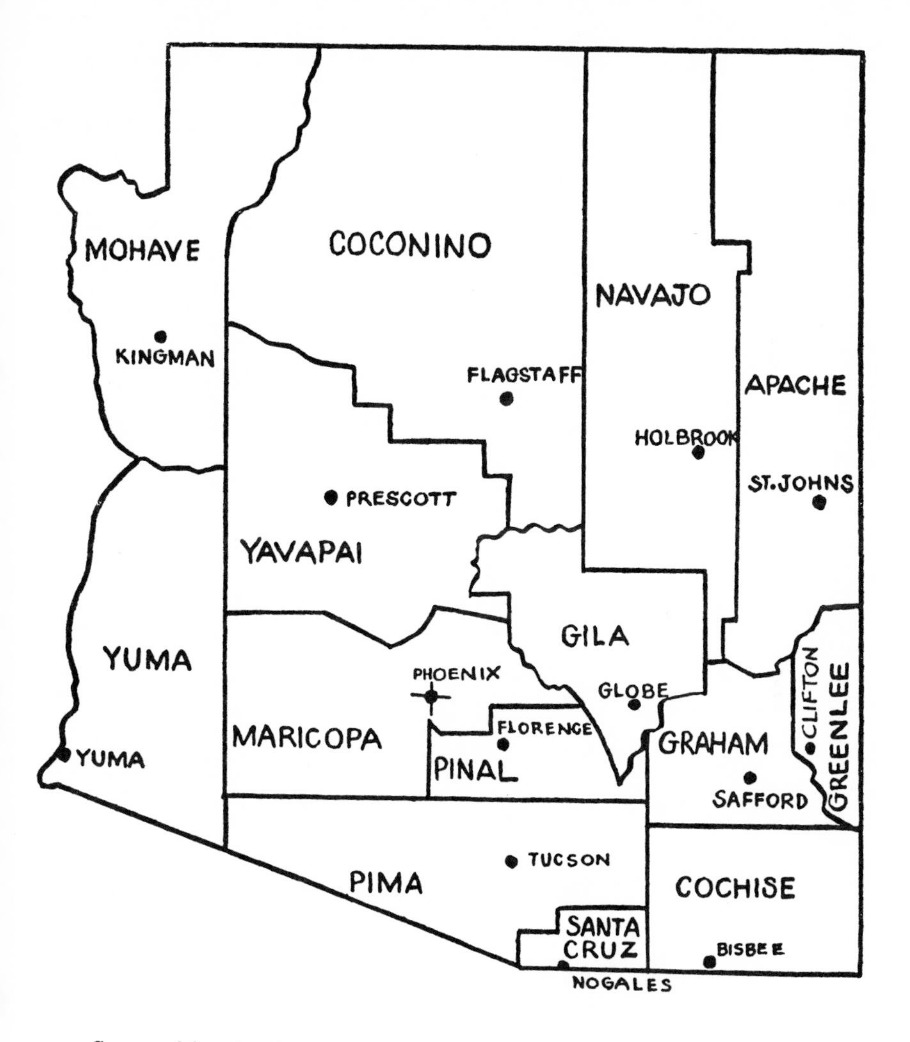

Some cities in the eastern and midwestern United States had long trouble with machines and bosses but such has not generally been the Arizona experience. Some feel that the national political parties have little meaning on the local level so therefore city officials are often chosen on a nonpartisan basis or under the banner of temporary political groups formed for local elections only. A "Charter government" ticket or slate of officers constitutes a political party. If Arizona has been free from bosses and machines, it unfortunately has not avoided the worst other features of this level of political life. City government is costly, makes mistakes and often commits great blunders. There are also excellent opportunities for graft and corruption to flourish which go largely unnoticed. People are simply not interested in local government unless unusual circumstances prevail, and therefore municipal officials go their merry way with very little supervision from the people they in theory serve.

A common problem of municipalities has been the fact that they were often under the thumb of state governments dominated by rural interests who have little regard for urban problems. At least this is the excuse offered by city governments for their lack of solving the problems of their area. Now with the reapportionment of the various state legislatures this will be changed, and city officials will no longer have this convenient excuse for covering up their lack of problem solving. Hopefully a bright new era of municipal government is soon to be at hand, and it had better be, for otherwise cities and towns will be innundated by unsolved problems. The urban movement is here to stay and will be accelerated until "megalopolis" welds giant communities into even larger populations living in tiny land areas with concentrations of people heretofore unknown. There will probably come a time when there is a "megalopolis" formed out of the area from Phoenix to Tucson. Municipal government is going to have to keep pace with events, once of course it has caught up with the twentieth century.

There is one other area of local government which is even less well known and observed than municipal government, and this is the special district which exists for various purposes. Typically special districts are concerned with such things as sewage and sanitation, irrigation and flood control. They may have boundaries which take in a part of a city, or may join together several cities. All districts have come into being to meet a particular need felt by a community or communities. Since they generally work well and have few problems they go almost unnoticed by the general public. □

24

FEDERAL RELATIONS

THE CONCEPT OF FEDERALISM can be traced back to the ancient Greek city states, but when the United States was created in 1789 it was the first modern nation with this governmental arrangement. The idea is to divide authority between a national government exercising power over affairs of concern to all and local units of government, in this case the states, which are concerned with local matters. Federalism was applied to this nation because it was absolutely necessary. It was next to impossible to get the states to give up what powers they did to the Federal government, let alone go out of business entirely as men such as Alexander Hamilton wanted. Then since we had the system, we began to look around for a justification for it, and several ideas were advanced.

It was said that federalism served local needs. In a nation as large as the United States, conditions and interests varied across the land, and one central government would produce a uniformity which was not desirable. The test tube function of federalism is also one commonly cited. If under a unitary government an experiment is tried and fails, all of the nation is the worse for it, but here one state may try something new and if it is a success all plus the Federal government may adopt it, but if it fails only one small part of the nation has suffered. Some have argued that federalism serves to safeguard individual rights from encroachment by the central government. The validity of this statement would, in the case of a resident of one of the Southern states, for example, depend largely whether he came equipped with a white or a black skin.

Federalism does create some problems and among other things it makes for an exceedingly complicated government which many people do not really understand. How does one tell whether this or that issue is a state matter, or a Federal matter, both or neither? Unfortunately state boundaries are often artificial, and population centers cut across the state lines and involve two or more states. In an age when all problems seem to be somehow national, people seemingly do not look anymore to the states for anything, or even care about them. Federalism also results in a lack of uniformity in laws on such matters as marriage and divorce, motor vehicles, the chartering of corporations, and other matters. Since people move about the nation with amazing frequency they may often find that they have inadvertently committed a crime which back home was no crime at all. In some states if a bank makes an error in reporting your money on deposit, and it affects you in some way, say your credit rating, you may sue and collect damages from the bank, while in other states there is no cause for action at all.

From 1789 on there has been a gradual drift in this country toward centralization of governmental power. The Supreme Court of the United States, often the arbiter of the divisions of power, was from 1801 to 1835 headed by that arch-Federalist John Marshall who was determined to enhance the power of the Federal government at the expense of the states. Then the Civil War accelerated this trend, and we truly became "one nation indivisible." Prior to that conflict when the United States signed a treaty with a foreign nation it began, "The United States are . . . ," while after 1865 the style was "The United States is . . ." It was probably in the late nineteenth century that people also began to lose faith in state government in general. Often incompetent, sometimes corrupt, and generally unresponsive to the needs of the people, the state was frequently ignored as the citizen looked more and more to Washington. That trend has been accelerated in the twentieth century until unless there are some major changes the states will ultimately wither and disappear from the scene. This is not due to a power grab from Washington, but simply because the states will not face up to their responsibilities.

Under the American constitutional system certain powers are specifically granted to the Federal government, and these are supplemented by the "necessary and proper" clause of the Constitution as well as the upholding of the implied powers idea by the Supreme Court. These include the power to declare war and conclude peace, the power to coin money and the power to control interstate and foreign commerce. Some powers are divided such as the power to tax and the power to borrow money; some powers are denied to one or both levels of government. Finally under the Tenth Amendment to the United States Constitution certain powers are reserved to the states. It is in this regard that there has been so much entry of the Federal government into areas once considered to be the preserve of the states. There are of course reasons why this has taken place. If the southern states had not denied the vote to a great group of their citizens, there would have been no need for Federal legislation in voting. If the states had been willing to finance their own public schools there would be less need for Federal laws in the area of education. Now admittedly some states are hard pressed to accomplish adequate financing of schools from local revenues, but on the other hand states such as Texas simply refuse to tax themselves to a reasonable degree.

One of the major problems of our time is the use of the Federal tax power and the distribution of revenue thus raised among the states. Largely in the twentieth century, the grant-in-aid programs have developed whereby the states and the Federal government join forces to accomplish a given end. Typical are the highways built partly out of state funds and partly with money from Washington. Over the years these programs have grown and today the states depend upon the Federal funds to meet the needs of their budgets. Some states receive under ten percent of their total budget money from the Federal treasury while others receive up to almost forty percent of their funds from the national source. It may well be argued that some form of equalization is working here because not all states are of equal wealth, and after all we are all a part of the same nation.

Still there remains the problem of some states taking Federal funds instead of taxing themselves as they should. Oddly enough it is the wealthy states who do tax themselves and pay high Federal taxes too who seem to least resent the Federal government while often it is the dependent states who get much more than their natural share of Federal handouts, who resent the Washington government. It has been recently suggested that the Federal treasury should share more of its revenue with the states on a no strings attached basis. This idea which is known as revenue sharing received its first test after President Nixon signed the bill in October of 1972 to put it into effect. During the first year Congress voted to distribute over five billion dollars among the states and cities. For the first time in our history we now have an arrangement whereby one level of government taxes and collects funds and another actually does the spending. This obviously creates a new dimension to federalism and one which may be increasingly important in future years. Arizona will benefit to a considerable degree from revenue sharing.

At the time of the writing of the Federal Constitution, there was a dispute over whether new states should be admitted to the union on an equal footing with the older units. This idea prevailed and now all states in the Federal arrangement are on an equal basis with all others. Once admitted a state has certain guarantees made to it by the Federal government. It will be protected against invasion and domestic violence. In the late nineteenth century it was established that the President of the United

States may send troops into a given area even over the violent protests of the governor of the state that they are unnecessary. While the concept may upset some states righters today, it seemed like a pretty good idea in the 1890's when the troops were used to break up a strike against the Pullman Company. Also the United States guarantees that a "republican form of government," shall be in operation in each state, but the President must decide what that means. This constitutional provision has generally been unimportant.

Once the states are members of the Union they also have obligations one to another. The "full faith and credit" clause of the Federal constitution means that legal acts, documents and orders of one state are valid in all states. Think of how much confusion would result if each time a husband and wife moved from one state to another, they had to be remarried because marriage is of course a matter left up to the states. However, with full faith and credit, marriage does not end at the state line, and in another area, wills made in a valid manner in one state will generally be valid in all states. The states must not abridge the privileges and immunities of the citizens of the various states. Thus California could not in the depression years legally bar the "Okies," who were migrating to the golden state to escape the dust bowl. There are some areas where states may legally discriminate in favor of their citizens. Thus a locally owned business may be taxed at a lower rate than one with headquarters out of state but doing the same amount of business within the taxing state as does the domestic corporation. Each state licenses its own professions and trades and determines for example, the qualifications of its teachers, physicians and lawyers. Nonresidents are generally charged a higher rate of tuition in state colleges and universities than are residents.

On occasion there are quarrels among the states as in the instance of Arizona and California fighting over the Colorado River, but generally the states live within the Federal union in relative harmony. Now and then they join together in some common project. The interstate compact which must be agreed to in these cases must also be approved by the United States Congress. To date some one hundred of these compacts have been utilized, the most famous probably being the New York - New Jersey agreement to operate a port authority.

Until recent decades the states had relations with one another and the Federal government and generally acted as agents for their local governments when dealing with Washington. Now, however, there is a trend much resented in the states, toward direct dealings between Washington and the local units of government. A city may, for example, negotiate a contract with the Federal government to build a housing project, a hospital, an airport or the like. However much the states may object to this, municipal officials usually think it is a grand idea.

In the last third of this century the states stand at crossroads. They are in danger of becoming mere historical curiosities or administrative units for a unitary national government. Federalism has been a positive good to this nation and it deserves to be rescued from oblivion. It should remain an important part of our governmental system. The mere chanting of the magical phrase, "states rights," over and over again will not do the trick. States rights has become a cry uttered by those who want no action taken. It should be utilized by those who want dynamic, popular state government. A political power vacuum will not long prevail. When problems must be solved people will turn to the most responsive government available. Will the states meet these challenges?

It is curious how some states have long traditions of solid, successful state government while others do not have such a fortunate record. If all states had the same high quality state government that New York has historically had then there would be less of a need for Federal activity in many areas. Some see the recent reapportionment of the state legislatures and the making of them more responsive to the majority of voters the last best hope of state government. Either this serves to revitalize the fifty state units or the cause is lost. What will be the story of state Federal relations from 1970 to 2070? □

25

ARIZONA SINCE 1912

THE ADMISSION OF ARIZONA into the Union in February of 1912 was the culmination of a long struggle to achieve that end. It came coincidentally at the peak of the Progressive era in American history, a period of intense reform which characterized not only the state but the nation as well. There was optimism abroad in the land that all social, economic and political problems could be and soon would be solved so as to give all the "good life." Sad to say the hopeful future of the "baby state" did not seem at once to materialize. The cost of running state government proved much more than most people had anticipated, and all of the ills of the world did not vanish at once. The economy of the state was still controlled by the "Eastern interests," and this continued to be resented. Arizona was not a very wealthy state; it was remote, the climate often left something to be desired, and yet most people were proud of their land.

One thing which has characterized Arizona since 1912 has been a steady growth in population. Just prior to statehood in 1910 the total population was 294,353; in 1920 it was 334,162; in 1930 it was 435,573; in 1940 it was 499,261; in 1950 it was 749,587; and by 1960 it had reached 1,302,161. Obviously the big jump in numbers took place following World War II, and it continues for by 1970 the total stood at 1,772,482. The trend continues for by mid 1975 it was estimated there had been a 25% increase since the last census and a total of 2,224,000 Arizonans.

Arizona hardly had time to become accustomed to its new status when World War I erupted. Locally it was at first feared that the conflict would cause widespread unemployment and economic dislocation. This proved to be an incorrect estimate of the situation and soon the copper industry in particular was booming. The United States entered the war in 1917 and patriotic fervor ran high in Arizona. As was true elsewhere these sentiments got out of hand as in the instance of the unfortunate man who was smeared with yellow paint in Phoenix because he was suspected of not buying Liberty Bonds. Most histories of the United States comment on the fact that organized labor cooperated in the "win the war" effort and that strikes were kept to a minimum. Such was not, however, the case in Arizona. Starting in 1915 a series of conflicts occupied the attention of Arizonans. The troubles reached a peak in 1917 with the Bisbee deportation when a group of vigilantes rounded up suspected members of the radical union, the Industrial Workers of the World, herded them into cattle cars and dumped them in New Mexico. News of this illegal action attracted nationwide attention and even incurred the wrath of the President of the United States.

There was great celebrating at the Armistice in November 1918, but the war ended in frustration, and the intolerance of the war period was carried on over into the post war period. Symptomatic of this was the Ku Klux Klan which would haunt Arizona through most of the 1920's. Immediately following World War I came the attempt of President Wilson to get the United States into the League of Nations, an idea generally supported in Arizona.

After a decade of solving the nation's problems and several years of attempting to set the world aright, Arizonans like most Americans were soon willing to forget idealism and crusades. The newspapers of an area probably reflect the ideals, aspirations and interests of the people, and whereas prior to about 1920 the press had been interested in largely local affairs, new topics of interest began to appear. The motion picture industry and the comings and goings of film personalities were good copy. So was the latest murder, especially if it had a sex angle. Prohibition was the law of the land, and it did not work any better here than elsewhere. The automobile arrived in force, and not only did the newspapers devote space to the new models, but cars made it much easier for Arizonans to get around in a rather large state. All in all Arizona seemed more interested in the outside world than in events within its own borders. Of course there were still state problems. Governor Hunt spent the 1920's attempting to save the Colorado or in attempting to block its useful development, according to one's views. Taxes seemed high and the costs of government went up and up. Still there was general prosperity, and if the state had few rich people it did have many middle class persons who were getting along.

By the middle of the 1920's playing the stock market became another aspect of life in Arizona. Every man was going to be a millionaire in time, and the spirit of the Babbitts and the boosters abounded. A Phoenix educator proclaimed that the service club was the greatest contribution to civilization in one hundred years, and a Presbyterian clergyman insisted that if only Jesus Christ were alive today he would be a Rotarian, or perhaps a member of the Kiwanis Club. It was all fun and the people who said these things were sincere and honest and hopeful, but unfortunately it did not last, and in the fall of 1929 the roaring twenties came crashing down.

Depression was abroad in the land, and by late 1930 or 1931, conditions were bad in Arizona and getting desperate. Unemployment abounded, banks failed, a bonus army walked across the state going east to stage a protest in Washington, and "Okies" came west also tramping across Arizona. Governor Stanford reflecting upon the years 1937 to 1939 later recalled that rarely was there a morning when he looked out of his window and failed to see at least one poor family camped on his front lawn. Relief rolls carried the names of once respectable self-supporting citizens who now found their secure world shattered. Arizonans generally strongly supported the New Deal program and its chief figure, Franklin D. Roosevelt.

Some believe that the New Deal restored prosperity, but it did not although it did save capitalism and restored general confidence in the American way of life. The second world war really ended unemployment, a rather sad commentary on the state of things. With the war effort, Arizona began to boom. Military installations were opened and were joined in time by prisoner of war camps and internment centers for the unfortunate Americans of Japanese ancestry. Oddly enough some Arizonans who would later spend their years wealthy and secure damning the horrible Federal government and its give-away programs first started to build their own pile of gold with the cost-plus contracts handed out by that same government during the period 1940 to 1945. Many phases of the economy of Arizona benefited by the war effort. Cotton farmers were encouraged to develop better and more produce, copper mines were producing to capacity, and jobs for all were plentiful.

World War II came to an end in 1945, and then the Arizona scene really began to boom. Many who had been stationed at the military bases in war time or had traversed the state on official junkets now resolved to make Arizona their home. California may have been the first and major golden land of those post war years, but Arizona received its share of the westward bound travellers. Once worthless desert lands abounded with housing projects and with the Federal government financing a good part of the whole thing, prosperity was at hand. Industry was earnestly sought, and a bright future was predicted for Arizona. When the state reached

SIDNEY P. OSBORN, only Arizona governor to die in office. Death came May 25, 1948, in his fourth term. During his tenure he led Arizona through the crucial years of World War II, through the turmoil of the immediate post-war years, and through the state's great population and industrial expansion.

the point of celebrating its semi-centennial in 1962, it did so with a feeling that it was almost too busy and in too much of a hurry to look back.

The decade following the celebration of the semi-centennial of statehood for Arizona continued to bring good times for most residents. There was general prosperity although perhaps people became more aware of the problems of those less fortunate within our society. The great civil rights crusades of the 1960's were felt in the southwest. The industrial revolution continued to make itself more and more a part of the Arizona economy. Citrus groves and cotton fields gave way to tract housing. The new majority political part, the Republican, embarked upon an extensive reorganization of Arizona government in all of its aspects. In the fall of 1973 a new problem of uncertain magnitude suddenly burst upon the scene. It was called the energy crisis and whether it was a serious threat to what most called the "Arizona way of life" or merely a temporary matter soon to be resolved awaited the unfolding of more time.

GOVERNORS OF ARIZONA

TERRITORIAL

Governor	Party	Term
John N. Goodwin (1824-1887)	*Republican*	1863-1865
Richard C. McCormick (1832-1901)	*Republican*	1865-1869
Anson P. K. Safford (1828?-1891)	*Republican*	1869-1877
John P. Hoyt (1841-1926)	*Republican*	1877-1878
John C. Fremont (1813-1890)	*Republican*	1878-1882
Frederick A. Tritle (1833-1906)	*Republican*	1882-1885
C. Meyer Zulick (1838-1926)	*Democrat*	1885-1889
Lewis Wolfley (1839-1910)	*Republican*	1889-1890
John N. Irwin (1845?-1905)	*Republican*	1890-1892
Nathan O. Murphy (1849-1908)	*Republican*	1892-1893
Louis C. Hughes (1842-1915)	*Democrat*	1893-1896
Benjamin J. Franklin (1839-1898)	*Democrat*	1896-1897
Myron H. McCord (1840-1908)	*Republican*	1897-1898
Nathan O. Murphy (1849-1908)	*Republican*	1898-1902
Alexander O. Brodie (1849-1918)	*Republican*	1902-1905
Joseph H. Kibbey (1853-1924)	*Republican*	1905-1909
Richard E. Sloan (1857-1933)	*Republican*	1909-1912

STATE

Governor	Party	Term
George W. P. Hunt (1859-1934)	*Democrat*	1912-1917
Thomas E. Campbell (1878-1944)	*Republican*	1917-
George W. P. Hunt (1859-1934)	*Democrat*	1917-1919
Thomas E. Campbell (1878-1944)	*Republican*	1919-1923
George W. P. Hunt (1859-1934)	*Democrat*	1923-1929
John C. Phillips (1870-1943)	*Republican*	1929-1931
George W. P. Hunt (1859-1934)	*Democrat*	1931-1933
Benjamin B. Moeur (1869-1937)	*Democrat*	1933-1937
Rawghlie C. Stanford (1878-1962)	*Democrat*	1937-1939
Robert T. Jones (1884-1958)	*Democrat*	1939-1941
Sidney P. Osborn (1884-1948)	*Democrat*	1941-1948
Dan E. Garvey (1886-1974)	*Democrat*	1948-1951
Howard Pyle (1906-)	*Republican*	1951-1955
Ernest W. McFarland (1894-)	*Democrat*	1955-1959
Paul Fannin (1907-)	*Republican*	1959-1965
Samuel P. Goddard (1919-)	*Democrat*	1965-1967
John R. ("Jack") Williams (1909-)	*Republican*	1967-1975
Raul H. Castro (1916-)	*Democrat*	1975-

ARIZONA TERRITORIAL DELEGATES TO CONGRESS

Charles D. Poston (1825-1902)	*Republican*	1864-1865
John N. Goodwin (1824-1887)	*Republican*	1865-1867
Coles Bashford (1816-1878)	*Independent*	1867-1869
Richard C. McCormick (1832-1901)	*Unionist*	1869-1875
Hiram S. Stevens (1832-1893)	*Democrat*	1875-1879
John G. Campbell (1827-1903)	*Democrat*	1879-1881
Granville H. Oury (1825-1891)	*Democrat*	1881-1885
Curtis C. Bean (1828-1904)	*Republican*	1885-1887
Marcus A. Smith (1851-1924)	*Democrat*	1887-1895
		1897-1899
		1901-1903
		1905-1909
Nathan O. Murphy (1849-1908)	*Republican*	1895-1897
John F. Wilson (1846-1911)	*Democrat*	1899-1901
		1903-1905
Ralph H. Cameron (1863-1953)	*Republican*	1909-1912

UNITED STATES SENATORS FROM ARIZONA

Marcus A. Smith (1851-1924)	*Democrat*	1912-1921
Henry F. Ashurst (1874-1962)	*Democrat*	1912-1941
Ralph H. Cameron (1863-1953)	*Republican*	1921-1927
Carl T. Hayden (1877-1972)	*Democrat*	1927-1969
Ernest W. McFarland (1894-)	*Democrat*	1941-1953
Barry M. Goldwater (1909-)	*Republican*	1953-1965
		1969-
Paul J. Fannin (1907-)	*Republican*	1965-

REPRESENTATIVES FROM ARIZONA

Carl T. Hayden (1877-1972)	*Democrat*	1912-1927
Lewis W. Douglas (1894-1974)	*Democrat*	1927-1933
Isabella S. Greenway (1886-1953) (later Mrs. King)	*Democrat*	1933-1937
John R. Murdock (1885-1972)	*Democrat*	1937-1953
Richard F. Harless (1905-1970)	*Democrat*	1943-1949
Harold A. Patten (1907-1969)	*Democrat*	1949-1955
John J. Rhodes (1916-)	*Republican*	1953-
Stewart L. Udall (1920-)	*Democrat*	1955-1961
Morris K. Udall (1922-)	*Democrat*	1961-
George F. Senner Jr. (1921-)	*Democrat*	1963-1967
Sam Steiger (1929-)	*Republican*	1967-
John B. Conlan (1930-)	*Republican*	1973-

CONSTITUTION of ARIZONA

CONTENTS

FACTS AND FIGURES

The Constitution of Arizona, in its original form, was adopted in the afternoon of December 9, 1910, as the Constitutional Convention by which the instrument was drafted concluded sixty-one days of earnest labor. Forty of the fifty-two delegates composing the body voted approval of the instrument, while twelve voiced opposition to its provisions—chiefly those establishing the Initiative, Referendum and Recall. Nevertheless, one of the members voting "no" appended his signature to the document.

Formulation of the Constitution was authorized by an Enabling Act of Congress which received the President's signature on June 20, 1910, after an historic struggle waged by the people of Arizona over more than a quarter of a century, for the right of local self-government and Arizona's recognition as a member of the Union of States.

Conclusion of the labors of the Constitutional Convention did not, however, automatically admit Arizona into the Union. That long sought end still depended upon ratification of the Constitution by the people of Arizona, and, in compliance with unusual requirements of the Enabling Act, its approval by the Congress and the President, or approval by the President in the event of the failure of Congress to act at the ensuing session of that body.

At an election held February 9, 1911, the people of Arizona ratified the Constitution by a vote of 12,187 to 3,302, and the Sixty-second Congress, after a protracted debate, adopted a resolution of approval. This, however, was on August 15, 1911, vetoed by President William H. Taft, who gave as a primary reason his unalterable opposition to the provision for the recall, by the people, of public officers, including judicial officers. A second resolution was thereupon adopted by Congress and approved by the President, which fixed as the price of statehood the holding of an election at which the people of Arizona should adopt an amendment removing judicial officers from the provisions of the Recall. The demand was complied with at an election held December 12, 1911, 14,963 votes being cast in favor of removal of the offending provision and 1,890 against. The significance of the vote was not that the people of Arizona opposed the recall of the judiciary but that they favored statehood. At the first election following that desired consummation, the provision was restored to its original form by a vote of 16,272 to 3,705.

On February 14, 1912, President Taft issued a proclamation declaring Arizona an equal State of the Union, thus giving effect to the Constitution amended at his behest.

CONSTITUTION of the STATE OF ARIZONA

PREAMBLE

We, the people of the State of Arizona, grateful to Almighty God for our liberties, do ordain this Constitution.

ARTICLE I.

STATE BOUNDARIES.

Sec. 1. The boundaries of the State of Arizona shall be as follows, namely: Beginning at a point on the Colorado River twenty English miles below the junction of the Gila and Colorado Rivers, as fixed by the Gadsden Treaty between the United States and Mexico, being in latitude thirty-two degrees, twenty-nine minutes, forty-four and forty-five one-hundredths seconds north and longitude one hundred fourteen degrees, forty-eight minutes, forty-four and fifty-three one-hundredths seconds west of Greenwich; thence along and with the international boundary line between the United States and Mexico in a southeastern direction to Monument Number 127 on said boundary line in latitude thirty-one degrees, twenty minutes north; thence east along and with said parallel of latitude, continuing on said boundary line to an intersection with the meridian of longitude one hundred nine degrees, two minutes, fifty-nine and twenty-five one-hundredths seconds west, being identical with the southwestern corner of New Mexico; thence north along and with said meridian of longitude and the west boundary of New Mexico to an intersection with the parallel of latitude thirty-seven degrees north, being the common corner of Colorado, Utah, Arizona, and New Mexico; thence west along and with said parallel of latitude and the south boundary of Utah to an intersection with the meridian of longitude one hundred fourteen degrees, two minutes, fifty-nine and twenty-five one-hundredths seconds west, being on the east boundary line of the State of Nevada; thence south along and with said meridian of longitude and the east boundary of said State of Nevada, to the center of the Colorado River; thence down the mid-channel of said Colorado River in a southern direction along and with the east boundaries of Nevada, California, and the Mexican Territory of Lower California, successively, to the place of beginning.

Sec. 2. The Legislature, in cooperation with the properly constituted authority of any adjoining State, is empowered to change, alter, and redefine the State boundaries, such change, alteration and redefinition to become effective only upon approval of the Congress of the United States.

ARTICLE II.

DECLARATION OF RIGHTS.

Sec. 1. A frequent recurrence to fundamental principles is essential to the security of individual rights and the perpetuity of free government.

Sec. 2 All political power is inherent in the people, and governments derive their just powers from the consent of the governed, and are established to protect and maintain individual rights.

Sec. 3. The Constitution of the United States is the supreme law of the land.

Sec. 4. No person shall be deprived of life, liberty, or property without due process of law.

Sec. 5. The right of petition, and of the people

peaceably to assemble for the common good, shall never be abridged.

Sec. 6. Every person may freely speak, write, and publish on all subjects, being responsible for the abuse of that right.

Sec. 7. The mode of administering an oath, or affirmation, shall be such as shall be most consistent with and binding upon the conscience of the person to whom such oath, or affirmation, may be administered.

Sec. 8. No person shall be disturbed in his private affairs, or his home invaded, without authority of law.

Sec. 9. No law granting irrevocably any privilege, franchise, or immunity shall be enacted.

Sec. 10. No person shall be compelled in any criminal case to give evidence against himself, or be twice put in jeopardy for the same offense.

Sec. 11. Justice in all cases shall be administered openly, and without unnecessary delay.

Sec. 12. The liberty of conscience secured by the provisions of this Constitution shall not be so construed as to excuse acts of licentiousness, or justify practices inconsistent with the peace and safety of the State. No public money or property shall be appropriated for or applied to any religious worship, exercise, or instruction, or to the support of any religious establishment. No religious qualification shall be required for any public office or employment, nor shall any person be incompetent as a witness or juror in consequense of his opinion on matters of religion, nor be questioned touching his religious belief in any court of justice to affect the weight of his testimony.

Sec. 13. No law shall be enacted granting to any citizen, class of citizens, or corporation other than municipal, privileges or immunities which, upon the same terms, shall not equally belong to all citizens or corporations.

Sec. 14. The privilege of the writ of habeas corpus shall not be suspended by the authorities of the State.

Sec. 15. Excessive bail shall not be required, nor excessive fines imposed, nor cruel and unusual punishment inflicted.

Sec. 16. No conviction shall work corruption of blood, or forfeiture of estate.

Sec. 17. Private property shall not be taken for private use, except for private ways of necessity, and for drains, flumes, or ditches, on or across the lands of others for mining, agricultural, domestic, or sanitary purposes. No private property shall be taken or damaged for public or private use without just compensation having first been made, paid into court for the owner, secured by bond as may be fixed by the court, or paid into the state treasury for the owner on such terms and conditions as the legislature may provide, and no right of way shall be appropriated to the use of any corporation other than municipal, until full compensation therefor be first made in money, or ascertained and paid into court for the owner, irrespective of any benefit from any improvement proposed by such corporation, which compensation shall be ascertained by a jury, unless a jury be waived as in other civil cases in courts of record, in the manner prescribed by law. Whenever an attempt is made to take private property for a use alleged to be public, the question whether the contemplated use be really public shall be a judicial question, and determined as such without regard to any legislative assertion that the use is public. (Amendment referred by the Legislature; approved at regular election Nov. 3, 1970; effective Nov. 27, 1970.)

Sec. 18. There shall be no imprisonment for debt, except in cases of fraud.

Sec. 19. Any person having knowledge or possession of facts that tend to establish the guilt of any other person or corporation charged with bribery or illegal rebating, shall not be excused from giving testimony or producing evidence, when legally called upon to do so, on the ground that it may tend to incriminate him under the laws of the State; but no person shall be prosecuted or subject to any penalty or forfeiture for, or on account of, any transaction, matter, or thing concerning which he may so testify or produce evidence.

Sec. 20. The military shall be in strict subordination to the civil power.

Sec. 21. All elections shall be free and equal, and no power, civil or military, shall at any time interfere to prevent the free exercise of the right of suffrage.

Sec. 22. All persons charged with crime shall be bailable by sufficient sureties, except for:

1. Capital offenses when the proof is evident or the presumption great.

2. Felony offenses, committed when the person charged is already admitted to bail on a separate felony charge and where the proof is evident or the presumption great as to the present charge. (Amendment referred to the Legislature; approved at regular election Nov. 3, 1970; effective Nov. 27, 1970.)

Sec. 23. The right of trial by jury shall remain inviolate. Juries in criminal cases in which a sentence of death or imprisonment for thirty years or more is authorized by law shall consist of twelve persons. In all criminal cases the unanimous consent of the jurors shall be necessary to render a verdict. In all other cases, the number of jurors, not less than six, and the number required to render a verdict, shall be specified by law.

(Amendment referred to the Legislature; approved at regular election Nov. 7, 1972; effective Dec. 1, 1972.)

Sec. 24. In criminal prosecutions, the accused shall have the right to appear and defend in person, and by counsel, to demand the nature and cause of the accusation against him, to have a copy thereof, to testify in his own behalf, to meet the witnesses against him face to face, to have compulsory process to compel the attendance of witnesses in his own behalf, to have a speedy public trial by an impartial jury of the county in which the offense is alleged to have been comitted, and the right to appeal in all cases; and in no instance shall any accused person before final judgment be compelled to advance money or fees to secure the rights herein guaranteed.

Sec. 25. No bill of attainder, ex-post-facto law, or law impairing the obligation of a contract, shall ever be enacted.

Sec. 26. The right of the individual citizen to bear arms in defense of himself or the State shall not be impaired, but nothing in this section shall be construed as authorizing individuals or corporations to organize, maintain, or employ an armed body of men.

Sec. 27. No standing army shall be kept up by this State in time of peace, and no soldier shall in time of peace be quartered in any house without the consent of its owner, nor in time of war except in the manner prescribed by law.

Sec. 28. Treason against the State shall consist only in levying war against the State, or adhering to its enemies, or in giving them aid and comfort. No person shall be convicted of treason unless on the testimony of two witnesses to the same overt act, or confession in open court.

Sec. 29. No hereditary emoluments, privileges, or powers shall be granted or conferred, and no law shall be enacted permitting any perpetuity or entailment in this State.

Sec. 30. No person shall be prosecuted criminally in any court of record for felony or misdemeanor, otherwise than by information or indictment; no person shall be prosecuted for felony by information without having had a preliminary examination before a magistrate or having waived such preliminary examination.

Sec. 31. No law shall be enacted in this State limiting the amount of damages to be recovered for causing the death or injury of any person.

Sec. 32. The provisions of this Constitution are mandatory, unless by express words they are declared to be otherwise.

Sec. 33. The enumeration in this Constitution of certain rights shall not be construed to deny others retained by the people.

Sec. 34. The State of Arizona and each municipal corporation within the State of Arizona shall have the right to engage in industrial pursuits. (Amendment referred by the Legislature; approved at regular election November 5, 1912; effective December 5, 1912.)

ARTICLE III.

DISTRIBUTION OF POWERS.

The powers of the government of the State of Arizona shall be divided into three separate departments, the Legislative, the Executive, and the Judicial; and, except as provided in this Constitution, such departments shall be separate and distinct, and no one of such departments shall exercise the powers properly belonging to either of the others.

ARTICLE IV.

LEGISLATIVE DEPARTMENT.

1. INITIATIVE AND REFERENDUM

Sec. 1. (1) The legislative authority of the State shall be vested in a Legislature, consisting of a Senate and a House of Representatives, but the people reserve the power to propose laws and amendments to the Constitution and to enact or reject such laws and amendments at the polls, independently of the Legislature; and they also reserve, for use at their own option, the power to approve or reject at the polls any Act, or item, section, or part of any Act, of the Legislature.

(2) The first of these reserved powers is the Initiative. Under this power ten per centum of the qualified electors shall have the right to propose any measure, and fifteen per centum shall have the right to propose any amendment to the Constitution.

(3) The second of these reserved powers is the Referendum. Under this power the Legislature, or five per centum of the qualified electors, may order the submission to the people at the polls of any measure, or item, section, or part of any meas-

ure, enacted by the Legislature, except laws immediately necessary for the preservation of the public peace, health, or safety, or for the support and maintenance of the departments of the State Government and State institutions; but to allow opportunity for Referendum Petitions, no Act passed by the Legislature shall be operative for ninety days after the close of the session of the Legislature enacting such measure, except such as require earlier operation to preserve the public peace, health, or safety, or to provide appropriations for the support and maintenance of the Departments of the State and of State institutions; Provided, that no such emergency measure shall be considered passed by the Legislature unless it shall state in a separate section why it is necessary that it shall become immediately operative, and shall be approved by the affirmative votes of two-thirds of the members elected to each House of the Legislature, taken by roll call of ayes and nays, and also approved by the Governor; and should such measure be vetoed by the Governor, it shall not become a law unless it shall be approved by the votes of three-fourths of the members elected to each House of the Legislature, taken by roll call of ayes and nays.

(4) All petitions submitted under the power of the Initiative shall be known as Initiative Petitions, and shall be filed with the Secretary of State not less than four months preceding the date of the election at which the measures so proposed are to be voted upon. All petitions submitted under the power of the Referendum shall be known as Referendum Petitions, and shall be filed with the Secretary of State not more than ninety days after the final adjournment of the session of the Legislature which shall have passed the measure to which the Referendum is applied. The filing of a Referendum Petition against any item, section, or part of any measure shall not prevent the remainder of such measures from becoming operative.

(5) Any measure or amendment to the Constitution proposed under the Initiative, and any measure to which the Referendum is applied, shall be referred to a vote of the qualified electors, and shall become law when approved by a majority of the votes cast thereon and upon proclamation of the Governor, and not otherwise.

(6) The veto power of the Governor, or the power of the Legislature, to repeal or amend, shall not extend to initiative or referendum measures approved by a majority vote of the qualified electors. (Amendment initiated by people; approved at regular election November 3, 1914; effective December 14, 1914.)

(7) The whole number of votes cast for all candidates for Governor at the general election last preceding the filing of any Initiative or Referendum petition on a State or county measure shall be the basis on which the number of qualified electors required to sign such petition shall be computed.

(8) The powers of the Initiative and the Referendum are hereby further reserved to the qualified electors of every incorporated city, town, and county as to all local, city, town, or county matters on which such incorporated cities, towns, and counties are or shall be empowered by general laws to legislate. Such incorporated cities, towns, and counties may prescribe the manner of exercising said powers within the restrictions of general laws. Under the power of the Initiative fifteen per centum of the qualified electors may propose measures on such local, city, town or county matters, and ten per centum of the electors may propose the Referendum on legislation enacted within and by such city, town, or county. Until provided by general law, said cities and towns may prescribe the basis on which said percentages shall be computed.

(9) Every Initiative or Referendum petition shall be addressed to the Secretary of State in the

case of petitions for or on State measures, and to the clerk of the Board of Supervisors, city clerk, or corresponding officer in the case of petitions for or on county, city, or town measures; and shall contain the declaration of each petitioner, for himself, that he is a qualified elector of the State (and in the case of petitions for or on city, town, or county measures, of the city, town, or county affected), his postoffice address, the street and number, if any, of his residence, and the date on which he signed such petition. Each sheet containing petitioners' signatures shall be attached to a full and correct copy of the title and text of the measure so proposed to be initiated or referred to the people, and every sheet of every such petition containing signatures shall be verified by the affidavit of the person who circulated said sheet or petition, setting forth that each of the names on said sheet was signed in the presence of the affiant and that in the belief of the affiant each signer was a qualified elector of the State, or in the case of a city, town, or county measure, of the city, town, or county affected by the measure so proposed to be initiated or referred to the people.

(10) When any Initiative or Referendum petition or any measure referred to the people by the Legislature shall be filed, in accordance with this section, with the Secretary of State, he shall cause to be printed on the official ballot at the next regular general election the title and number of said measure, together with the words "Yes" and "No" in such manner that the electors may express at the polls their approval or disapproval of the measure.

(11) The text of all measures to be submitted shall be published as proposed amendments to the Constitution are published, and in submitting such measures and proposed amendments the Secretary of State and all other officers shall be guided by the general law until legislation shall be especially provided therefor. (Method of publication superseded by statute. See section 19-123, Arizona Revised Statutes.)

(12) If two or more conflicting measures or amendments to the Constitution shall be approved by the people at the same election, the measure or amendment receiving the greatest number of affirmative votes shall prevail in all particulars as to which there is conflict.

(13) It shall be the duty of the Secretary of State, in the presence of the Governor and the Chief Justice of the Supreme Court, to canvass the votes for and against each such measure or proposed amendment to the Constitution within thirty days after the election, and upon the completion of the canvass the Governor shall forthwith issue a proclamation, giving the whole number of votes cast for and against each measure or proposed amendment, and declaring such measures or amendments as are approved by a majority of those voting thereon to be law.

(14) This section shall not be construed to deprive the Legislature of the right to enact any measure.

(15) This section of the Constitution shall be, in all respects, self-executing.

Sec. 2. The Legislature shall provide a penalty for any wilful violation of any of the provisions of the preceding section.

2. THE LEGISLATURE.

Sec. 1. (1) The Senate shall be composed of one member elected from each of the thirty legislative districts established by the Legislature.

The House of Representatives shall be composed of two members elected from each of the thirty legislative districts established by the Legislature.

(2) Upon the presentation to the Governor of a petition bearing the signatures of not less than two-thirds of the members of each House, requesting that he call a special session of the Legislature and designating the date of convening, the Governor shall forthwith call a special session to assemble on the date specified. At a special session so called the subjects which may be considered by the Legislature shall not be limited.

(Amendment referred by the Legislature; approved at regular election Nov. 7, 1972; effective Dec. 1, 1972.)

2(a) and 2(b). Relating to the compensation and expenses of members of the Legislature, are repealed. (Amendment referred by the Legislature; approved at regular election Nov. 3, 1970; effective Nov. 27, 1970.)

Sec. 2. No person shall be a member of the Legislature unless he shall be a citizen of the United States at the time of his election, nor unless he shall be at least twenty-five years of age, and shall have been a resident of Arizona at least three years and of the county from which he is elected at least one year before his election.

Sec. 3. The sessions of the Legislature shall be held annually at the Capitol of the State, and shall commence on the second Monday of January of each year. The Governor may call a special session, whenever in his judgment it is advisable. In calling a special session, the Governor shall specify the subjects to be considered, and at such special session no laws shall be enacted except such as relate to the subjects mentioned in the call. (Amendment referred by the Legislature; approved at special election September 12, 1950; effective October 2, 1950.)

Sec. 4. No person holding any public office of profit or trust under the authority of the United States, or of this State, shall be a member of the Legislature; Provided, that appointments in the State militia and the offices of notary public, justice of the peace, United States commissioner, and postmaster of the fourth class, shall not work disqualification for membership within the meaning of this section.

Sec. 5. No member of the Legislature, during the term for which he shall have been elected or appointed shall be eligible to hold any other office or be otherwise employed by the State of Arizona or, any county or incorporated city or town thereof. This prohibition shall not extend to the office of school trustee, nor to employment as a teacher or instructor in the public school system. (Amendment initiated by the people; approved at regular election November 8, 1938; effective December 14, 1938.)

Sec. 6. Members of the Legislature shall be privileged from arrest in all cases except treason, felony, and breach of the peace, and they shall not be subject to any civil process during the session of the Legislature, nor for fifteen days next before the commencement of each session.

Sec. 7. No member of the Legislature shall be

liable in any civil or criminal prosecution for words spoken in debate.

Sec. 8. Each House, when assembled, shall choose its own officers, judge of the election and qualification of its own members, and determine its own rules of procedure.

Sec. 9. The majority of the members of each House shall constitute a quorum to do business, but a smaller number may meet, adjourn from day to day, and compel the attendance of absent members, in such manner and under such penalties as each House may prescribe. Neither House shall adjourn for more than three days, nor to any place other than that in which it may be sitting, without the consent of the other.

Sec. 10. Each House shall keep a journal of its proceedings, and at the request of two members the ayes and nays on roll call on any question shall be entered.

Sec. 11. Each House may punish its members for disorderly behavior, and may, with the concurrence of two-thirds of its members, expel any member.

Sec. 12. Every bill shall be read by sections on three different days, unless in case of emergency, two-thirds of either House deem it expedient to dispense with this rule. The vote on the final passage of any bill or joint resolution shall be taken by ayes and nays on roll call. Every measure when finally passed shall be presented to the Governor for his approval or disapproval.

(Amendment referred by the Legislature; approved at regular election Nov. 7, 1972; effective Dec. 1, 1972.)

Sec. 13. Every Act shall embrace but one subject and matters properly connected therewith, which subject shall be expressed in the title; but if any subject shall be embraced in an Act which shall not be expressed in the title, such Act shall be void only as to so much thereof as shall not be embraced in the title.

Sec. 14. No Act or section thereof shall be revised or amended by mere reference to the title of such Act, but the Act or section as amended shall be set forth and published at full length.

Sec. 15. A majority of all members elected to each House shall be necessary to pass any bill, and all bills so passed shall be signed by the presiding officer of each House in open session.

Sec. 16. Any member of the Legislature shall have the right to protest and have the reasons of his protest entered on the journal.

Sec. 17. The Legislature shall never grant any extra compensation to any public officer, agent, servant or contractor, after the services shall have been rendered or the contract entered into, nor shall the compensation of any public officer, other than a justice of the peace, be increased or diminished during his term of office; provided, however, that when any legislative increase or decrease in compensation of the members of any court or the clerk thereof, or of any board or commission composed of two or more officers or persons whose respective terms of office are not coterminous, has heretofore or shall hereafter become effective as to any member or clerk of such court, or any member of such board or commission, it shall be effective from such date as to each thereof. (Amendment referred by the Legislature; approved at special election September 29, 1953; effective October 31, 1953.)

Sec. 18. The Legislature shall direct by law in what manner and in what courts suits may be brought against the State.

Sec. 19. No local or special laws shall be enacted in any of the following cases, that is to say:

1. Granting divorces.

2. Locating or changing county seats.

3. Changing rules of evidence.

4. Changing the law of descent or succession.

5. Regulating the practice of courts of justice.

6. Limitation of civil actions or giving effect to informal or invalid deeds.

7. Punishment of crimes and misdemeanors.

8. Laying out, opening, altering, or vacating roads, plats, streets, alleys, and public squares.

9. Assessment and collection of taxes.

10. Regulating the rate of interest on money.

11. The conduct of elections.

12. Affecting the estates of deceased persons or of minors.

13. Granting to any corporation, association, or individual, any special or exclusive privileges, immunities, or franchises.

14. Remitting fines, penalties, and forfeitures.

15. Changing names of persons or places.

16. Regulating the jurisdiction and duties of justices of the peace.

17. Incorporation of cities, towns, or villages, or amending their charters.

18. Relinquishing any indebtedness, liability, or obligation to this State.

19. Summoning and empanelling of juries.

20. When a general law can be made applicable.

Sec. 20. The general appropriation bill shall embrace nothing but appropriations for the different departments of the State, for State institutions, for public schools, and for interest on the public debt. All other appropriations shall be made by separate bills, each embracing but one subject.

Sec. 21. The members of the first Legislature shall hold office until the first Monday in January, 1913. The terms of office of the members of succeeding Legislatures shall be two years.

Sec. 22. (Section 22, prescribing compensation of members of the Legislature, repealed November 8, 1932. See sub-section (2), section 1.)

Sec. 23. It shall not be lawful for any person holding public office in this State to accept or use a pass or to purchase transportation from any railroad or other corporation, other than as such transportation may be purchased by the general public; Provided, that this shall not apply to members of the National Guard of Arizona traveling under orders. The Legislature shall enact laws to enforce this provision.

Sec. 24. The enacting clause of every bill enacted by the Legislature shall be as follows: "Be it enacted by the Legislature of the State of Arizona," or when the Initiative is used: "Be it enacted by the People of the State of Arizona."

Sec. 25. The legislature, in order to insure continuity of state and local governmental operations in periods of emergency resulting from disasters caused by enemy attack, shall have the power and the immediate duty to:

1. Provide for prompt and temporary succession to the powers and duties of public offices, of whatever nature and whether filled by election or appointment, the incumbents of which may become unavailable for carrying on the powers and duties of such offices.

2. Adopt such other measures as may be necessary and proper for insuring the continuity of governmental operations.

In the exercise of the powers hereby conferred, the legislature shall in all respects conform to the requirements of this constitution except to the extent that in the judgment of the legislature so to do would be impracticable or would admit of undue delay.

(Amendment referred by the Legislature; approved at regular election November 6, 1962; effective November 26, 1962.)

ARTICLE V.

EXECUTIVE DEPARTMENT.

Sec. 1. The Executive Department shall consist of Governor, Secretary of State, State Auditor, State Treasurer, Attorney General, and Superintendent of Public Instruction, each of whom shall hold his office for four years beginning on the first Monday of January, 1971 next after the regular general election in 1970.

The persons, respectively, having the highest number of votes cast for the office voted for shall be elected, but if two or more persons shall have an equal and the highest number of votes for any one of said offices, the two Houses of the Legislature at its next regular session shall elect forthwith, by joint ballot, one of such persons for said office.

The officers of the Executive Department during their terms of office shall reside at the seat of government where they shall keep their offices and the public records, books, and papers. They shall perform such duties as are prescribed by the Constitution and as may be provided by law. (Amendment referred by the Legislature; approved at regular election November 5, 1968; effective December 4, 1968.)

Sec. 1. The Executive Department shall consist of Governor, Secretary of State, State Treasurer, Attorney General, and Superintendent of Public Instruction, each of whom shall hold his office for two years beginning on the first Monday of January next after his election.

The persons, respectively, having the highest number of votes cast for the office voted for shall be elected, but if two or more persons shall have an equal and the highest number of votes for any one of said offices. the two Houses of the Legislature at its next regular session shall elect forthwith, by joint ballot, one of such persons for said office.

The officers of the Executive Department during their terms of office shall reside at the seat of government where they shall keep their offices and the public records, books, and papers. They shall perform such duties as are prescribed by the Constitution and as may be provided by law. (Amendment referred by the Legislature; approved at regular election November 5, 1968; effective December 4, 1968.)

(Since the people have abolished the State Auditor's office, we hold that Art. 5, Sec. 1 has been amended by the adoption of Proposition No. 108 and No. 104 to read:)

"Sec. 1. The Executive Department shall consist of Governor, Secretary of State, State Treasurer, Attorney General, and Superintendent of Public Instruction, each of whom shall hold his office for four years beginning on the first Monday of January, 1971 next after the regular general election in 1970." (Supreme Court decision No. 9480.)

Sec. 2. No person shall be eligible to any of the offices mentioned in Section 1 of this article except a male person of the age of not less than twenty-five years, who shall have been for ten years next preceding his election a citizen of the United States, and for five years next preceding his election a citizen of Arizona.

Sec. 3. The Governor shall be commander-in-chief of the military forces of the State, except when such forces shall be called into the service of the United States.

Sec. 4. The Governor shall transact all executive business with the officers of the Government, civil and military, and may require information in writing from the officers in the Executive Department upon any subject relating to the duties of their respective offices. He shall take care that the laws be faithfully executed. He may convene the Legislature in extraordinary session. He shall communicate, by message, to the Legislature at every session the condition of the State, and recommend such matters as he shall deem expedient.

Sec. 5. The Governor shall have power to grant reprieves, commutation, and pardons, after convictions, for all offenses except treason and cases of impeachment, upon such conditions and with such restrictions and limitiations as may be provided by law.

Sec. 6. In the event of the death of the Governor, or his resignation, removal from office, or permanent disability to discharge the duties of the office, the Secretary of State, if holding by election, shall succeed to the office of Governor until his successor shall be elected and shall qualify. If the Secretary of State be holding otherwise than by election, or shall fail to qualify as Governor, the Attorney General, the State Treasurer, or the Superintendent of Public Instruction, if holding by election, shall, in the order named, succeed to the office of Governor. The taking of the oath of office as Governor by any person specified in this section shall constitute resignation from the office by virtue of the holding of which he qualifies as Governor. Any successor to the office shall become Governor in fact and entitled to all of the emoluments, powers and duties of Governor upon taking the oath of office.

In the event of the impeachment of the Governor, his absence from the State, or other temporary disability to discharge the duties of the office, the powers and duties of the office of Governor shall devolve upon the same person as in case of vacancy, but only until the disability ceases. (Amendment referred by the Legislature; approved at regular election November 5, 1968; effective December 4, 1968.)

Sec. 7. Every bill passed by the Legislature, before it becomes a law, shall be presented to the Governor. If he approve, he shall sign it, and it shall become a law as provided in this Constitution. But if he disapprove, he shall return it, with his objections, to the House in which it originated, which shall enter the objections at large on the journal. If after reconsideration it again passes both Houses by an aye and nay vote on roll call of two-thirds of the members elected to each House, it shall become a law as provided in this Constitution, notwithstanding the Governor's objections. This Section shall not apply to emergency measures as referred to in Section 1 of the Article on the Legislative Department.

If any bill be not returned within five days after it shall have been presented to the Governor (Sunday excepted) such bill shall become a law in like manner as if he had signed it, unless the Legislature by its final adjournment prevents its return, in which case it shall be filed with his objections in the office of the Secretary of State within ten days after such adjournment (Sundays excepted) or become a law as provided in this Constitution. After the final action by the Governor, or following the adoption of a bill notwithstanding his objection, it shall be filed with the Secretary of State.

If any bill presented to the Governor contains several items of appropriations of money, he may object to one or more of such items, while approving other portions of the bill. In such case he shall append to the bill at the time of signing it, a statement of the item or items which he declines to approve, together with his reasons therefor, and such item or items shall not take effect unless passed over the Governor's objections as in this section provided.

The veto power of the Governor shall not extend to any bill passed by the Legislature and referred to the people for adoption or rejection.

Sec. 8. When any office shall, from any cause, become vacant, and no mode shall be provided by the Constitution or by law for filling such vacancy, the Governor shall have the power to fill such vacancy by appointment.

Sec. 9. The powers and duties of Secretary of State, State Treasurer, Attorney-General, and Superintendent of Public Instruction shall be as prescribed by law. (Amendment referred by the Legislature; approved at regular election November 5, 1968; effective December 4, 1968.)

Sec. 10. No person shall be eligible to succeed himself to the office of State Treasurer for the succeeding two years after the expiration of the term for which he shall have been elected.

Sec. 11. The returns of the election for all State officers shall be canvassed, and certificates of election issued by the Secretary of State, in such manner as may be provided by law.

Sec. 12. All commissions shall issue in the name of the State, and shall be signed by the Governor, sealed with the seal of the State, and attested by the Secretary of State.

Sec. 13. The salaries of those holding elective state offices shall be as established by law from time to time, subject to the limitations of article 6, section 33 and to the limitations of article 4, part 2, section 17. Such salaries as are presently established may be altered from time to time by the procedure established in this section or as otherwise provided by law, except that legislative salaries may be altered only by the procedures established in this section.

A commission to be known as the commission on salaries for elective state officers is authorized to be established by the legislature. The commission shall be composed of five members appointed from private life, two of whom shall be appointed by the governor and one each by the president of the senate, the speaker of the house of representatives, and the chief justice. At such times as may be directed by the legislature, the commission shall report to the governor with recommendations concerning the rates of pay of elected state officers. The governor shall upon the receipt of such report make recommendations to the legislature with respect to the exact rates of pay which he deems advisable for those offices and positions other than for rates of pay of members of the legislature. Such recommendations shall become effective at a time established by the legislature after the transmission of the recommendation of the governor without aid of further legislative action unless, within such period of time, there has been enacted into law a statute which establishes rates of pay other than those proposed by the governor, or unless either house of the legislature specifically disapproves all or part of the governor's recommendation. The recommendations of the governor, unless disapproved or altered within the time provided by law, shall be effective; and any 1971 recommendations shall be effective as to all offices on the first Monday in January of 1973. In case of either a legislative enactment or disapproval by either house, the recommendations shall be effective only insofar as not altered or disapproved. The recommendations of the commission as to legislative salaries shall be certified by it to the secretary of state and the secretary of state shall submit to the qualified electors at the next regular general election the question, "Shall the recommendations of the commission on salaries for elective state officers concerning legislative salaries be accepted? ☐ Yes ☐ No." Such recommendations if approved by the electors shall become effective at the beginning of the next regular legislative session without any other authorizing legislation. All recommendations which become effective under this section shall supersede all laws enacted prior to their effective date relating to such salaries. (Amendment referred by the Legislature; approved at regular election Nov. 3, 1970; effective Nov. 27, 1970.)

ARTICLE VI.

JUDICIAL DEPARTMENT.

Sec. 1. The judicial power shall be vested in an integrated judicial department consisting of a Supreme Court, such intermediate appellate courts as may be provided by law, a superior court, such courts inferior to the superior court as may be provided by law, and justice courts.

Sec. 2. The Supreme Court shall consist of not less than five justices. The number of justices may be increased or decreased by law, but the court shall at all times be constituted of at least five justices.

The Supreme Court shall sit in accordance with rules adopted by it, either in banc or in divisions of not less than three justices, but the court shall not declare any law unconstitutional except when sitting in banc. The decisions of the court shall be in writing and the grounds stated.

The court shall be open at all times, except on nonjudicial days, for the transaction of business.

Sec. 3. The Supreme Court shall have administrative supervision over all the courts of the state. Justices of the Supreme Court shall elect from their number a chief justice to preside over the court and a vice chief justice to preside in the absence or incapacity of the chief justice.

The chief justice, or in his absence or incapacity, the vice chief justice, shall exercise the court's administrative supervision over all the courts of the state. He may assign judges of intermediate appellate courts, superior courts, or courts inferior to the superior court to serve in other courts or counties.

Sec. 4. Justices of the Supreme Court shall be elected by the qualified electors of the state at the general election. They shall hold office for a term of six years from and after the first Monday in January next succeeding their election, and until their successors are elected and qualify. The names of all candidates for justice of the Supreme Court shall be placed on the regular ballot without partisan or other designation except the term and title of the office.

The Governor shall fill any vacancy by appointing a person to serve until the election and qualification of a successor. At the next succeeding general election following the appointment of a person to fill a vacancy, a justice shall be elected to serve for the remainder of the unexpired term.

Sec. 5. The Supreme Court shall have:

1. Original jurisdiction of habeas corpus, and quo warranto, mandamus, injunction and other extraordinary writs to state officers.

2. Original and exclusive jurisdiction to hear and determine causes between counties concerning disputed boundaries and surveys thereof or concerning claims of one county against another.

3. Appellate jurisdiction in all actions and proceedings except civil and criminal actions originating in courts not of record, unless the action involves the validity of a tax, impost, assessment, toll, statute or municipal ordinance.

4. Power to issue injunctions and writs of mandamus, review, prohibition, habeas corpus, certiorari, and all other writs necessary and proper to the complete exercise of its appellate and revisory jurisdiction.

5. Power to make rules relative to all procedural matters in any court.

6. Such other jurisdiction as may be provided by law.

Each justice of the Supreme Court may issue writs of habeas corpus to any part of the state upon petition by or on behalf of a person held in actual custody, and may make such writs returnable before himself, the Supreme Court, appellate court or superior court, or judge thereof.

Sec. 6. A justice of the Supreme Court shall be a person of good moral character and admitted to the practice of law in and a resident of the State of Arizona for ten years next preceding his taking office.

Sec. 7. The Supreme Court shall appoint a clerk of the court and assistants thereto who shall serve at its pleasure, and who shall receive such compensation as may be provided by law.

The Supreme Court shall appoint an administrative director and staff to serve at its pleasure to assist the chief justice in discharging his administrative duties. The director and staff shall receive such compensation as may be provided by law.

Sec. 8. Provision shall be made by law for the speedy publication of the opinions of the Supreme Court, and they shall be free for publication by any person.

Sec. 9. The jurisdiction, powers, duties and composition of any intermediate appellate court shall be as provided by law.

Sec. 10. There shall be in each county at least one judge of the superior court. There shall be in each county such additional judges as may be provided by law, but not exceeding one judge for each thirty thousand inhabitants or majority fraction thereof. The number of inhabitants in a county for purposes of this section may be determined by census enumeration or by such other method as may be provided by law.

Sec. 11. There shall be in each county a presiding judge of the superior court. In each county in which there are two or more judges, the Supreme Court shall appoint one of such judges presiding judge. Presiding judges shall exercise administrative supervision over the superior court and judges thereof in their counties, and shall have such other duties as may be provided by law or by rules of the Supreme Court.

Sec. 12. Judges of the superior court shall be elected by the qualified electors of their counties at the general election. They shall hold office for a term of four years from and after the first Monday in January next succeeding their election, and until their successors are elected and qualify. The names of all candidates for judge of the superior court shall be placed on the regular ballot without partisan or other designation except the division and title of the office.

The Governor shall fill any vacancy by appointing a person to serve until the election and qualification of a successor. At the next succeeding general election following the appointment of a person to fill a vacancy, a judge shall be elected to serve for the remainder of the unexpired term.

Sec. 13. The superior courts provided for in this article shall constitute a single court, composed of all the duly elected or appointed judges in each of the counties of the state. The legislature may classify counties for the purpose of fixing salaries of judges or officers of the court.

The judgments, decrees, orders and proceedings of any session of the superior court held by one or more judges shall have the same force and effect as if all the judges of the court had presided.

The process of the court shall extend to all parts of the state.

Sec. 14. The superior court shall have original jurisdiction of:

1. Cases and proceedings in which exclusive jurisdiction is not vested by law in another court.
2. Cases of equity and at law which involve the title to or possession of real property, or the legality of any tax, impost, assessment, toll or municipal ordinance.
3. Other cases in which the demand or value of property in controversy amounts to one thousand dollars or more, exclusive of interest and costs.
4. Criminal cases amounting to felony, and cases of misdemeanor not otherwise provided for by law.
5. Actions of forcible entry and detainer.
6. Proceedings in insolvency.
7. Actions to prevent or abate nuisance.
8. Matters of probate.
9. Divorce and for annulment of marriage.
10. Naturalization and the issuance of papers therefor.

11. Special cases and proceedings not otherwise provided for, and such other jurisdiction as may be provided by law.

(Amendment referred by the Legislature; approved at regular election Nov. 7, 1972; effective Dec. 1, 1972.)

Sec. 15. The superior court shall have exclusive original jurisdiction in all proceedings and matters affecting dependent, neglected, incorrigible or delinquent children, or children accused of crime, under the age of eighteen years. The judges shall hold examinations in chambers for all such children concerning whom proceedings are brought, in advance of any criminal prosecution of such children, and may, in their discretion, suspend criminal prosecution of such children. The powers of the judges to control such children shall be as provided by law.

Sec. 16. The superior court shall have appellate jurisdiction in cases arising in justice and other courts inferior to the superior court as may be provided by law.

Sec. 17. The superior court shall be open at all times, except on nonjudicial days, for the determination of non-jury civil cases and the transaction of business. For the determination of civil causes and matters in which a jury demand has been entered, and for the trial of criminal causes, a trial jury shall be drawn and summoned from the body of the county, as provided by law. The right of jury trial as provided by this constitution shall remain inviolate, but trial by jury may be waived by the parties in any civil cause or by the parties with the consent of the court in any criminal cause. Grand juries shall be drawn and summoned only by order of the superior court.

Sec. 18. The superior court or any judge thereof may issue writs of mandamus, quo warranto, review, certiorari, prohibition, and writs of habeas corpus on petition by or on behalf of a person held in actual custody within the county. Injunctions, attachments, and writs of prohibition and habeas corpus may be issued and served on legal holidays and non-judicial days.

Sec. 19. A judge of the superior court shall serve in another county at the direction of the chief justice of the Supreme Court or may serve in another county at the request of the presiding judge of the superior court thereof.

Sec. 20. Any retired justice of the Supreme Court or judge of an intermediate appellate court or superior court who is drawing retirement pay may serve as a Supreme Court justice, intermediate appellate or superior court judge. When serving outside his county of residence, any such retired justice or judge shall receive his necessary traveling and subsistence expenses.

Sec. 21. Every matter submitted to a judge of the superior court for his decision shall be decided within sixty days from the date of submission thereof. The Supreme Court shall by rule provide for the speedy disposition of all matters not decided within such period.

Sec. 22. Judges of the superior court, intermediate appellate courts or courts inferior to the superior court having jurisdiction in civil cases of one thousand dollars or more, exclusive of interest and costs, established by law under the provisions of section 1 of this article, shall be at least thirty years of age, of good moral character, and admitted to the practice of law in and a resident of the state for five years next preceding their taking office.

(Amendment referred by the Legislature; approved at regular election Nov. 7, 1972; effective Dec. 1, 1972.)

Sec. 23. There shall be in each county a clerk of the superior court. The clerk shall be elected by the qualified electors of his county at the general election and shall hold office for a term of four years from and after the first Monday in January next succeeding his election. The clerk shall have such powers and perform such duties as may be provided by law or by rule of the Supreme Court or superior court. He shall receive such compensation as may be provided by law.

Sec. 24. Judges of the superior court may appoint court commissioners, masters and referees in their respective counties, who shall have such powers and perform such duties as may be provided by law or by rule of the Supreme Court. Court commissioners, masters and referees shall receive such compensation as may be provided by law.

Sec. 25. The style of process shall be "The State of Arizona", and prosecutions shall be conducted in the name of the state and by its authority.

Sec. 26. Each justice, judge and justice of the peace shall, before entering upon the duties of his office, take and subscribe an oath that he will support the Constitution of the United States and the Constitution of the State of Arizona, and that he will faithfully and impartially discharge the duties of his office to the best of his ability.

The oath of all judges of courts inferior to the superior court and the oath of justices of the peace shall be filed in the office of the county recorder, and the oath of all other justices and judges shall be filed in the office of the Secretary of State.

Sec. 27. Judges shall not charge juries with respect to matters of fact, nor comment thereon, but shall declare the law. No cause shall be reversed for technical error in pleadings or proceedings when upon the whole case it shall appear that substantial justice has been done.

Sec. 28. Justices and judges of courts of record shall not be eligible to any public office or public employment during their term of office, except that they may assume another judicial office, and upon qualifying therefor, the office formerly held shall become vacant. No justice or judge of any court of record shall practice law during his continuance in office.

Sec. 29. Relating to salaries of justices of the supreme court and judges of the superior court, is repealed. (Amendment referred by the Legislature; approved at regular election Nov. 3, 1970; effective Nov. 27, 1970.)

Sec. 30. The Supreme Court and the superior court shall be courts of record. Other courts of record may be established by law, but justice courts shall not be courts of record.

Sec. 31. The legislature may provide for the appointment of members of the bar having the qualifications provided in section 22 of this article as judges **pro tempore** of courts inferior to the Supreme Court. When serving, any such person shall have all the judicial powers of a regularly elected judge of the court to which he is appointed. A person so appointed shall receive such compensation as may be provided by law. The population limitation of section 10 of this article shall not apply to the appointment of judges **pro tempore** of the superior court.

Sec. **32**. The number of justices of the peace to be elected in precincts shall be as provided by law. Justices of the peace may be police justices of incorporated cities and towns.

The jurisdiction, powers and duties of courts inferior to the superior court and of justice courts, and the terms of office of judges of such courts and justices of the peace shall be as provided by law. The legislature may classify counties and precincts for the purpose of fixing salaries of judges of courts inferior to the superior court and of justices of the peace.

The civil jurisdiction of courts inferior to the superior court and of justice courts shall not exceed the sum of two thousand five hundred dollars, exclusive of interest and costs. Criminal jurisdiction shall be limited to misdemeanors. The jurisdiction of such courts shall not encroach upon the jurisdiction of courts of record but may be made concurrent therewith, subject to the limitations provided in this section.

Sec. 33. No change made by the legislature in the number of justices or judges shall work the removal of any justice or judge from office. The salary of any justice or judge shall not be reduced during the term of office for which he was elected or appointed.

Sec. 34. Any judicial officer except a retired justice or judge who absents himself from the state for more than sixty consecutive days shall be deemed to have forfeited his office, but the Governor may extend the leave of absence for such time as reasonable necessity therefor exists.

Sec. 35. All justices, judges, justices of the peace and officers of any court holding office by election or appointment at the time of the adoption of this article shall continue in office for their respective terms, and until their successors are elected and qualify. The continued existence of any office heretofore legally established or held shall not be abolished or repealed by the adoption of this article. The statutes and rules relating to the authority, jurisdiction, practice and procedure of courts, judicial officers and offices in force at the time of the adoption of this article and not inconsistent herewith, shall, so far as applicable, apply to and govern such courts, judicial officers and offices until amended or repealed.

(Initiative Petition of the People. Amended Regular Election November 8, 1960. Effective December 9, 1960.)

ARTICLE VI.I.

COMMISSION ON JUDICIAL QUALIFICATIONS.

1. Composition; appointment; terms; vacancies

Sec. 1. A commission on judicial qualifications is created to be composed of nine persons consisting of two judges of the court of appeals, two judges of the superior court and one justice of the peace, who shall be appointed by the supreme court, two members of the state bar of Arizona, who shall be appointed by the governing body of such bar association, and two citizens who are not judges, retired judges nor members of the state bar of Arizona, who shall be appointed by the governor subject to confirmation by the senate.

Terms of members of the commission shall be four years, except that if a member ceases to hold the position that qualified him for appointment his membership on the commission terminates. An appointment to fill a vacancy for an unexpired term shall be made for the remainder of the term by the appointing power of the original appointment.

2. Disqualification of judge

Sec. 2. A judge is disqualified from acting as a judge, without loss of salary, while there is pending an indictment or an information charging him in the United States with a crime punishable as a felony under Arizona or federal law, or a recommendation to the supreme court by the commission on judicial qualifications for his removal or retirement.

3. Suspension or removal of judge

Sec. 3. On recommendation of the commission on judicial qualifications, or on its own motion, the supreme court may suspend a judge from office without salary when, in the United States, he pleads guilty or no contest or is found guilty of a crime punishable as a felony under Arizona or federal law or of any other crime that involves moral turpitude under such law. If his conviction is reversed the suspension terminates, and he shall be paid his salary for the period of suspension. If he is suspended and his conviction becomes final the supreme court shall remove him from office.

4. Retirement of judge

Sec. 4. On recommendation of the commission on judicial qualifications, the supreme court may retire a judge for disability that seriously interferes with the performance of his duties and is or is likely to become permanent, and may censure or remove a judge for action by him that constitutes wilful misconduct in office, wilful and persistent failure to perform his duties, habitual intemperance or conduct prejudicial to the administration of justice that brings the judicial office into disrepute.

A judge retired by the supreme court shall be considered to have retired voluntarily. A judge removed by the supreme court is ineligible for judicial office in this state.

5. Definitions and rules implementing article

Sec. 5. The term "judge" as used in this constitutional amendment shall apply to all justices of the peace, judges of the superior court, judges of the court of appeals and justices of the supreme court. The supreme court shall make rules implementing this article and providing for confidentiality of proceedings. A judge who is a member of the commission or supreme court shall not participate as a member in any proceedings hereunder involving his own censure, removal or involuntary retirement.

6. Article self-executing

Sec. 6. The provisions of this article shall be self-executing.

ARTICLE VII.

SUFFRAGE AND ELECTIONS.

Sec. 1. All elections by the people shall be by ballot, or by such other method as may be prescribed by law; Provided, that secrecy in voting shall be preserved.

Sec. 2. No person shall be entitled to vote at any general election, or for any office that now is, or hereafter may be, elective by the people, or upon any question which may be submitted to a vote of the people, unless such person be a citizen of the United States of the age of twenty-one years or over, and shall have resided in the State one year immediately preceding such election, provided that qualifications for voters at a general election for the purpose of electing presidential electors shall be as prescribed by law. The word "citizen" shall include persons of the male and female sex.

The rights of citizens of the United States to

vote and hold office shall not be denied or abridged by the state, or any political division or municipality thereof, on account of sex, and the right to register, to vote and to hold office under any law now in effect, or which may hereafter be enacted, is hereby extended to, and conferred upon males and females alike.

No person under guardianship, non compos mentis, or insane, shall be qualified to vote at any election, nor shall any person convicted of treason or felony, be qualified to vote at any election unless restored to civil rights.

(Amendment referred by the Legislature; approved at regular election November 6, 1962; effective November 26, 1962.)

Sec. 3. For the purpose of voting, no person shall be deemed to have gained or lost a residence by reason of his presence or absence while employed in the service of the United States, or while a student at any institution of learning, or while kept at any alms-house or other asylum at public expense, or while confined in any public jail or prison.

Sec. 4. Electors shall in all cases, except treason, felony, or breach of the peace, be privileged from arrest during their attendance at any election, and in going thereto and returning therefrom.

Sec. 5. No elector shall be obliged to perform military duty on the day of an election, except in time of war or public danger.

Sec. 6. No soldier, seaman, or marine, in the army or navy of the United States shall be deemed a resident of this State in consequence of his being stationed at any military or naval place within this State.

Sec. 7. In all elections held, by the people, in this State, the person, or persons, receiving the highest number of legal votes shall be declared elected.

Sec. 8. Qualifications for voters at school elections shall be as are now, or as may hereafter be, provided by law.

Sec. 9. For the purpose of obtaining an advisory vote of the people, the Legislature shall provide for placing the names of candidates for United States Senator on the official ballot at the general election next preceding the election of a United States Senator.

Sec. 10. The Legislature shall enact a direct primary election law, which shall provide for the nomination of candidates for all elective State, county, and city offices, including candidates for United States Senator and for Representative in Congress.

Sec. 11. There shall be a general election of Representatives in Congress, and of State, county, and precinct officers on the first Tuesday after the first Monday in November of the first even numbered year after the year in which Arizona is admitted to Statehood and biennially thereafter.

Sec. 12. There shall be enacted registration and other laws to secure the purity of elections and guard against abuses of the elective franchise.

Sec. 13. Questions upon bond issues or special assessments shall be submitted to the vote of real property tax payers, who shall also in all respects be qualified electors of this State, and of the political subdivisions thereof affected by such question. (Amendment referred by the Legislature; approved at regular election November 4, 1930; effective December 1, 1930.)

Sec. 14. No fee shall ever be required in order to have the name of any candidate placed on the official ballot for any election or primary.

Sec. 15. Every person elected or appointed to any elective office of trust or profit under the authority of the state, or any political division or any municipality thereof, shall be a qualified elector of the political division or municipality in which such person shall be elected.

(Amendment referred by the Legislature; approved at regular election Nov. 7, 1972; effective Dec. 1, 1972.)

Sec. 16. The Legislature, at its first session, shall enact a law providing for a general publicity, before and after election, of all campaign contributions to, and expenditures of campaign committees and candidates for public office.

Sec. 17. There shall be a primary and general election as prescribed by law, which shall provide for nomination and election of a candidate for United States Senator and for Representative in Congress when a vacancy occurs through resignation or any other cause.

(Amendment referred by the Legislature; approved at regular election November 6, 1962; effective November 26, 1962.)

ARTICLE VIII.

REMOVAL FROM OFFICE.

1. RECALL OF PUBLIC OFFICERS.

Sec. 1. Every public officer in the State of Arizona, holding an elective office, either by election or appointment, is subject to recall from such office by the qualified electors of the electoral district from which candidates are elected to such office. Such electoral district may include the whole State. Such number of said electors as shall equal twenty-five per centum of the number of votes cast at the last preceding general election for all of the candidates for the office held by such officer, may by petition, which shall be known as a Recall Petition, demand his recall. (Amendment referred by the Legislature, approved at regular election, November 5, 1912; effective December 5, 1912.)

Sec. 2. Every Recall Petition must contain a general statement, in not more than two hundred words, of the grounds of such demand, and must be filed in the office in which petitions for nominations to the office held by the incumbent are required to be filed. The signatures to such Recall Petition need not all be on one sheet of paper, but each signer must add to his signature the date of his signing said petition, and his place of residence, giving his street and number, if any, should he reside in a town or city. One of the signers of each sheet of such petition, or the person circulating such sheet, must make and subscribe an oath on said sheet, that the signatures thereon are genuine.

Sec. 3. If said officer shall offer his resignation it shall be accepted, and the vacancy shall be filled as may be provided by law. If he shall not resign within five days after a Recall Petition is filed, a special election shall be ordered to be held, not less than twenty, nor more than thirty days after such order, to determine whether such officer shall be recalled. On the ballots at said election shall be printed the reasons as set forth in the petition for demanding his recall, and, in not more than two hundred words, the officer's justification of his course in office. He shall continue to perform the duties of his office until the result of said election shall have been officially declared.

Sec. 4. Unless he otherwise request, in writing, his name shall be placed as a candidate on the official ballot without nomination. Other candidates for the office may be nominated to be voted for at said election. The candidate who shall receive the highest number of votes, shall be declared elected for the remainder of the term. Unless the incumbent receive the highest number of votes, he shall be deemed to be removed from office, upon qualification of his successor. In the event that his successor shall not qualify within five days after the result of said election shall have been declared, the said office shall be vacant, and may be filled as provided by law.

Sec. 5. No Recall Petition shall be circulated against any officer until he shall have held his office for a period of six months, except that it may be filed against a member of the Legislature at any time after five days from the beginning of the first session after his election. After one Recall Petition and election, no further Recall Petition shall be filed against the same officer during the term for which he was elected, unless petitioners signing such petition shall first pay into the public treasury which has paid such election expenses, all expenses of the preceding election.

Sec. 6. The general election laws shall apply to recall elections in so far as applicable. Laws necessary to facilitate the operation of the provisions of this article shall be enacted, including provision for payment by the public treasury of the reasonable special election campaign expenses of such officer.

2. IMPEACHMENT.

Sec. 1. The House of Representatives shall have the sole power of impeachment. The concurrence of a majority of all the members shall be necessary to an impeachment. All impeachments shall be tried by the Senate, and, when sitting for that purpose, the Senators shall be upon oath or affirmation to do justice according to law and evidence, and shall be presided over by the Chief Justice of the Supreme Court. Should the Chief Justice be on trial, or otherwise disqualified, the Senate shall elect a judge of the Supreme Court to preside.

Sec. 2. No person shall be convicted without a concurrence of two-thirds of the Senators elected. The Governor and other State and judicial officers, except justices of courts not of record, shall be liable to impeachment for high crimes, misdemeanors, or malfeasance in office, but judgment in such cases shall extend only to removal from office and disqualification to hold any office of honor, trust, or profit in the State. The party, whether convicted or acquitted, shall, nevertheless, be liable to trial and punishment according to law.

ARTICLE IX.

PUBLIC DEBT, REVENUE, AND TAXATION.

Sec. 1. The power of taxation shall never be surrendered, suspended, or contracted away. All taxes shall be uniform upon the same class of property within the territorial limits of the authority levying the tax, and shall be levied and collected for public purposes only.

Sec. 2. There shall be exempt from taxation all federal, state, county and municipal property. Property of educational, charitable and religious associations or institutions not used or held for profit may be exempt from taxation by law. Public debts, as evidenced by the bonds of Arizona, its counties, municipalities, or other subdivisions, shall also be exempt from taxation. All household goods owned by the user thereof and used solely for noncommercial purposes shall be exempt from taxation, and such person entitled to such exemption shall not be required to take any affirmative action to receive the benefit of such exemption. Stocks of raw or finished materials, unassembled parts, work in process of finished products constituting the inventory of a retailer or wholesaler located within the state and principally engaged in the resale of such materials, parts or products, whether or not for resale to the ultimate consumer shall be exempt from taxation. There shall be further exempt from taxation the property of widows, honorably discharged soldiers, sailors, United States marines, members of revenue marine service, nurse corps, or of the components of auxiliaries of any thereof, residents of this state, not exceeding the amount of two thousand dollars, where the total assessment of such widow and such other persons named herein does not exceed five thousand dollars; provided, that no such exemption shall be made for such persons other than widows unless they shall have served at least sixty days in the military or naval service of the United States during time of war, and shall have been residents of this state prior to September 1, 1945. All property in the state not exempt under the laws of the United States or under this constitution, or exempt by law under the provisions of this section shall be subject to taxation, to be ascertained as provided by law. This section shall be self-executing. (Amendment referred by the Legislature; approved at regular election November 5, 1968; effective December 4, 1968.)

Sec. 2(A). There shall be exempt from taxation all federal, state, county and municipal property. Property of educational, charitable and religious associations or institutions not used or held for profit may be exempt from taxation by law. Public debts, as evidenced by the bonds of Arizona, its counties, municipalities, other subdivisions, shall also be exempt from taxation. Stocks of raw or finished materials, unassembled parts, work in process or finished products constituting the inventory of a retailer or wholesaler located within the state and principally engaged in the resale of such materials, parts or products, whether or not for resale to the ultimate consumer shall be exempt from taxation. This section shall be self-executing. As amended, election November 5, 1968.

Sec. 2(B). There shall be further exempt from taxation the property of each widow, and each honorably discharged airman, soldier, sailor, United States marine, member of revenue marine service, nurse corps or of the component of auxiliary of any thereof, resident of this state, not exceeding the amount of two thousand dollars, where the total assessment of such widow and such other person does not exceed five thousand dollars; provided, that no such exemption shall be made for such person other than a widow unless such person shall have served at least sixty days in the military or naval service of the United States during World War I or prior wars, and shall have been a resident of this state prior to September 1, 1945.

There shall be further exempt from taxation the property of each honorably discharged airman, soldier, sailor, United States marine, member of revenue marine service, nurse corps, or of the component of auxiliary of any thereof, resident of this state, not exceeding the amount of two thousand dollars for the tax year 1969, the amount of one thousand five hundred dollars for the tax year 1970, the amount of one thousand dollars for the tax year 1971, and the amount of five hundred dollars for the tax year 1972, where the total assessment of such person named herein does not exceed five thousand dollars; provided, that no such exemption shall be made for such person unless he shall have served at least sixty days in the military or naval service of the United States during time of war after World War I, and shall have been a resident of this state prior to September 1, 1945; provided, that no such exemption shall be made for such person after the tax year 1972.

There shall be further exempt from taxation as herein provided the property of each honorably discharged airman, soldier, sailor, United States marine, member of revenue marine service, nurse corps or of the component of auxiliary of any thereof, resident of this state, where such person has a service-connected disability as determined by the United States veterans administration, and where the total assessment of such person does not exceed five thousand dollars; provided, that no such exemption shall be made for such person unless he shall have been a resident of this state prior to September 1, 1945, or unless he shall have been a resident of this state for at least four years prior to his original entry into service as an airman, soldier, sailor, United States marine, member of revenue marine service, nurse corps or of the component of auxiliary of any thereof. The property of such person having a compensable service-connected disability exempt from taxation as herein provided shall be determined as follows: (1) If such person's service-connected disability as determined by the United States veterans administration is sixty per cent or less, the property of such person exempt from taxation shall be determined by such person's percentage of disability multiplied by the assessment of such person not exceeding the amount of two thousand dollars; (2) If such person's service-connected disability as determined by the United States veterans administration is more than sixty per cent, the property of such person exempt from taxation shall not exceed the amount of two thousand dollars.

There shall be further exempt from taxation the property of each honorably discharged airman, soldier, sailor, United States marine, member of revenue marine service, nurse corps or of the component of auxiliary of any thereof; resident of this state, not exceeding the amount of two thousand dollars, where such person has a nonservice-connected total and permanent disability, physical or mental, as so certified by the United States veterans administration, and where the total assessment of such person does not exceed five thousand dollars; provided, that no such exemption shall be made for such person unless he shall have served at least sixty days in the military or naval service of the United States during time of war after World War I, and shall have been a resident of this state prior to September 1, 1945.

No property shall be exempt which has been conveyed to evade taxation. The total exemption from taxation granted to property owned by a person who qualifies for any exemption in accordance with the terms of this section 2(B) shall not exceed two thousand dollars. This section shall be self-executing. As amended, election November 5, 1968.

Sec. 2(C). All property in the state not exempt under the laws of the United States or under this constitution, or exempt by law under the provisions of this section shall be subject to taxation to be ascertained as provided by law. This section shall be self-executing. As amended, election November 5, 1968.

(Amendments 2(A), 2(B) and 2(C) referred by the Legislature; approved at regular election November 5, 1968; effective December 4, 1968.)

Sec. 2(A). There shall be exempt from taxation all federal, state, county and municipal property. Property of educational, charitable and religious associations or institutions not used or held for profit may be exempt from taxation by law Public debts, as evidenced by the bonds of Arizona its counties, municipalities, or other subdivisions, shall also be exempt from taxation. Stocks of raw or finished materials, unassembled parts, work in process or finished products constituting the inventory of a retailer or wholesaler located within the state and principally engaged in the resale of such materials, parts or products, whether or not for resale to the ultimate consumer shall be exempt from taxation. This section shall be self-executing. As amended, election November 5, 1968.

Sec. 2(B). There shall be further exempt from taxation the property of each honorably discharged soldier, sailor, United States marine, member of revenue marine service, nurse corps, or of the component of auxiliary of any thereof, resident of this state, not exceeding the amount of two thousand dollars, where the total assessment of such person does not exceed five thousand dollars; provided, that no such exemption shall be made for such person unless he shall have served at least sixty days in the military or naval service of the United States during time of war, and shall have been a resident of this state prior to September 1, 1945.

There shall be further exempt from taxation the property of each widow, resident of this state, not exceeding the amount of two thousand dollars, where the total assessment of such widow does not exceed five thousand dollars; provided, that the income from all sources of such widow, together with the income from all sources of all children of such widow residing with her in such widow's residence in the year immediately preceding the year for which such widow applies for exemption, did not exceed (1) $3,500, if none of the widow's children under the age of twenty-one years resided with her in such widow's residence, or (2) $5,000, if one or more of the widow's children residing with her in such widow's residence was under the age of twenty-one years, or was totally and permanently disabled, physically or mentally, as certified by competent medical authority as provided by law; and provided, further that such widow resided with her last husband in this state at the time of his death if she was not a widow and a resident of this state prior to January 1, 1969.

No property shall be exempt which has been conveyed to evade taxation. The total exemption from taxation granted to property owned by a person who qualifies for any exemption in accordance with the terms of this section 2(B) shall not exceed two thousand dollars. This section shall be self-executing. As amended, election November 5, 1968.

Sec. 2(C). All property in the state not exempt under the laws of the United States or under this constitution, or exempt by law under the provisions of this section shall be subject to taxation to be ascertained as provided by law. This section shall be self-executing. As amended, election November 5, 1968.

(Amendments 2(A), 2(B) and 2(C) referred by the Legislature; approved at regular election November 5, 1968; effective December 4, 1968.)

Sec. 3. The Legislature shall provide by law for an annual tax sufficient, with other sources of revenue, to defray the necessary ordinary expenses of the State for each fiscal year. And for the purpose of paying the State debt, if there be any, the Legislature shall provide for levying an annual tax sufficient to pay the annual interest and the principal of such debt within twenty-five years from the final passage of the law creating the debt.

No tax shall be levied except in pursuance of law, and every law imposing a tax shall state distinctly the object of the tax, to which object only it shall be applied.

All taxes levied and collected for State purposes shall be paid into the State treasury in money only.

Sec. 4. The fiscal year shall commence on the first day of July in each year. An accurate statement of receipts and expenditures of the public money shall be published annually, in such manner as shall be provided by law. Whenever the expenses of any fiscal year shall exceed the income, the Legislature may provide for levying a tax for the ensuing fiscal year sufficient, with other sources of income, to pay the deficiency, as well as the estimated expenses of the ensuing fiscal year.

Sec. 5. The State may contract debts to supply the casual deficits or failures in revenues, or to meet expenses not otherwise provided for; but the aggregate amount of such debts, direct and contingent, whether contracted by virtue of one or more laws, or at different periods of time, shall never exceed the sum of three hundred and fifty thousand dollars; and the money arising from the creation of such debts shall be applied to the purpose for which it was obtained or to repay the debts so contracted, and to no other purpose.

In addition to the above limited power to contract debts the State may borrow money to repel invasion, suppress insurrection, or defend the State in time of war; but the money thus raised shall be applied exclusively to the object for which the loan shall have been authorized or to the repayment of the debt thereby created. No money shall be paid out of the State treasury, except in the manner provided by law.

Sec. 6. Incorporated cities, towns, and villages may be vested by law with power to make local improvements by special assessments, or by special taxation of property benefited. For all corporate purposes, all municipal corporations may be vested with authority to assess and collect taxes.

Sec. 7. Neither the State, nor any county, city, town, municipality, or other subdivision of the State shall ever give or loan its credit in the aid of, or make any donation or grant, by subsidy or otherwise, to any individual, association, or corporation, or become a subscriber to, or a shareholder in, any company or corporation, or become a joint owner with any person, company, or corporation, except as to such ownerships as may accrue to the State by operation or provision of law.

Sec. 8. No county, city, town, school district, or other municipal corporation shall for any purpose become indebted in any manner to an amount exceeding four per centum of the taxable property in such county, city, town, school district, or other municipal corporation, without the assent of a majority of the property taxpayers, who must also in all respects be qualified electors, therein voting at an election provided by law to be held for that purpose, the value of the taxable property therein to be ascertained by the last assessment for State and county purposes, previous to incurring such indebtedness; except, that in incorporated cities and towns assessments shall be taken from the last assessment for city or town purposes; Provided, that under no circumstances shall any county or school district become indebted to an amount exceeding ten per centum of such taxable property, as shown by the last assessment roll thereof; and Provided further, that any incorporated city or town, with such assent, may be allowed to become indebted to a larger amount, but not exceeding fifteen per centum additional, for supplying such city or town with water, artificial light, or sewers, when the works for supplying such water, light, or sewers are or shall be owned and controlled by the municipality, and for the acquisition and development by the incorporated city or town of land or interests therein for open space preserves, parks, playgrounds and recreational facilities.

(Amendment referred by the Legislature; approved at regular election Nov. 7, 1972; effective Dec. 1, 1972.)

Sec. 9. **Every law** which imposes, **continues, or revives a tax shall distinctly state the tax and the objects for which it shall be applied; and it shall not be sufficient to refer to any other law to fix such tax or object.**

Sec. 10. **No tax shall be laid or appropriation of public money made in aid of any church, or private or sectarian school, or any public service corporation.**

Sec. 11. The manner, method and mode of assessing, equalizing and levying taxes in the State of Arizona shall be such as is prescribed by law.

Beginning January 1, 1941, a license tax is hereby imposed on vehicles registered for operation upon the highways in Arizona, which license tax shall be in lieu of all ad valorem property taxes on any vehicle subject to such license tax. Such license tax shall be collected annually by the registering officer at the time of application for and before registration of the vehicle each year and shall be (a) at a rate equal to the average ad valorem rate for all purposes in the several taxing districts of the state for the preceding year, but in no event to exceed a rate of four dollars on each one hundred dollars in value, and (b) during the first calendar year of the life of the vehicle upon a value equal to sixty percent of the manufacturer's list price of such vehicle, and during each succeeding calendar year upon a value twenty-five per cent less than the value for the preceding calendar year.

In the event that a vehicle is destroyed after the beginning of a registration year, the license tax paid for such year on such vehicle may be reduced as provided by law.

Beginning January 1, 1969, mobile homes, as defined by law for tax purposes, shall not be subject to the license tax imposed under the provisions of this section but shall be subject to ad valorem property taxes on any mobile homes in the manner provided by law. Distribution of the proceeds derived from such tax shall be as provided by law.

In the event application is made after the beginning of the registration year for registration of a vehicle not previously registered in the state, the license tax for such year on such vehicle shall be reduced by one-twelfth for each full month of the registration year already expired.

The Legislature shall provide for the distribution of the proceeds from such license tax to the state, counties, school districts, cities and towns.

The provisions of this section shall expire at midnight on December 31, 1973.

(Amendment referred by the Legislature; approved at regular election Nov. 7, 1972; effective Dec. 1, 1972.)

Sec. 11. From and after December 31, 1973, the manner, method and mode of assessing, equalizing and levying taxes in the State of Arizona shall be such as is prescribed by law.

From and after December 31, 1973, a license tax is hereby imposed on vehicles registered for operation upon the highways in Arizona, which license tax shall be in lieu of all ad valorem property taxes on any vehicle subject to such license tax. Such license tax shall be collected as provided by law. To facilitate an even distribution of the registration of vehicles and the collection of the license tax imposed by this section, the Legislature may provide for different times or periods of registration between and within the several classes of vehicles.

In the event that a vehicle is destroyed after the beginning of a registration year, the license tax paid for such year on such vehicle may be reduced as provided by law.

From and after December 31, 1973, mobile homes, as defined by law for tax purposes, shall not be subject to the license tax imposed under the provisions of this section but shall be subject to ad valorem property taxes on any mobile homes in the manner provided by law. Distribution of the proceeds derived from such tax shall be as provided by law.

From and after December 31, 1973, the Legislature shall provide for the distribution of the proceeds from such license tax to the state, counties, school districts, cities and towns.

(Amendment referred by the Legislature; approved at regular election Nov. 7, 1972; effective Dec. 1, 1972.)

Sec. 12. The law-making power shall have authority to provide for the levy and collection of license, franchise, gross revenue, excise, income, collateral and direct inheritance, legacy, and succession taxes, also graduated income taxes, graduated collateral and direct inheritance taxes, graduated legacy and succession taxes, stamp, registration, production, or other specific taxes.

Sec. 13. No tax shall be levied on raw or unfinished materials, unassembled parts, work in process or finished products, constituting the inventory of a manufacturer or manufacturing establishment located within the state and principally engaged in the fabrication, production and manufacture of products, wares and articles for use, from raw or prepared materials, imparting thereto new forms, qualities, properties and combinations, which materials, parts, work in process or finished products are not consigned or billed to any other party. (Amendment referred by the Legislature; approved at special election September 12, 1950; effective October 2, 1950.)

Sec. 14. No moneys derived from fees, excises, or license taxes relating to registration, operation, or use of vehicles on the public highways or streets or to fuels or any other energy source used for the propulsion of vehicles on the public highways or streets, shall be expended for other than highway and street purposes including the cost of administering the state highway system and the laws creating such fees, excises, or license taxes, statutory refunds and adjustments provided by law, payment of principal and interest on highway and street bonds and obligations, expenses of state enforcement of traffic laws and state administration of traffic safety programs, payment of costs of publication and distribution of Arizona highways magazine, state costs of construction, reconstruction, maintenance or repair of public highways, streets or bridges, cost of rights of way acquisitions and expenses related thereto, roadside development, and for distribution to counties, incorporated cities and towns to be used by them solely for highway and street purposes including costs of rights of way acquisitions and expenses related thereto, construction, reconstruction, maintenance, repair, roadside development, of county, city and town roads, streets, and bridges and payment of principal and interest on highway and street bonds. As long as the total highway user revenues derived equals or exceeds the total derived in the fiscal year ending June 30, 1970, the state and any county shall not receive from such revenues for the use of each and for distribution to cities and towns, fewer dollars than were received and distributed in such fiscal year. This section shall not apply to moneys derived from the automobile license tax imposed under section 11 of article IX of the Constitution of Arizona. All moneys collected in accordance with this section shall be distributed as provided by law. (Amendment referred by the Legislature; approved at regular election Nov. 3, 1970; effective Nov. 27, 1970.)

Sec. 15. Commencing January 1, 1965, a license tax is imposed on aircraft registered for operation in Arizona, which license tax shall be in lieu of all ad valorem property taxes on any aircraft subject thereto, but nothing in this section shall be deemed to apply to:

1. Regularly scheduled aircraft operated by an air line company for the primary purpose of carrying persons or property for hire in interstate, intrastate, or international transportation.

2. Aircraft owned and held by an aircraft dealer solely for purposes of sale.

3. Aircraft owned by a nonresident who operates aircraft for a period not in excess of ninety days in any one calendar year, provided that such aircraft are not engaged in any intrastate commercial activity.

4. Aircraft owned and operated exclusively in the public service by the state or by any political subdivision thereof, or by the civil air patrol.

The amount, manner, method and mode of assessing, equalizing and levying such license tax and the distribution of the proceeds therefrom shall be prescribed by law. (Amendment referred by the Legislature; approved at regular election November 3, 1964; effective December 3, 1964.)

Sec. 16. Commencing January 1, 1967, all watercraft registered for operation in Arizona, excluding watercraft owned and operated for any commercial purpose, is exempt from ad valorem property taxes. Watercraft exempt from ad valorem property taxes shall be subject to or exempt from a license tax, as may be prescribed by law.

"Watercraft", as used in this section, shall be defined as provided by law. (Amendment referred by the Legislature; approved at regular election November 8, 1966; effective November 29, 1966.)

ARTICLE X.

STATE AND SCHOOL LANDS.

Sec. 1. All lands expressly transferred and confirmed to the State by the provisions of the Enabling Act approved June 20, 1910, including all lands granted to the State and all lands heretofore granted to the Territory of Arizona, and all lands otherwise acquired by the State, shall be by the State accepted and held in trust to be disposed of in whole or in part, only in manner as in the said Enabling Act and in this Constitution provided, and for the several objects specified in the respective granting and confirmatory provisions. The natural products and money proceeds of any of said lands shall be subject to the same trusts as the lands producing the same.

Sec. 2. Disposition of any of said lands, or of any money or thing of value directly or indirectly derived therefrom, for any object other than that for which such particular lands (or the lands from which such money or thing of value shall have been derived) were granted or confirmed, or in any manner contrary to the provisions of the said Enabling Act, shall be deemed a breach of trust.

Sec. 3. No mortgage or other encumbrance of the said lands, or any part thereof, shall be valid in favor of any person or for any purpose or under any circumstances whatsoever. Said lands shall not be sold or leased, in whole or in part, except to the highest and best bidder at a public auction to be held at the county seat of the county wherein the lands to be affected, or the major portion thereof, shall lie, notice of which public auction shall first have been duly given by advertisement, which shall set forth the nature, time and place of the transaction to be had, with a full description of the lands to be offered, and be published once each week for not less than ten successive weeks in a newspaper of general circulation published regularly at the state capital, and in that newspaper of like circulation which shall then be regularly published nearest to the location of the lands so offered; nor shall any sale or contract for the sale of any timber or other natural product of such lands be made, save at the place, in the manner, and after the notice by publication provided for sales and leases of the lands themselves. Nothing herein, or elsewhere in article X contained, shall prevent:

1. The leasing of any of the lands referred to in this article in such manner as the Legislature may prescribe, for grazing, agricultural, commercial and homesite purposes, for a term of ten years or less, without advertisement;

2. The leasing of any of said lands, in such manner as the Legislature may prescribe, whether or not also leased for grazing and agricultural purposes, for mineral purposes, other than for the exploration, development, and production of oil, gas and other hydrocarbon substances, for a term of twenty years or less, without advertisement, or, 3. the leasing of any of said lands, whether or not also leased for other purposes, for the exploration, development, and production of oil, gas and other hydrocarbon substances on, in or under said lands for an initial term of twenty (20) years or less and as long thereafter as oil, gas or other hydrocarbon substance may be procured therefrom in paying quantities, the leases to be made in any manner, with or without advertisement, bidding, or appraisement, and under such terms and provisions, as the Legislature may prescribe, the terms and provisions to include a reservation of a royalty to the state of not less than twelve and one-half per cent of production. (Amendment referred by the Legislature; approved at special election September 12, 1950; effective date October 2, 1950.) (The U. S. Congress, by amendment of the Arizona Enabling Act, gave its consent to the provisions of the above amendment to the Constitution of Arizona. See Public Law 44, 82nd Congress, first session, Chapter 120, approved June 2, 1951.)

Sec. 4. All lands, lease-holds, timber, and other products of land, before being offered, shall be appraised at their true value, and no sale or other disposal thereof shall be made for a consideration less than the value so ascertained, nor in any case less than the minimum price hereinafter fixed, nor upon credit unless accompanied by ample security, and the legal title shall not be deemed to have passed until the consideration shall have been paid.

Sec. 5. No lands shall be sold for less than three dollars per acre, and no lands which are or shall be susceptible of irrigation under any projects now or hereafter completed or adopted by the United States under legislation for the reclamation of lands, or under any other project for the reclamation of lands, shall be sold at less than twenty-five dollars per acre; Provided, that the State, at the request of the Secretary of the Interior, shall from time to time relinquish such of its lands to the United States as at any time are needed for irrigation works in connection with any such Government project, and other lands in lieu thereof shall be selected from lands of the character named and in the manner prescribed in Section Twenty-four of the said Enabling Act.

Sec. 6. No lands reserved and excepted of the lands granted to this State by the United States, actually or prospectively valuable for the development of water powers or power for hydro-electric use or transmission, which shall be ascertained and designated by the Secretary of the Interior within five years after the proclamation of the President declaring the admission of the State, shall be subject to any disposition whatsoever by the State or by any officer of the State, and any conveyance or transfer of such lands made within said five years shall be null and void.

Sec. 7. A separate fund shall be established for each of the several objects for which the said grants are made and confirmed by the said Enabling Act to the State, and whenever any moneys shall be in any manner derived from any of said lands, the same shall be deposited by the State Treasurer in the fund corresponding to the grant under which the particular land producing such moneys was, by said Enabling Act, conveyed or confirmed. No moneys shall ever be taken from one fund for deposit in any other, or for any object other than that for which the land producing the same was granted or confirmed. The State Treasurer shall keep all such moneys invested in safe, interest-bearing securities, which securities shall be approved by the Governor and Secretary of State, and shall at all times be under a good and sufficient bond or bonds conditioned for the faithful performance of his duties in regard thereto.

Sec. 8. Every sale, lease, conveyance, or contract of or concerning any of the lands granted or confirmed, or the use thereof or the natural products thereof made to this State by the said Enabling Act, not made in substantial conformity with the provisions thereof, shall be null and void.

Sec. 9. All lands expressly transferred and confirmed to the State, by the provisions of the Enabling Act approved June 20, 1910, including all lands granted to the State, and all lands heretofore granted to the Territory of Arizona, and all lands otherwise acquired by the State, may be sold or leased by the State in the manner, and on the conditions, and with the limitations, prescribed by the said Enabling Act and this Constitution, and as may be further prescribed by law; Provided, that the Legislature shall provide for the separate appraisement of the lands and of the improvements on school and university lands which have been held under lease prior to the adoption of this Constitution, and for reimbursement to the actual bona fide residents or lessees of such lands upon which such improvements are situated, as prescribed by Title 65, Civil Code of Arizona, 1901, and in such cases only as permit reimbursements to lessees in said Title 65.

Sec. 10. The legislature shall provide by proper laws for the sale of all state lands or the lease of such lands, and shall further provide by said laws for the protection of the actual bona fide residents and lessees of said lands, whereby such residents and lessees of said lands shall be protected in their rights to their improvements (including water rights) in such manner that in case of lease to other parties the former lessee shall be paid by the succeeding lessee the value of such improvements and rights and actual bona fide residents and lessees shall have preference to a renewal of their leases at a reassessed rental to be fixed as provided by law. (Amendment initiated by the people; approved at regular election November 5, 1918; effective December 5, 1918.)

Sec. 11. No individual, corporation or association shall be allowed to purchase more than one hundred sixty (160) acres of agricultural land or more than six hundred forty (640) acres of grazing land. (Amendment initiated by the people; approved at regular election November 5, 1918; effective December 5, 1918.)

ARTICLE XI.

EDUCATION.

Sec. 1. The Legislature shall enact such laws as shall provide for the establishment and maintenance of a general and uniform public school system, which system shall include kindergarten schools, common schools, high schools, normal schools, industrial schools, and a university (which shall include an agricultural college, a school of mines, and such other technical schools as may be essential, until such time as it may be deemed advisable to establish separate State institutions of such character.) The Legislature shall also enact such laws as shall provide for the education and care of the deaf, dumb, and blind.

Sec. 2. The general conduct and supervision of the public school system shall be vested in a State Board of Education, a State Superintendent of Public Instruction, county school superintendents, and such governing boards for the State institutions as may be provided by law.

Sec. 3. The State Board of Education shall be composed of the following members: the Superintendent of Public Instruction, the President of a State University or a State College, three lay members, a member of the State Junior College Board, a superintendent of a high school district, a classroom teacher and a county school superintendent. Each member, other than the Superintendent of Public Instruction, to be appointed by the Governor with the consent of the Senate. The powers, duties, compensation and expenses, and the terms of office of the Board shall be such as may be prescribed by law. (Amendment referred by the Legislature; approved at regular election November 3, 1964; effective December 3, 1964.)

Sec. 4. The State Superintendent of Public Instruction shall be a member, and secretary, of the State Board of Education, and, ex-officio, a member of any other board having control of public instruction in any State institution. His powers and duties shall be prescribed by law.

Sec. 5. The regents of the University, and the governing boards of other State educational institutions, shall be appointed by the Governor, except that the Governor shall be, ex-officio, a member of the board of regents of the University.

Sec. 6. The University and all other State educational institutions shall be open to students of both sexes, and the instruction furnished shall be as nearly free as possible.

The Legislature shall provide for a system of common schools by which a free school shall be established and maintained in every school district for at least six months in each year, which school shall be open to all pupils between the ages of six and twenty-one years.

Sec. 7. No sectarian instruction shall be imparted in any school or State educational institution that may be established under this Constitution, and no religious or political test or qualification shall ever be required as a condition of admission into any public educational institution of the State, as teacher, student, or pupil; but the liberty of conscience hereby secured shall not be so construed as to justify practices or conduct inconsistent with the good order, peace, morality, or safety of the State, or with the rights of others.

Sec. 8. A permanent State school fund for the use of the common schools shall be derived from the sale of public school lands or other public lands specified in the Enabling Act approved June 20, 1910; from all estates or distributive shares of estates that may escheat to the State; from all unclaimed shares and dividends of any corporation incorporated under the laws of Arizona; and from all gifts, devises, or bequests made to the State for general educational purposes.

The income derived from the investment of the permanent State school fund, and from the rental derived from school lands, with such other funds as may be provided by law shall be apportioned only for common and high school education in Arizona, and in such manner as may be prescribed by law. (Amendment initiated by the people; approved at regular election November 3, 1964; effective December 3, 1964.)

Sec. 9. The amount of this apportionment shall become a part of the county school fund, and the Legislature shall enact such laws as will provide for increasing the county fund sufficiently to maintain all the public schools of the county for a minimum term of six months in every school year. The laws of the State shall enable cities and towns to maintain free high schools, industrial schools, and commercial schools.

Sec. 10. The revenue for the maintenance of the respective State educational institutions shall be derived from the investment of the proceeds of the sale, and from the rental of such lands as have been set aside by the Enabling Act approved June 20, 1910, or other legislative enactment of the United States, for the use and benefit of the respective State educational institutions. In addition to such income the Legislature shall make such appropriations, to be met by taxation, as shall insure the proper maintenance of all State educational institutions, and shall make such special appropriations as shall provide for their development and improvement.

ARTICLE XII.

COUNTIES.

Sec. 1. Each county of the State, now or hereafter organized, shall be a body politic and corporate.

Sec. 2. The several counties of the Territory of Arizona as fixed by statute at the time of the adoption of this Constitution are hereby declared to be the counties of the State until changed by law.

Sec. 3. There are hereby created in and for each organized County of the State the following officers who shall be elected by the qualified electors thereof: a Sheriff, a County Attorney, a Recorder, a Treasurer, an Assessor, a Superintendent of Schools and at least three Supervisors, each of whom shall be elected and hold his office for a term of four (4) years beginning on the first of January next after his election, which number of Supervisors is subject to increase by law. The Supervisors shall be nominated and elected from districts as provided by law.

The candidates for these offices elected in the general election of November 3, 1964 shall take office on the first day of January, 1965 and shall serve until the first day of January, 1969. (Amendment initiated by the people; approved at regular election November 3, 1964; effective December 3, 1964.)

Sec. 4. The duties, powers, and qualifications of such officers shall be as prescribed by law. The Board of Supervisors of each county is hereby empowered to fix salaries for all county and precinct officers within such county for whom no compensation is provided by law, and the salaries so fixed shall remain in full force and effect until changed by general law.

ARTICLE XIII.

MUNICIPAL CORPORATIONS.

Sec. 1. Municipal corporations shall not be created by special laws, but the Legislature, by general laws, shall provide for the incorporation and organization of cities and towns and for the classification of such cities and towns in proportion to population, subject to the provisions of this Article.

Sec. 2. Any city containing, now or hereafter, a population of more than three thousand five hundred may frame a charter for its own government consistent with, and subject to, the Constitution and the laws of the State, in the following manner: A board of freeholders composed of fourteen qualified electors of said city may be elected at large by the qualified electors thereof, at a general or special election, whose duty it shall be, within ninety days after such election, to prepare and propose a charter for such city. Such proposed charter shall be signed in duplicate by the members of such board, or a majority of them, and filed, one copy of said proposed charter with the chief executive officer of such city and the other with the county recorder of the county in which said city shall be situated. Such proposed charter shall then be published in one or more newspapers published, and of general circulation, within said city for at least twenty-one days if in a daily paper, or in three consecutive issues if in a weekly paper, and the first publication shall be made within twenty days after the completion of the proposed charter. Within thirty days, and not earlier than twenty days, after such publication, said proposed charter shall be submitted to the vote of the qualified electors of said city at a general or special election. If a majority of such qualified electors voting thereon shall ratify such proposed charter, it shall thereupon be submitted to the Governor for his approval, and the Governor shall approve it if it shall not be in conflict with this Constitution or with the laws of the State. Upon such approval said charter shall become the organic law of such city and supersede any charter then existing (and all amendments thereto), and all ordinances inconsistent with said new charter. A copy of such charter, certified by the chief executive officer, and authenticated by the seal, of such city, together with a statement similarly certified and authenticated setting forth the submission of such charter to the electors and its ratification by them, shall, after the approval of such charter by the Governor, be made in duplicate and filed, one copy in the office of the Secretary of State and the other in the archives of the city after being recorded in the office of said County Recorder. Thereafter all courts shall take judicial notice of said charter.

The charter so ratified may be amended by amendments proposed and submitted by the legislative authority of the city to the qualified electors thereof (or by petition as hereinafter provided), at a general or special election, and ratified by a majority of the qualified electors voting thereon and approved by the Governor as herein provided for the approval of the charter.

Sec. 3. An election of such board of freeholders may be called at any time by the legislative authority of any such city. Such election shall be called by the chief executive officer of any such city within ten days after there shall have been filed with him a petition demanding such election, signed by a number of qualified electors residing within such city equal to twenty-five per centum of the total number of votes cast at the next preceding general municipal election. Such election shall be held not later than thirty days after the call therefor. At such election a vote shall be taken upon the question whether further proceedings toward adopting a charter shall be had in pursuance to the call, and unless a majority of the qualified electors voting thereon shall vote to proceed further, no further proceedings shall be had, and all proceedings up to the time of said election shall be of no effect.

Sec. 4. No municipal corporation shall ever grant, extend, or renew a franchise without the approval of a majority of the qualified electors residing within its corporate limits who shall vote thereon at a general or special election, and the legislative body of any such corporation shall submit any such matter for approval or disapproval to such electors at any general municipal election, or call a special election for such purpose at any time upon thirty days' notice. No franchise shall be granted, extended, or renewed for a longer time than twenty-five years.

Sec. 5. Every municipal corporation within this State shall have the right to engage in any business or enterprise which may be engaged in by a person, firm, or corporation by virtue of a franchise from said municipal corporation.

Sec. 6. No grant, extension, or renewal of any franchise or other use of the streets, alleys, or other public grounds, or ways, of any municipality shall divest the State or any of its subdivisions of its or their control and regulation of such use and enjoyment; nor shall the power to regulate charges for public services be surrendered; and no exclusive franchise shall ever be granted.

Sec. 7. Irrigation, power, electrical, agricultural improvement, drainage, and flood control districts, and tax levying public improvement districts, now or hereafter organized pursuant to law, shall be political subdivisions of the State, and vested with all the rights, privileges and benefits, and entitled to the immunities and exemptions granted municipalities and political subdivisions under this Constitution or any law of the State or of the United States; but all such districts shall be exempt from the provisions of sections 7 and 8 of Article IX of this Constitution. (Initiated by the people; approved at regular election November 5, 1940; effective November 27, 1940.)

ARTICLE XIV.

CORPORATIONS OTHER THAN MUNICIPAL.

Sec. 1. The term "corporation," as used in this Article, shall be construed to include all associations and joint stock companies having any powers or privileges of corporations not possessed by individuals or co-partnerships, and all corporations shall have the right to sue and shall be subject to be sued, in all courts, in like cases as natural persons.

Sec. 2. Corporations may be formed under general laws, but shall not be created by special Acts. Laws relating to corporations may be altered, amended, or repealed at any time, and all corporations doing business in this State may, as to such business, be regulated, limited, and restrained by law.

Sec. 3. All existing charters under which a bona fide organization shall not have taken place and business commenced in good faith within six months from the time of the approval of this Constitution shall thereafter have no validity.

Sec. 4. No corporation shall engage in any business other than that expressly authorized in its charter or by the law under which it may have been or may hereafter be organized.

Sec. 5. No corporation organized outside of the limits of this State shall be allowed to transact business within this State on more favorable conditions than are prescribed by law for similar corporations organized under the laws of this State; and no foreign corporation shall be permitted to transact business within this State unless said foreign corporation is by the laws of the country, state, or territory under which it is formed permitted to transact a like business in such country, state, or territory.

Sec. 6. No corporation shall issue stock, except to bona fide subscribers therefor or their assignees; nor shall any corporation issue any bond, or other obligation, for the payment of money, except for money or property received or for labor done. The stock of corporations shall not be increased, except in pursuance of a general law, nor shall any law authorize the increase of stock of any corporation without the consent of the person or persons holding the larger amount in value of the stock of such corporation, nor without due notice of the proposed increase having been given as may be prescribed by law. All fictitious increase of stock or indebtedness shall be void.

Sec. 7. No corporation shall lease or alienate any franchise so as to relieve the franchise, or property held thereunder, from the liabilities of the lessor, or grantor, lessee, or grantee, contracted or incurred in the operation, use, or enjoyment of such franchise or of any of its privileges.

Sec. 8. No domestic or foreign corporation shall do any business in this State without having filed its articles of incorporation or a certified copy thereof with the Corporation Commission, and without having one or more known places of business and an authorized agent, or agents, in the State upon whom process may be served. Suit may be maintained against a foreign corporation in the county where an agent of such corporation may be found, or in the county where the cause of action may arise.

Sec. 9. The right of exercising eminent domain shall never be so abridged or construed as to prevent the State from taking the property and the franchises of incorporated companies and subjecting them to public use the same as the property of individuals.

Sec. 10. In all elections for directors or managers of any corporation, each shareholder shall have the right to cast as many votes in the aggregate as he shall be entitled to vote in said company under its charter multiplied by the number of directors or managers to be elected at such election; and each shareholder may cast the whole number of votes, either in person or by proxy, for one candidate, or distribute such votes among two or more such candidates; and such directors or managers shall not be elected otherwise.

Sec. 11. **Liability of stockholders.** The shareholders or stockholders of every banking or insurance corporation or association shall be held individually responsible, equally and ratably, and not one for another, for all contracts, debts, and engagements of such corporation or association, to the extent of the amount of their stock therein, at the par value thereof, in addition to the amount invested in such shares or stock; provided, however, that the shareholders or stockholders of any banking corporation or association which is a member of the federal deposit insurance corporation or any successor thereto or other insuring instrumentality of the United States in accordance with the provisions of any applicable law of the United States of America, shall not be liable for any amount in addition to the amount already invested in such shares or stock.

Sec. 12. Any president, director, manager, cashier, or other officer of any banking institution who shall receive, or assent to, the reception of any deposits after he shall have knowledge of the fact that such banking institution is insolvent or in failing circumstances shall be individually responsible for such deposits.

Sec. 13. No persons acting as a corporation under the laws of Arizona shall be permitted to set up, or rely upon, the want of a legal organization as a defense to any action which may be brought against them as a corporation, nor shall any person or persons who may be sued on a contract now or hereafter made with such corporation, or sued for any injury now or hereafter done to its property, or for a wrong done to its interests, be permitted to rely upon such want of legal organization in his or their defense.

Sec. 14. This Article shall not be construed to deny the right of the legislative power to impose other conditions upon corporations than those herein contained.

Sec. 15. Monopolies and trusts shall never be allowed in this State and no incorporated company, co-partnership or association of persons in this State shall directly or indirectly combine or make any contract, with any incorporated company, foreign or domestic, through their stockholders or the trustees or assigns of such stockholders or with any co-partnership or association of persons, or, in any manner whatever, to fix the prices, limit the production, or regulate the transportation of any product or commodity. The Legislature shall enact laws for the enforcement of this Section by adequate penalties, and in the case of incorporated companies, if necessary for that purpose, may, as a penalty declare a forfeiture of their franchises.

Sec. 16. The records, books, and files of all public service corporations, State banks, building and loan associations, trust, insurance, and guaranty companies shall be at all times liable and subject to the full visitorial and inquisitorial powers of the State, notwithstanding the immunities and privileges secured in the Declaration of Rights of this Constitution to persons, inhabitants, and citizens of this State.

Sec. 17. Provisions shall be made by law for the payment of a fee to the State by every domestic corporation, upon the grant, amendment, or extension of its charter, and by every foreign corporation upon its obtaining a license to do business in this State; and also for the payment, by every domestic corporation and foreign corporation doing business in this State, of an annual registration fee of not less than ten dollars, which fee shall be paid irrespective of any specific license or other tax imposed by law upon such company for the privilege of carrying on its business in this State, or upon its franchise or property; and for the making, by every such corporation, at the time of paying such fee, of such report to the Corporation Commission of the status, business, or condition of such corporation, as may be prescribed by law. No foreign corporation, except insurers, shall have authority to do business in this State, until it shall have obtained from the Corporation Commission a license to do business in the State, upon such terms as may be prescribed by law. The Legislature may relieve any purely charitable, social, fraternal, benevolent, or religious institution from the payment of such annual registration fee. (Amendment referred by the Legislature; approved at regular election November 5, 1968; effective January 28, 1968.)

Sec. 18. It shall be unlawful for any corporation, organized or doing business in this State, to make any contribution of money or anything of value for the purpose of influencing any election or official action.

Sec. 19. Suitable penalties shall be prescribed by law for the violation of any of the provisions of this Article.

ARTICLE XV.

THE CORPORATION COMMISSION.

Sec. 1. A Corporation Commission is hereby created to be composed of three persons, who shall be elected at the general election to be held under the provisions of the Enabling Act approved June 20, 1910, and whose term of office shall be co-terminous with that of the Governor of the State elected at the same time, and who shall maintain their chief office, and reside, at the State Capital. At the first general State election held under this Constitution at which a Governor is voted for, three commissioners shall be elected who shall, from and after the first Monday in January next succeeding said election, hold office as follows:

The one receiving the highest number of votes shall serve six years, and the one receiving the second highest number of votes shall serve four years, and the one receiving the third highest number of votes shall serve two years. And one commissioner shall be elected every two years thereafter. In case of vacancy in said office, the Governor shall appoint a commissioner to fill such vacancy. Such appointed commissioner shall fill such vacancy until a commissioner shall be elected at a general election as provided by law, and shall qualify. The qualifications of commissioners may be prescribed by law.

Sec. 2. All corporations other than municipal engaged in carrying persons or property for hire; or in furnishing gas, oil, or electricity for light, fuel, or power; or in furnishing water for irrigation, fire protection, or other public purposes; or in furnishing, for profit, hot or cold air or steam for heating or cooling purposes; or in transmitting messages or furnishing public telegraph or telephone service, and all corporations other than municipal, operating as common carriers, shall be deemed public service corporations.

Sec. 3. The Corporation Commission shall have full power to, and shall, prescribe just and reasonable classifications to be used and just and reasonable rates and charges to be made and collected, by public service corporations within the State for service rendered therein, and make reasonable rules, regulations, and orders, by which such corporations shall be governed in the transaction of business within the State, and may prescribe the forms of contracts and the systems of keeping accounts to be used by such corporations in transacting such business, and make and enforce reasonable rules, regulations, and orders for the convenience, comfort, and safety, and the preservation of the health, of the employees and patrons of such corporations; Provided, that incorporated cities and towns may be authorized by law to exercise supervision over public service corporations doing business therein, including the regulation of rates and charges to be made and collected by such corporations; Provided further, that classifications, rates, charges, rules, regulations, orders, and forms or systems prescribed or made by said Corporation Commission may from time to time be amended or repealed by such Commission.

Sec. 4. The Corporation Commission, and the several members thereof, shall have power to inspect and investigate the property, books, papers, business, methods, and affairs of any corporation whose stock shall be offered for sale to the public and of any public service corporation doing business within the State, and for the purpose of the Commission, and of the several members thereof, shall have the power of a court of general jurisdiction to enforce the attendance of witnesses and the production of evidence by subpoena, attachment, and punishment, which said power shall extend throughout the State. Said Commission shall have power to take testimony under commission or deposition either within or without the State.

Sec. 5. The Corporation Commission shall have the sole power to issue certificates of incorporation to companies organizing under the laws of this State, and to issue licenses to foreign corporations to do business in this State, except as insurers, as may be prescribed by law.

Domestic and foreign insurers shall be subject to licensing, control and supervision by a department of insurance as prescribed by law. A director of the department of insurance shall be appointed by the governor subject to approval by the senate for a term which may be prescribed by law. (Amendment referred by the Legislature; approved at regular election November 5, 1968; effective January 28, 1968.)

Sec. 6. The law-making power may enlarge the powers and extend the duties of the Corporation Commission, and may prescribe rules and regulations to govern proceedings instituted by and before it; but, until such rules and regulations are provided by law, the Commission may make rules and regulations to govern such proceedings.

Sec. 7. Every public service corporation organized or authorized under the laws of the State to do any transportation or transmission business within the State shall have the right to construct and operate lines connecting any points within the State, and to connect at the State boundaries with like lines; and every such corporation shall have the right with any of its lines to cross, intersect, or connect with, any lines of any other public service corporation.

Sec. 8. Every public service corporation doing a transportation business within the State shall receive and transport, without delay or discrimination, cars loaded or empty, property, or passengers delivered to it by any other public service corporation doing a similar business, and deliver cars, loaded or empty, without delay or discrimination, to other transportation corporations, under such regulations as shall be prescribed by the Corporation Commission, or by law.

Sec. 9. Every public service corporation engaged in the business of transmitting messages for profit shall receive and transmit, without delay or discrimination, any messages delivered to it by any other public service corporation engaged in the business of transmitting messages for profit, and shall, with its lines, make physical connection with the lines of any public service corporation engaged in the business of transmitting messages for profit, under such rules and regulations as shall be prescribed by the Corporation Commission, or by law; Provided, that such public service corporations shall deliver messages to other such corporations, without delay or discrimination, under such rules and regulations as shall be prescribed by the Corporation Commission, or by law.

Sec. 10. Railways heretofore constructed, or that may hereafter be constructed, in this State, are hereby declared public highways, and all railroad, car, express, electric, transmission, telegraph, telephone, or pipeline corporations, for the transportation of persons, or of electricity, messages, water, oil, or other property for profit, are declared to be common carriers and subject to control by law.

Sec. 11. The rolling stock and all other movable property belonging to any public service corporation in this State, shall be considered personal property, and its real and personal property, and every part thereof, shall be liable to attachment, execution, and sale in the same manner as the property of individuals; and the law-making power shall enact no laws exempting any such property from attachment, execution, or sale.

Sec. 12. All charges made for service rendered, or to be rendered, by public service corporations within this State shall be just and reasonable, and no discrimination in charges, service, or facilities shall be made between persons or places for rendering a like and contemporaneous service, except that the granting of free or reduced rate transportation may be authorized by law, or by the Corporation Commission, to the classes of persons described in the Act of Congress approved February 11, 1887, entitled An Act to Regulate Commerce, and the amendments thereto, as those to whom free or reduced rate transportation may be granted.

Sec. 13. All public service corporations and corporations whose stock shall be offered for sale to the public shall make such reports to the Corporation Commission, under oath, and provide such information concerning their acts and operations as may be required by law, or by the Corporation Commission.

Sec. 14. The Corporation Commission shall, to aid it in the proper discharge of its duties, ascertain the fair value of the property within the State of every public service corporation doing business therein; and every public service corporation doing business within the State shall furnish to the Commission all evidence in its possession, and all assistance in its power, requested by the Commission in aid of the determination of the value of the property within the State of such public service corporation.

Sec. 15. No public service corporation in existence at the time of the admission of this State into the Union shall have the benefit of any future legislation except on condition of complete acceptance of all provisions of this Constitution applicable to public service corporations.

Sec. 16. If any public service corporation shall violate any of the rules, regulations, orders, or decisions of the Corporation Commission, such corporation shall forfeit and pay to the State not less than one hundred dollars nor more than five thousand dollars for each such violation, to be recovered before any court of competent jurisdiction.

Sec. 17. Nothing herein shall be construed as

denying to public service corporations the right of appeal to the courts of the State from the rules, regulations, orders, or decrees fixed by the Corporation Commission, but the rules, regulations, orders, or decrees so fixed shall remain in force pending the decision of the courts.

Sec. 18. Relating to salaries of the Corporation Commissioners, is repealed. (Amendment referred by the Legislature; approved at regular election Nov. 3, 1970; effective Nov. 27, 1970.)

Sec. 19. The Corporation Commission shall have the power and authority to enforce its rules, regulations, and orders by the imposition of such fines as it may deem just, within the limitations prescribed in Sec. 16 of this Article.

ARTICLE XVI.

MILITIA.

Sec. 1. The militia of the State of Arizona shall consist of all able-bodied male citizens of the State between the ages of eighteen and forty-five years, and of those between said ages who shall have declared their intention to become citizens of the United States, residing therein, subject to such exemptions as now exist, or as may hereafter be created, by the laws of the United States or of this State.

Sec. 2. The organized militia shall be designated "The National Guard of Arizona," and shall consist of such organized military bodies as now exist under the laws of the Territory of Arizona or as may hereafter be authorized by law.

Sec. 3. The organization, equipment, and discipline of the National Guard shall conform as nearly as shall be practicable to the regulations for the government of the armies of the United States.

ARTICLE XVII.

WATER RIGHTS.

Sec. 1. The common law doctrine of riparian water rights shall not obtain or be of any force or effect in the State.

Sec. 2. All existing rights to the use of any of the waters in the State for all useful or beneficial purposes are hereby recognized and confirmed.

ARTICLE XVIII.

LABOR.

Sec. 1. Eight hours and no more, shall constitute a lawful day's work in all employment by, or on behalf of, the State or any political subdivision of the State. The Legislature shall enact such laws as may be necessary to put this provision into effect, and shall prescribe proper penalties for any violations of said laws.

Sec. 2. No child under the age of fourteen years shall be employed in any gainful occupation at any time during the hours in which the public schools of the district in which the child resides are in session; nor shall any child under sixteen years of age be employed underground in mines, or in any occupation injurious to health or morals or hazardous to life or limb; nor for more than eight hours in any day.

(Amendment referred by the Legislature; approved at regular election Nov. 7, 1972; effective Dec. 1, 1972.)

Sec. 3. It shall be unlawful for any person, company, association, or corporation to require of its servants or employees as a condition of their employment, or otherwise, any contract or agreement whereby such person, company, association, or corporation shall be released or discharged from liability or responsibility on account of personal injuries which may be received by such servants or employees while in the service or employment of such person, company, association, or corporation, by reason of the negligence of such person, company, association, corporation, or the agents or employees thereof; and any such contract or agreement if made, shall be null and void.

Sec. 4. The common law doctrine of fellow servant, so far as it affects the liability of a master for injuries to his servant resulting from the acts or omissions of any other servant or servants of the common master is forever abrogated.

Sec. 5. The defense of contributory negligence or of assumption of risk shall, in all cases whatsoever, be a question of fact and shall, at all times, be left to the jury.

Sec. 6. The right of action to recover damages for injuries shall never be abrogated, and the amount recovered shall not be subject to any statutory limitation.

Sec. 7. To protect the safety of employees in all hazardous occupations, in mining, smelting, manufacturing, railroad or street railway transportation, or any other industry the Legislature shall enact an Employer's Liability law, by the terms of which any employer, whether individual, association, or corporation shall be liable for the death or injury, caused by any accident due to a condition or conditions of such occupation, of any employee in the service of such employer in such hazardous occupation, in all cases in which such death or injury of such employee shall not have been caused by the negligence of the employee killed or injured.

Sec. 8. The Legislature shall enact a Workmen's Compensation Law applicable to workmen engaged in manual or mechanical labor in all public employment whether of the State, or any political sub-division or municipality thereof as may be defined by law and in such private employments as the Legislature may prescribe by which compensation shall be required to be paid to any such workman, in case of his injury and to his dependents, as defined by law, in case of his death, by his employer, if in the course of such employment personal injury to or death of any such workman from any accident arising out of and in the course of, such employment, is caused in whole, or in part, or is contributed to, by a necessary risk or danger of such employment, or a necessary risk or danger inherent in the nature thereof, or by failure of such employer, or any of his or its agents or employee or employees to exercise due care, or to comply with any law affecting such employment; provided that it shall be optional with any employee engaged in any such private employment to settle for such compensation, or to retain the right to sue said employer as provided by this Constitution; and, provided further, in order to assure and make certain a just and humane compensation law in the State of Arizona, for the relief and protection of such workmen, their widows, children or dependents, as defined by law, from the burdensome, expensive and litigious remedies for injuries to or death of such workmen, now existing in the State of Arizona, and producing uncertain and unequal compensation therefor, such employee, engaged in such private employment, may exercise the option to settle for compensation by failing to reject the provisions of such Workmen's Compensation Law prior to the injury.

The percentages and amounts of compensation provided in House Bill No. 227 enacted by the Seventh Legislature of the State of Arizona, shall never be reduced nor any industry included within the provision of said House Bill No. 227 eliminated except by initiated or referred measure as provided by this Constitution. (Amendment referred by the Legislature; approved at special election September 29, 1925; effective November 2, 1925.)

Sec. 9. The exchange, solicitation, or giving out of any labor "black list," is hereby prohibited, and suitable laws shall be enacted to put this provision into effect.

Sec. 10. No person not a citizen or ward of the United States shall be employed upon or in connection with any state, county or municipal works or employment; provided, that nothing herein shall be construed to prevent the working of prisoners by the state or by any county or municipality thereof on street or road work or other public work and that the provisions of this section shall not apply to the employment of any teacher, instructor, or professor authorized to teach in the United States under the teacher exchange program as provided by federal statutes enacted by the Congress of the United States or the employment of university or college faculty members. The legislature shall enact laws for the enforcement and shall provide for the punishment of any violation of this section.

(Referred to the People by the Legislature. As Amended General Election November 8, 1960. Effective date December 9, 1960.)

ARTICLE XIX.

MINES.

The office of Mine Inspector is hereby established. The Legislature, at its first session, shall enact laws so regulating the operation and equipment of all mines in the State as to provide for the health and safety of workers therein and in connection therewith, and fixing the duties of said office. Upon approval of such laws by the Governor, the Governor, with the advice and consent of the Senate, shall forthwith appoint a Mine Inspector, who shall serve until his successor shall have been elected at the first general election thereafter and shall qualify. Said successor and all subsequent incumbents of said office shall be elected at general elections, and shall serve for two years.

ARTICLE XX.

ORDINANCE.

The following ordinance shall be irrevocable without the consent of the United States and the people of this State:

First. Perfect toleration of religious sentiment shall be secured to every inhabitant of this State, and no inhabitant of this State shall ever be molested in person or property on account of his or her mode of religious worship, or lack of the same.

Second. Polygamous or plural marriages, or polygamous co-habitation, are forever prohibited within this State.

Third. The introduction of intoxicating liquors for resale purposes into Indian country is prohibited within this State until July 1, 1957. (Amendment referred by the Legislature; approved at regular election November 2, 1954; effective November 23, 1954.)

Fourth. The people inhabiting this State do agree and declare that they forever disclaim all right and title to the unappropriated and ungranted public lands lying within the boundaries thereof and to all lands lying within said boundaries owned or held by any Indian or Indian tribes, the right or title to which shall have been acquired through or from the United States or any prior sovereignty, and that, until the title of such Indian or Indian tribes shall have been extinguished, the same shall be, and remain, subject to the disposition and under the absolute jurisdiction and control of the Congress of the United States.

Fifth. The lands and other property belonging to citizens of the United States residing without this State shall never be taxed at a higher rate than the lands and other property situated in this State belonging to residents thereof, and no taxes shall be imposed by this State on any lands or other property within an Indian Reservation owned or held by any Indian; but nothing herein shall preclude the State from taxing as other lands and other property are taxed, any lands and other property outside of an Indian Reservation owned or held by any Indian, save and except such lands as have been granted or acquired as aforesaid, or as may be granted or confirmed to any Indian or Indians under any act of Congress. (Amendment referred by the Legislature; approved at special election May 31, 1927; effective June 27, 1927.)

Sixth. The debts and liabilities of the Territory of Arizona, and the debts of the counties thereof, valid and subsisting at the time of the passage of the Enabling Act approved June 20, 1910, are hereby assumed and shall be paid by the State of Arizona, and the State of Arizona shall, as to all such debts and liabilities, be subrogated to all the rights, including rights of indemnity and reimbursement, existing in favor of said Territory or of any of the several counties thereof, at the time of the passage of the said Enabling Act: Provided, that nothing in this ordinance shall be construed as validating or in any manner legalizing any Territorial, county, municipal, or other bonds, obligations, or evidences of indebtedness of said Territory or the counties or municipalities thereof which now are or may be invalid or illegal at the time the said State of Arizona is admitted as a State, and the Legislature or the people of the State of Arizona shall never pass any law in any manner validating or legalizing the same.

Seventh. Provisions shall be made by law for the establishment and maintenance of a system of public schools which shall be open to all the children of the State and be free from sectarian control, and said schools shall always be conducted in English.

The State shall never enact any law restricting or abridging the right of suffrage on account of race, color, or previous condition of servitude.

Eighth. The ability to read, write, speak, and understand the English language sufficiently well to conduct the duties of the office without the aid of an interpreter, shall be a necessary qualification for all State officers and members of the State Legislature.

Ninth. The capital of the State of Arizona, until changed by the electors voting at an election provided for by the Legislature for that purpose shall be at the City of Phoenix, but no such election shall be called or provided for prior to the thirty-first day of December, nineteen hundred and twenty-five.

Tenth. Repealed.

Eleventh. Repealed.

Twelfth. The State of Arizona and its people hereby consent to all and singular the provisions of the Enabling Act approved June 20, 1910, concerning the lands thereby granted or confirmed to the State, the terms and conditions upon which said grants and confirmations are made, and the means and manner of enforcing such terms and conditions, all in every respect and particular as in the aforesaid Enabling Act provided.

Thirteenth. This ordinance is hereby made a part of the Constitution of the State of Arizona, and no future Constitutional amendment shall be made which in any manner changes or abrogates this ordinance in whole or in part without the consent of Congress.

ARTICLE XXI.

MODE OF AMENDING.

Sec. 1. Any amendment or amendments to this Constitution may be proposed in either House of the Legislature, or by Initiative Petition signed by a number of qualified electors equal to fifteen per centum of the total number of votes for all candidates for Governor at the last preceding general election. (See section 19-123 Arizona Revised Statutes.)

Any proposed amendment or amendments which shall be introduced in either House of the Legislature, and which shall be approved by a majority of the members elected to each of the two Houses, shall be entered on the journal of each House, together with the ayes and nayes thereon. When any proposed amendment or amendments shall be thus passed by a majority of each House of the Legislature and entered on the respective journals thereof, or when any elector or electors shall file with the Secretary of State any proposed amendment or amendments together with a petition therefor signed by a number of electors equal to fifteen per centum of the total number of votes for all candidates for Governor in the last preceding general election, the Secretary of State shall submit such proposed amendment or amendments to the vote of the people at the next general election (except when the Legislature shall call a special election for the purpose of having said proposed amendment or amendments voted upon, in which case the Secretary of State shall submit such proposed amendment or amendments to the qualified electors at said special election,) and if a majority of the qualified electors voting thereon shall approve and ratify such proposed amendment or amendments in said regular or special election, such amendment or amendments shall become a part of this Constitution. Until a method of publicity is otherwise provided by law, the Secretary of State shall have such proposed amendment or amendments published for a period of at least ninety days previous to the date of said election in at least one newspaper in every county of the State in which a newspaper shall be published, in such manner as may be prescribed by law. If more than one proposed amendment shall be submitted at any election, such proposed amendments shall be submitted in such manner that the electors may vote for or against such proposed amendments separately.

Sec. 2. No Convention shall be called by the Legislature to propose alterations, revisions, or amendments to this Constitution, or to propose a new Constitution, unless laws providing for such Convention shall first be approved by the people on a Referendum vote at a regular or special election, and any amendments, alterations, revisions, or new Constitution proposed by such Convention shall be submitted to the electors of the State at a general or special election and be approved by the majority of the electors voting thereon before the same shall become effective.

ARTICLE XXII.

SCHEDULE AND MISCELLANEOUS.

Sec. 1. No rights, actions, suits, proceedings, contracts, claims, or demands, existing at the time of the admission of this State into the Union, shall be affected by a change in the form of government, from Territorial to State, but all shall continue as if no change had taken place; and all process which may have been issued under the authority of the Territory of Arizona, previous to its admission into the Union, shall be as valid as if issued in the name of the State.

Sec. 2. All laws of the Territory of Arizona now in force, not repugnant to this Constitution, shall remain in force as laws of the State of Arizona until they expire by their own limitations or are altered or repealed by law; Provided, that wherever the word Territory, meaning the Territory of Arizona, appears in said laws, the word State shall be substituted.

Sec. 3. All debts, fines, penalties, and forfeitures which have accrued, or may hereafter accrue, to the Territory of Arizona shall inure to the State of Arizona.

Sec. 4. All recognizances heretofore taken, or which may be taken, before the change from a Territorial to a State government, shall remain valid, and shall pass to and may be prosecuted in the name of the State, and all bonds executed to the Territory of Arizona, or to any county or municipal corporation, or to any officer, or court, in his or its official capacity, shall pass to the State authorities and their successors in office for the uses therein expressed, and may be sued for and recovered accordingly; and all the estate, real, personal, and mixed, and all judgments, decrees, bonds, specialties, choses in action, and claims, demands or debts of whatever description, belonging to the Territory of Arizona, shall inure to and vest in the State of Arizona, and may be sued for and recovered by the State of Arizona in the same manner, and to the same extent, as the same might or could have been by the Territory of Arizona.

Sec. 5. All criminal prosecutions and penal actions which may have arisen, or which may arise, before the change from a Territorial to a State government, and which shall then be pending, shall be prosecuted to judgment and execution in the name of the State. All offenses committed against the laws of the Territory of Arizona before the change from a Territorial to a State government, and which shall not be prosecuted before such change, may be prosecuted in the name, and by the authority, of the State of Arizona, with like effect as though such change had not taken place, and all penalties incurred and punishments inflicted shall remain the same as if this Constitution had not been adopted. All actions at law and suits in equity, which may be pending in any of the courts, of the Territory of Arizona at the time of the change from a Territorial to a State government, shall be continued and transferred to the court of the State, or of the United States, having jurisdiction thereof.

Sec. 6. All Territorial, district, county, and precinct officers who may be in office at the time of the admission of the State into the Union shall hold their respective offices until their successors shall have qualified, and the official bonds of all such officers shall continue in full force and effect while such officers remain in office.

Sec. 7. Whenever the judge of the superior court of any county, elected or appointed under the provisions of this Constitution, shall have qualified, the several causes then pending in the district court of the Territory, and in and for such county, except such causes as would have been within the exclusive jurisdiction of the United States courts, had such courts existed at the time of the commencement of such causes within such county, and the records, papers, and proceedings of said district court, and other property pertaining thereto, shall pass into the jurisdiction and possession of the superior court of such county.

It shall be the duty of the clerk of the district court having custody of such papers, records, and property, to transmit to the clerk of said superior court the original papers in all cases pending in such district and belonging to the jurisdiction of said superior court, together with a transcript, or transcripts, of so much of the record of said district court as shall relate to the same; and until the district courts of the Territory shall be superseded in manner aforesaid, and as in this Constitution provided, the said district courts, and the judges thereof, shall continue with the same jurisdiction and powers, to be exercised in the same judicial district, respectively, as heretofore, and now, constituted.

Sec. 8. When the State is admitted into the Union, and the superior courts, in their respective counties, are organized, the books, records, papers, and proceedings of the probate court in each county, and all causes and matters of administration pending therein, shall pass into the jurisdiction and possession of the superior court of the same county created by this Constitution, and the said court shall proceed to final judgment or decree, order, or other determination, in the several matters and causes with like effect as the probate court might have done if this Constitution had not been adopted.

Sec. 9. Whenever a quorum of the judges of the Supreme Court of the State shall have been elected, and qualified, and shall have taken office, under this Constitution, the causes then pending in the Supreme Court of the Territory, except such causes as would have been within the exclusive jurisdiction of the United States courts, had such courts existed at the time of the commencement of such causes, and the papers, records, and proceedings of said court, and the seal and other property pertaining thereto, shall pass into the jurisdiction and possession of the Supreme Court of the State, and until so superseded, the Supreme Court of the Territory, and the judges thereof, shall continue, with like powers and jurisdiction as if this Constitution had not been adopted, or the State admitted into the Union; and all causes pending in the Supreme Court of the Territory at said time, and which said causes would have been within the exclusive jurisdiction of the United States courts, had such courts existed, at the time of the commencement of such causes, and the papers, records, and proceedings of said court, relating thereto, shall pass into the jurisdiction of the United States courts, all as in the Enabling Act approved June 20, 1910, provided.

Sec. 10. Until otherwise provided by law, the seal now in use in the Supreme Court of the Territory, shall be the seal of the Supreme Court of the State, except that the word "State", shall be substituted for the word "Territory" on said seal. The seal of the superior courts of the several counties of the State, until otherwise provided by law, shall be the vignette of Abraham Lincoln, with the words "Seal of the Superior Court of.................... County, State of Arizona", surrounding the vignette. The seal of municipalities, and of all county officers, in the Territory, shall be the seals of such municipalities and county officers, respectively, under the State, until otherwise provided by law, except that the word "Territory", or "Territory of Arizona", be changed to read "State" or "State of Arizona", where the same may appear on any such seals.

Sec. 11. The provisions of this Constitution shall be in force from the day on which the President of the United States shall issue his proclamation declaring the State of Arizona admitted into the Union.

Sec. 12. One Representative in the Congress of the United States shall be elected from the State at large, and at the same election at which officers shall be elected under the Enabling Act, approved June 20. 1910, and, thereafter, at such times and in such manner as may be prescribed by law. (Congressional representation amended by Act of Congress and this section superseded by statute. See section 16-727 Arizona Revised Statutes.)

Sec. 13. The term of office of every officer to be elected or appointed under this Constitution or the laws of Arizona shall extend until his successor shall be elected and shall qualify.

Sec. 14. Any law which may be enacted by the Legislature under this Constitution may be enacted by the people under the Initiative. Any law which may not be enacted by the Legislature under this Constitution shall not be enacted by the people.

Sec. 15. Reformatory and penal institutions, and institutions for the benefit of the insane, blind, deaf, and mute, and such other institutions as the public good may require, shall be established and supported by the State in such manner as may be prescribed by law.

Sec. 16. It shall be unlawful to confine any minor under the age of eighteen years, accused or convicted of crime, in the same section of any jail or prison in which adult prisoners are confined. Suitable quarters shall be prepared for the confinement of such minors.

Sec. 17. All State and county officers (except notaries public) and all justices of the peace and constables, whose precinct includes a city or town or part thereof, shall be paid fixed and definite salaries, and they shall receive no fees for their own use.

Sec. 18. Relating to the office of the State Examiner, is repealed. (Amendment referred by the Legislature; approved at regular election November 5, 1968; effective December 4, 1968.)

Sec. 19. The Legislature shall enact laws and adopt rules prohibiting the practice of lobbying on the floor of either House of the Legislature, and further regulating the practice of lobbying.

Sec. 20. The seal of the State shall be of the following design: In the background shall be a range of mountains, with the sun rising behind the peaks thereof, and at the right side of the range of mountains there shall be a storage reservoir and a dam, below which in the middle distance are irrigated fields and orchards reaching into the foreground, at the right of which are cattle grazing. To the left in the middle distance on a mountain side is a quartz mill in front of which and in the foreground is a miner standing with pick and shovel. Above this device shall be the motto: "Ditat Deus." In a circular band surrounding the whole device shall be inscribed: "Great Seal of The State of Arizona", with the year of admission of the State into the Union.

Sec. 21. The Legislature shall enact all necessary laws to carry into effect the provisions of this Constitution.

Sec. 22. The judgment of death shall be inflicted by administering lethal gas. The execution shall take place within the limits of the State prison. (Amendment referred by the Legislature; approved at special election October 3, 1933; effective October 28, 1933.)

ARTICLE XXIII.

PROHIBITION.

(Initiated by the people; approved at regular election November 3, 1914; effective December 14, 1914. Repealed by amendment initiated by the people; approved at regular election November 8, 1932.)

ARTICLE XXIV.

PROHIBITION.

(Initiated by the people; approved at regular election November 7, 1916; effective December 8, 1916. Repealed by amendment initiated by the people; effective November 28, 1932.)

ARTICLE XXV.

No person shall be denied the opportunity to obtain or retain employment because of non-membership in a labor organization, nor shall the State or any subdivision thereof, or any corporation, individual or association of any kind enter into any agreement, written or oral, which excludes any person from employment or continuation of employment because of non-membership in a labor organization. (Amendment initiated by the people; approved at regular election November 5, 1946; effective November 25, 1946.)

ARTICLE XXVI.

Sec. 1. Any person holding a valid license as a real estate broker or a real estate salesman regularly issued by the Arizona State Real Estate Department when acting in such capacity as broker or salesman for the parties, or agent for one of the parties to a sale, exchange, or trade, or the renting and leasing of property, shall have the right to draft or fill out and complete, without charge, any and all instruments incident thereto including, but not limited to, preliminary purchase agreements and earnest money receipts, deeds, mortgages, leases, assignments, releases, contracts for sale of realty, and bills of sale. (Amendment initiated by the people; approved at regular election November 6, 1962; effective November 26, 1962.)

Revised: January, 1973

DELEGATES to THE CONSTITUTIONAL CONVENTION of 1910

Baker, Albert C. — Democrat from Maricopa County
Lawyer, Chief Justice of the Territory, 1893-1897,
Justice of the State Supreme Court, 1919-1921

Bolan, John — Democrat from Cochise County
Miner

Bradner, Samuel B. — Democrat from Cochise County
Railroad switchman, Speaker of the House of Representatives,
First State Legislature

Cassidy, Lysander — Democrat from Maricopa County
Lawyer

Cobb, Lamar — Democrat from Graham-Greenlee County
Surveyor and mining engineer, First State Engineer

Coker, E. W. — Democrat from Pinal County
Lawyer

Colter, Fred T. — Democrat from Apache County
Rancher, member of the state legislature, candidate for
governor, served on several state boards and commissions

Connelly, Patrick F. — Democrat from Cochise County
Railroad engineer

Cooper, William F. — Republican from Pima County
Newspaperman, lawyer

Crutchfield, James E. — Democrat from Maricopa County
Methodist minister

Cunniff, Michael G. — Democrat from Yavapai County
Former editor of WORLD'S WORK, *New York, member of the Arizona state legislature*

Cunningham, Donnell L. — Democrat from Cochise County
Justice of the State Supreme Court, 1912-1921

Curtis, Bracey — Republican from Santa Cruz County
Banker, active in chamber of commerce

Doe, Edward M. — Republican from Coconino County
Lawyer, Justice of the Territorial Supreme Court, 1909-1912

Ellinwood, Everett E. — Democrat from Cochise County
United States Attorney for Arizona, 1893-1898, candidate for governor

Feeney, Thomas — Democrat from Cochise County
Machinist

Franklin, Alfred — Democrat from Maricopa County
Lawyer, Justice of the State Supreme Court, 1912-1918

Goldwater, Morris — Democrat from Yavapai County
Vice President of the Convention
Merchant and banker, mayor of Prescott, member of the state legislature

Hunt, George W. P. — Democrat from Gila County
President of the Convention
Businessman, member of the territorial legislature, Governor of Arizona, 1912-1917, 1917-1919, 1923-1929, 1931-1933

Hutchinson, Charles C. — Republican from Coconino County
Cattleman, banker

Ingraham, Fred — Democrat from Yuma County
Lawyer, judge of the superior court

Jacome, Carlos C. — Republican from Pima County
Merchant

Jones, Albert M. — Democrat from Yavapai County
Sheep Rancher

Jones, Francis A. — Democrat from Maricopa County
Railroad traffic expert

Keegan, John J. — Democrat from Gila County
Saloon owner, member of the state fair commission

Kingan, Samuel L. Republican from Pima County
Lawyer

Kinney, Alfred Democrat from Gila County
Businessman, mine owner, member of the state legislature

Langdon, John Republican from Gila County
Master Mechanic for mining company

Lovin, Henry Democrat from Mohave County
Merchant, cattleman, county sheriff

Lynch, Andrew R. Democrat from Graham-Greenlee County
County school superintendent, member of the state legislature

Moeur, Benjamin B. Democrat from Maricopa County
Physician, Governor of Arizona, 1933-1937

Moore, A. A. ("Lank") Democrat from Yavapai County
Rancher, member of the territorial and state legislatures

Morgan, William Democrat from Navajo County
Sheep rancher, member of the territorial legislature

Orme, John P. Democrat from Maricopa County
Farmer, President of the Salt River Valley Water Users' Association

Osborn, Sidney P. Democrat from Maricopa County
Newspaperman, Arizona Secretary of State, 1912-1919,
Governor of Arizona, 1941-1948

Parsons, Andrew F. Democrat from Cochise County
Lawyer

Pusch, George Republican from Pima County
Cattleman

Roberts, Charles M. Democrat from Cochise County
Miner, stockman, banker, member of the state legislature

Scott, James Republican from Navajo County
Cattleman

Short, E. L. Democrat from Yuma County
Merchant

Simms, Mit Democrat from Graham-Greenlee County
Rancher, farmer, candidate for governor, State Treasurer,
1915-1917 and 1931-1933, Arizona Secretary of State
1919-1921, member of the corporation commission

Sims, Robert B. Democrat from Cochise County
Rancher, businessman, warden of the state prison,
member state industrial commission

Standage, Orrin — Democrat from Maricopa County
Farmer

Tovrea, Edward A. — Democrat from Cochise County
Meat packer, stockyards owner

Tuthill, Alexander M. — Democrat from Graham-Greenlee County
Physician, commanding officer of the Arizona National Guard

Webb, Wilfred T. — Democrat from Graham-Greenlee County
Rancher, businessman, member of the state legislature

Weinberger, Jacob — Democrat from Gila County
Lawyer, appointed by President Truman, Judge of the United States Court, Southern District of California, 1946

Wells, Edmund W. — Republican from Yavapai County
Lawyer, banker, Justice of the Territorial Supreme Court, 1891-1893, first Republican nominee for governor, 1911

White, James C. — Republican from Pima County
Railroad man

Willis, Thomas N. — Democrat from Pima County
Rancher

Winsor, Mulford — Democrat from Yuma County
Newspaperman, member of the state legislature, served in various state agencies, first head of the Department of Library and Archives

Wood, Homer R. — Democrat from Yavapai County
Pharmacist, mining man, member of the state legislature and state fair commission

□

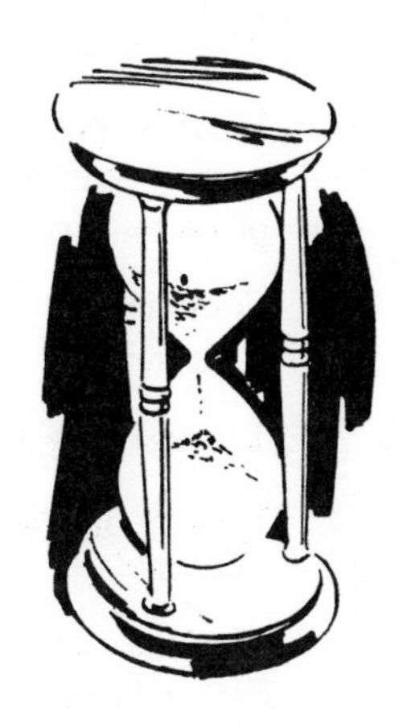

ARIZONA CHRONOLOGY

15,000 to 10,000 years before present	Man arrives in the New World. This is a conservative estimate and some would place the arrival at 30,000 to 40,000 years ago.
circa 2,000 B.C.	Cochise Man flourishes
Start of the Christian Era	Arizona inhabitants divide into three different cultures, Anasazi (plateau people), Hohokam (desert people) and Mogollon (plateau people).
1400-1500 A.D.	Cataclysmic events cause great changes in living patterns in the Arizona area; modern tribal systems begin to emerge and new tribes arrive from other areas.
1519	Cortez begins his conquest of Mexico.
1539	Fray Marcos de Niza goes north from Mexico in search of Seven Cities of Cibola.
1540	Start of Coronado's expedition.
1598-1607	Juan de Onate explores Arizona and founds a colony in New Mexico.

1691-1711	The age of Father Kino in Arizona.
1730's	Silver deposits found in Mexico and the name "Arissona" or "Arizonac" first applied to a geographical area.
1752	Founding of Tubac, first presidio on Arizona soil.
1768-1781	The age of Father Garces in Arizona.
1776	Spanish garrison moved from Tubac to Tucson.
1810	Mexican independence first advocated by Father Hidalgo.
1821	Mexico achieves its independence.
1821	Opening of the Santa Fe trade between the United States and residents of the southwest.
1825-1840	Era of the mountain men.
1846	Outbreak of the Mexican War; Kearney's Army of the West and Cooke's Mormon Battalion cross Arizona.
1848	Treaty of Guadalupe Hidalgo; Arizona north of the Gila transferred to the United States.
1848-1849	Gold rush to California and Arizona receives some of the surplus population.
1850	Creation of the Territory of New Mexico with capital at Santa Fe.
1850's	Surveyors at work in Arizona, forts built and camels tried for transportation.
1853-1854	Gadsden Purchase treaty adds southern Arizona to the United States.
1856	First request for a separate territory by Arizonans.

1857	"Jackass Mail," San Antonio-San Diego Mail Line begins service across Arizona.
1860	Residents of Arizona form unofficial provisional territorial government at Tucson.
1860-1861	Southern states secede from Union and military posts in Arizona abandoned.
1862	Confederate territory of Arizona created; battle of Picacho Pass takes place and Union forces again control Arizona.
1863	Enactment of the Organic Act and arrival of first territorial officials.
1864	Capital moved to Prescott; First Territorial Legislature enacts Howell Code.
1865-1885	Arizona is troubled by frequent Indian wars.
1867	Capital moved to Tucson.
1869	The Powell expedition down the Colorado River.
1869-1877	The administration of Governor Safford; school system organized and eastern mining capital invested in Arizona.
1877	Capital moved back to Prescott.
1877-1885	Two transcontinental railroads built across Arizona.
1881	Tucson has territory's first telephone system.
1886	Electric lights installed in Phoenix.
1898	Arizona's Bucky O'Neill of the Rough Riders killed in Spanish American War.
1900	First automobile in Arizona Territory.
1902-1906	Joint statehood with New Mexico discussed and defeated.

1902	Enactment of the Newlands Act which leads to the construction of Theodore Roosevelt Dam.
1910	Enabling Act at last passed by Congress; Arizona constitution written.
1912	Arizona becomes the forty-eighth state.
1912-1933	The Hunt era in Arizona politics.
1917	The Bisbee Deportation takes place and alleged radical union members are run out of the state by vigilantes.
1922	Santa Fe Compact signed to divide Colorado River waters; Arizona refuses to ratify.
1928	Congress authorizes the building of Hoover Dam much opposed by Arizona.
1934	Reorganization of federal Indian policies and renewed emphasis placed on tribal system.
1941-1948	The Osborn era in Arizona politics.
1941	United States enters World War II and military bases in Arizona are expanded.
1945	Real start of the industrial revolution in Arizona as manufacturing becomes increasingly important; new "pioneers" begin to swell the state's population.
1964	Native son Barry M. Goldwater is Republican nominee for President of the United States.
1966	In state elections Republicans for the first time in history win majority in state legislature.
1968	Congress authorizes building of Central Arizona Project long sought by Senator Hayden. □

NATIONAL FORESTS, PARKS, MONUMENTS HISTORIC SITES AND MEMORIALS IN ARIZONA

National Forests:

Apache		1,191,800 acres
Coconino		1,810,097 acres
Coronado		1,721,049 acres
Kaibab		1,719,610 acres
Prescott		1,248,537 acres
Sitgreaves		807,833 acres
Tonto		2,885,227 acres
	Total	11,384,153 acres

National Parks:

Grand Canyon 673,203 acres

Arizona's most famous natural wonder

Petrified Forest 94,189 acres

Located in northern Arizona this is the site of the famous petrified logs and includes the painted desert

National Monuments:

Canyon de Chelly 83,840 acres

Ancient dwelling site on the Navajo Reservation in the northeastern part of the state

Chiricachua 10,633 acres

Unusual rock formations in southeastern Arizona

Grand Canyon 193,019 acres

Lands located to the west of the national park

Marble Canyon 26,080 acres

Arizona's newest national monument located northeast of the park section of Grand Canyon

Montezuma Castle 783 acres

Ancient dwelling site and "Montezuma's Well" located in central Arizona

Navajo 360 acres

Pueblo "apartments" in caves located on the Navajo Reservation

Organ Pipe Cactus 328,691 acres

The famous cactus and other desert plants, located on the Mexican border west of the Papago Indian Reservation

Pipe Spring 40 acres

Memorial to Mormon pioneers located in the far north of Arizona west of Fredonia

Saguaro 77,132 acres

Near Tucson several different "life zones" of plant and animal life are revealed to the visitor

Sunset Crater 3,040 acres

An ancient extinct volcano located northeast of Flagstaff

Tonto 1,120 acres

Ancient dwellings near Roosevelt Dam

Tumacacori 43 acres

The Spanish mission between Tucson and Nogales

Tuzigoot 10 acres

Ancient dwelling near Clarkdale

Walnut Canyon 1,642 acres

Home of the Sinagua near Flagstaff

Wupatki 53,233 acres

Several ancient dwellings located northeast of Flagstaff

NATIONAL HISTORIC SITES:

Fort Bowie 900 acres

Site of the old military installation in southeastern Arizona

Hubbell Trading Post 152 acres

J. Lorenzo Hubbell operated this famous post at Ganado in northeastern Arizona

NATIONAL MEMORIAL:

Coronado 2,834 acres

In memory of the Spanish explorer and located in southern Arizona

INDIAN RESERVATIONS IN ARIZONA

RESERVATION	TRIBES	AREA	POPULATION*
Ak-Chin (Maricopa)	*Maricopa, Pima, Papago*	21,840 acres	230
Camp Verde	*Yavapai, Apache*	578	690
Cocopah	*Cocopah*	528	100
Colorado River	*Mohave, Chemehuevi*	225,996	1,680
Fort Apache	*Apache*	1,664,872	6,000
Fort McDowell	*Yavapai, Pima*	24,680	330
Gila Bend	*Papago*	10,297	260
Gila River	*Pima, Maricopa*	371,929	7,420
Havasupai	*Havasupai*	3,058	370
Hopi	*Hopi*	2,472,216	5,940
Hualapai	*Hualapai*	991,680	1,030
Kaibab	*Paiutes*	120,413	140
Navajo (Arizona part)	*Navajo*	8,968,828	68,700
Papago	*Papago*	2,773,596	5,290
Salt River	*Pima, Maricopa*	46,591	2,260
San Carlos	*Apache*	1,854,801	4,650
San Xavier	*Papago*	71,044	660
Yavapai	*Yavapai*	1,399	90
Ft. Yuma (located in California on west bank of Colorado River)	*Yuma*	—	1,220

*Population estimates are based on Bureau of Indian Affairs figures, September 1968. The B.I.A. considers an individual to be an "Indian" if he lives on or near the reservation lands and is eligible for Bureau services. Based on this criteria there were approximately 105,900 Arizona "Indians" in 1968. The census bureau, on the other hand regards as an Indian anyone who so regards himself.

REGISTERED VOTERS IN ARIZONA — 1912 and 1972

	1912	*1972*
Apache County	382	11,783
Cochise County	5,834	25,133
Coconino County	1,218	24,358
Gila County	2,585	14,724
Graham County	1,172	8,721
Greenlee County	1,432	5,307
Maricopa County	6,494	482,245
Mohave County	1,096	13,531
Navajo County	926	17,930
Pima County	2,463	179,950
Pinal County	836	27,574
Santa Cruz	355	5,847
Yavapai County	3,205	22,573
Yuma County	1,306	22,136
Totals	29,304	861,812

STANDING COMMITTEES OF THE ARIZONA LEGISLATURE

House of Representatives	*Senate*
Agriculture	Agriculture, Commerce and Labor
Appropriations	Appropriations
Banking and Insurance	Education
Commerce	Finance
Counties and Municipalities	Government
Education	Health and Welfare
Government Operations	Judiciary
Health	Natural Resources
Human Resources	Rules
Judiciary	Transportation
Natural Resources	
Rules	
Transportation	
Ways and Means	

SALARIES OF ARIZONA OFFICIALS

	1912	*1976*
Governor	$ 4,000	$40,000
Secretary of state	3,500	24,000
Attorney general	2,500	35,000
Treasurer	3,000	22,500
Superintendent of Public Instruction	2,500	27,500
Mine inspector	3,000	20,000
Supreme court justices	5,000	32,000
Appeals court judges	——	30,000
Superior court judges	3,000 to 4,000	28,000
Corporation commission members	3,000	30,000
Legislators	7.00 per day	6,000

The Cactus Wren, Arizona State Bird

SOME SUGGESTED READING

Ashurst, Henry F., *A Many-Colored Toga, The Diary of Henry Fountain Ashurst,* edited by George F. Sparks. Tucson, 1962
Bancroft, Hubert Howe, *History of Arizona and New Mexico, 1530-1888.* Reprinted, Albuquerque, N.M., 1962
Barnes, Will C., *Arizona Place Names,* revised by Byrd H. Granger. Tucson, 1960
Bolton, Herbert E., *Coronado, Knight of Pueblos and Plains.* New York, 1949
...., *Rim of Christendom,* New York, 1936
Brandes, Ray, *Frontier Military Posts of Arizona.* Globe, 1960
Brinckerhoff, Sidney B. and Odie B. Faulk, *Lancers for the King.* Phoenix, 1965
Colton, Ray C., *The Civil War in the Western Territories.* Norman, Oklah., 1959
Cross, Jack L., *et al, Arizona, Its People and Resources.* Tucson, 1960
Darrah, William C., *Powell of the Colorado.* Princeton, N.J., 1951
Davis, Britton, *The Truth About Geronimo.* New Haven, Conn., 1929
Dunbier, Roger, *The Sonoran Desert.* Tucson, 1968
Farish, Thomas E., *History of Arizona.* 8 vols., San Francisco, 1914-1918
Favour, Alpheus H., *Old Bill Williams, Mountain Man.* Chapel Hill, N.C., 1936
Forbes, Jack D., *Apache, Navajo, and Spaniard.* Norman, Oklah., 1960
...., *Warriors of the Colorado.* Norman, Oklah., 1965
Gladwin, Harold Sterling, *A History of the Ancient Southwest.* Portland, Maine, 1957
Goff, John S., *George W. P. Hunt and His Arizona,* Pasadena, Calif., 1973
Gressinger, A. W., *Charles D. Poston, Sunland Seer.* Globe, 1961
Henson, Pauline, *Founding a Wilderness Capital. Prescott, A. T., 1864.* Flagstaff, 1965
Hill, Myles E., and John S. Goff, *Arizona, Past and Present,* Cave Creek, Ariz., 1971
Hollon, W. Eugene, *The Southwest: Old and New.* New York, 1961
Lamar, Howard R., *The Far Southwest, 1846-1912: A Territorial History.* New Haven, Conn., 1966
Lockwood, Frank C., *Life in Old Tucson, 1854-1864.* Tucson, 1943
McClintock, James H., *Arizona.* 3 vols., Chicago, 1916
...., *Mormon Settlement in Arizona.* Phoenix, 1921
McDowell, Edwin, *Barry Goldwater, Portrait of an Arizonan.* Chicago, 1964
Mann, Dean E., *The Politics of Water in Arizona.* Tucson, 1963
Mason, Bruce B. and Heinz R. Hink, *Constitutional Government in Arizona.* Tempe, 1968
Martin, Douglas D., *An Arizona Chronology, Statehood, 1913-1936.* Tucson, 1966
...., *An Arizona Chronology, The Territorial Years, 1846-1912.* Tucson, 1963
Miller, Joseph, *Arizona, The Grand Canyon State.* New York, 1966
Peplow, Edward H., *History of Arizona.* 3 vols., Phoenix, 1958
Powell, Donald M., *The Peralta Grant.* Norman, Oklah., 1960
Quebbeman, Frances, *Medicine in Territorial Arizona.* Phoenix, 1965
Richards, J. Morris, *The Birth of Arizona.* Phoenix, 1940
Sacks, B., *Be It Enacted: The Creation of The Territory of Arizona.* Phoenix, 1964
Sloan, Richard E. and Ward R. Adams, *History of Arizona.* 4 vols., Phoenix, 1930
Theobald, John and Lillian, *Arizona Territory, Post Office & Postmasters.* Phoenix, 1961
Van Petten, Donald R., *The Constitution and Government of Arizona.* Phoenix, 1960
Wagoner, Jay J., *Arizona Territory, 1863-1912, A Political History.* Tucson, 1970
Wallace, Andrew F., editor, *Sources and Readings in Arizona History.* Tucson, 1965
Wallace, Edward S., *The Great Reconnaissance, Soldiers, Artists and Scientists on the Frontier, 1848-1861.* Boston, 1955
Wyllys, Rufus K., *Arizona, The History of a Frontier State.* Phoenix, 1950

INDEX

ACKNOWLEDGMENT . .
Historical photographs reproduced through the courtesy of the Department of Library and Archives, Phoenix.

House of Representatives Wing of the State Capitol, Phoenix